WRESTLING REALITY

WRESTLING REALITY

THE LIFE AND MIND OF CHRIS KANYON, WRESTLING'S GAY SUPERSTAR

CHRIS KANYON and RYAN CLARK

ECW

Copyright © Ryan Clark and Ken Klucsarits, 2011

Published by ECW PRESS
2120 Queen Street East, Suite 200, Toronto, Ontario, Canada M4E 1E2
416-694-3348 / info@ecwpress.com

All rights reserved. No part of this publication may be reproduced, stored in a retrieval system, or transmitted in any form by any process — electronic, mechanical, photocopying, recording, or otherwise — without the prior written permission of the copyright owners and ECW Press. The scanning, uploading, and distribution of this book via the Internet or via any other means without the permission of the publisher is illegal and punishable by law. Please purchase only authorized electronic editions, and do not participate in or encourage electronic piracy of copyrighted materials. Your support of the authors' rights is appreciated.

"Former Gay Pro Wrestler Chris Klucsarits a.k.a. 'Chris Kanyon' Found in Apparent Suicide."
© Daily news, L.P. (New York). Used with permission.

LIBRARY AND ARCHIVES CANADA CATALOGUING IN PUBLICATION

Kanyon, Chris
Wrestling reality : the life and mind of Chris Kanyon, wrestling's gay superstar / Chris Kanyon and Ryan Clark.

ISBN 978-1-77041-028-2
ALSO ISSUED AS: 978-1-77090-068-4 (PDF); 978-1-77090-067-7 (EPUB)

1. Kanyon, Chris. 2. Wrestlers--United States--Biography.
3. Gay athletes--United States--Biography.
I. Clark, Ryan, 1979- II. Title.

GV1196.K36A3 2011   796.812092   C2011-902846-8

Editor for the press: Michael Holmes
Cover design: Marijke Friesen
Cover image: Emanuel Melo
Text Design and Typesetting: Ingrid Paulson
ECW PRESS Printing: Transcontinental 1 2 3 4 5
ecwpress.com

PRINTED AND BOUND IN CANADA

MIX
Paper from responsible sources
FSC FSC® C011825
www.fsc.org

CONTENTS

Preface / ix
Introduction, by Jim Mitchell / xii

Prologue: September 14, 2003 / 1

I   THE RISE OF KANYON
1. Growing Up in Sunnyside / 09
2. Waiting for Fireworks / 16
3. The Long Skate Home / 21
4. Culture Shock / 25
5. It's So Fake / 30
6. Redemption / 35
7. Roman Candles / 38
8. The Turnbuckle of My Dreams / 43
9. My College Education / 47
10. Chasing My Dream / 52
11. Secrets and Steven Tyler / 58
12. Pete and the Lower East Side Wrestling Gym / 65
13. The Debut of Chris Morgan / 73
14. My "Faggy" Wrestling Costume / 78
15. The Land of Trailers and Freaks / 83
16. Mistakes / 95

17	Awe and Disgust in the Mirror / 103
18	Smoky Mountain High / 108
19	Screwed but Moving On / 116
20	Say Hello to Afa / 127
21	Relationships, Personality and My Gimmick / 138
22	Party in Memphis / 144
23	Out of a Job, on to the Power Plant / 154

II THE FALL OF CHRIS

24	Diamond Dallas Page / 165
25	The Strange Life of a Single Gay Wrestler / 170
26	California Dreaming and Making My Name / 177
27	Success as Mortis, Overshadowed by nWo / 184
28	The Online Dating Scene / 193
29	Negotiations / 201
30	Death on the Autobahn? / 206
31	The Return of Kidman, the Debut of Blood Runs Cold / 211
32	Heels, Sullivan and the Bucket / 216
33	Frustrations / 223
34	Injecting the Needle / 232
35	From Mortis to Kanyon / 238
36	To Hollywood and Toronto — and Back / 245
37	The WWF and the Effect of 9/11 / 271
38	Did Vince Really Want to Hurt Me? / 288

III THE BATTLE FOR CHRIS KANYON

39	Fighting Back Outside the Ring / 295
40	Kanyon Vs. Flair / 300
41	Enjoy the Journey, Enjoy Your Life / 303

Epilogue: April 2, 2010 / 307

Acknowledgments / 311

To our parents and families—you gave us everything, and we thank you from the bottom of our hearts.

PREFACE

I'll never forget the day I met Chris Kanyon. I was a newspaper journalist, sent to cover National Coming Out Day in 2006 at the local university. The day — October 11 each year — was one of celebration for those who wanted to announce their sexuality and celebrate their choice while feeling comfortable and confident among peers in a supportive environment.

Kanyon was speaking at Northern Kentucky University, and I was there to cover the speech for the local newspaper, the *Cincinnati Enquirer.* Why was Kanyon so important? In the late '90s he had been one of the most famous wrestlers on the planet. He'd appeared on national television multiple times a week, made more than a million dollars and even had his own action figure. He was a legend in the professional wrestling world.

That is, until 2004 when he let everyone in on his secret: He was gay.

He was a gay professional wrestler.

Kanyon spoke to a large group at the university that day, and his story was riveting. I am not a gay man, and I am not a huge fan of wrestling, but I know a good story when I hear one, and Kanyon's was full of passion and rage and sadness and something else — hope. Kanyon wanted others to avoid the pain he had endured. He wanted those who are gay to be honest with themselves and others, to celebrate who they are and not have to live in fear of the repercussions.

I approached him afterward. He was tall, and still fit even though he'd been away from wrestling professionally for a couple of years. He had long, black hair, pulled back into a shiny ponytail. But the first thing you noticed was his easy smile. Kanyon could talk to you and make you feel important. He was someone who didn't seem like he'd ever been famous — he looked like he could be your lifelong friend.

I complimented him on his speech and asked him where his book was — surely, I said, anyone with a story this good had a book in the works. He told me he was talking to several people about writing a book. I gave him my card and said I wanted to write it. I'd already been involved in writing another sports book, and I have friends who are editors in the publishing world. I told him we could have a deal done that week. We parted ways, and he promised he would keep in touch.

Over the next few months we kept in touch via email, and it led to us agreeing to write his book. For the next 18 months, both in person and over the phone, Kanyon shared his life story with me. I recorded much of what he said and took notes on the rest. Together we crafted his story, which I quickly realized was going to be a tragedy. Even though Kanyon grew up to achieve his dreams, he was destined to fall, because his success was dependent on being someone he wasn't. He was trapped in a world of false realities. In his professional life he played a role, and in his personal life he played another role. Rarely, if ever, could he truly be himself. To make matters worse, he began to realize he suffered from manic depression, a serious mental affliction that swung him between high points of energy and happiness and the lowest lows of severe depression.

Even after revealing his secret, Kanyon was still dealing with the new life of being an out gay man in a society that is anything but comfortable with such honesty. For decades Kanyon had kept his secret to himself, for fear that he would lose his job within the ultra-macho world of pro wrestling — and that's exactly what happened. Before coming out, he was forced to participate in skits mocking gays, and when he did announce he was gay he was let go from his job in World Wrestling Entertainment. Kanyon always said he was shunned because he was finally honest about being gay. The rejection by the industry he'd dedicated his life to fueled his illness, leading to madness and suicidal impulses.

On April 2, 2010, Chris Kanyon committed suicide. Just a few months prior he and I had agreed that his book was finished. He seemed in good spirits;

he talked of starting a wrestling school. Sadly, Kanyon became another of a long line of wrestlers to die tragically by age 40. Whether felled by suicide, heart attacks, strokes or drug overdoses, an alarming number of wrestlers hadn't reached that age.

Not only did I lose someone I now count as a friend, but of much lesser importance, I wondered what we should do with his book. It's written in the first-person, and the story's tragic conclusion threatened to shift the focus from one of courage and determination to one of defeat.

But no. That isn't Kanyon's legacy. It isn't about the last lost battle, but about the fight itself. The fight against depression and the fight to be honest about who you are.

Even now, I'm haunted by a question: If Kanyon had felt more comfortable about coming out sooner in his life, would he still be alive today? There's no way to be sure, but I know it would have given him more of a chance. This is the chance he wants to pass onto others struggling with their sexuality.

These are Kanyon's last words — his story, in his voice, the way he wanted it told on the page. Finally, he got to define his own reality. I only wish he'd had more time to enjoy it.

— Ryan Clark, August 2010

INTRODUCTION, *by Jim Mitchell*

For 18 years I had the privilege of experiencing Chris Kanyon's friendship. Though we initially met through our mutual love of and involvement in professional wrestling, our roots would go far deeper than that. Kanyon was the one person I knew I could always count on, regardless of the miles between us or how difficult and inconvenient the situation at hand may have been.

I told Chris early on, as many people did, that he was too nice of a guy to be in the wrestling business. He was honest, generous to fault, loyal and had an incredible degree of personal integrity. He stood up for deserving underdogs, despite what it may have cost him, because he innately felt it was the right thing to do.

Kanyon was directly responsible for making my childhood dream of being involved in wrestling on a national stage materialize, in addition to my professional success outside of wrestling. I once told him I felt guilty that I couldn't possibly return the favor in kind on the same grand scale. He told me, "I don't expect you to. You're my best friend. I did what I did because that's what friends are supposed to do."

It's impossible to fully articulate my gratitude for the positive impact his friendship and selflessness made on my life.

At times we fought and argued like wild animals, often to hilarious extremes. Despite that, our bond remained unbreakable.

Many of the secrets Kanyon revealed to the public in recent years had been shared with me long ago. I was honored that, out of his many friends, he chose to confide in me early on. Chris dealt with a level of internal torment most people will never be able to grasp. To see someone I cared for experiencing that kind of ongoing anguish was painful beyond description at times, yet insignificant compared to what he endured.

The last time I saw Kanyon in person he told me that he planned to leave us. It was a matter of "when," not "if." He wasn't sad. He wasn't angry. If nothing else, he seemed to be at peace with himself. As I had done countless times before over the years, I tried to convince him that he had plenty to live for and listed all of the people who loved him and would be devastated by his passing. He told me that I was being selfish because I was more worried about my own pain than his. He said that he had no control over wrestling politics or his mental health, but the one thing he could control was his own existence. He felt no one had the right to insist that he go on living when he found doing so to be unbearable.

I knew I was seeing Chris for the final time when he summed up his feelings by quoting part of Morgan Freeman's closing monologue from one of his favorite movies, *The Shawshank Redemption*:

"Some birds aren't meant to be caged. Their feathers are just too bright. And when they fly away, the part of you that knows it was a sin to lock them up does rejoice." Now that he's gone, those words have a profound and surprisingly comforting resonance.

All I could do was to give Kanyon a tearful hug and thank him for being such a truly wonderful friend. Kanyon left Freeman's final two lines off of the quote he shared with me that night. I can think of no better way to describe the void his absence has left in my life than to close with them:

"But still, the place you live in is that much more drab and empty that they're gone. I guess I just miss my friend."

— Jim Mitchell, Summer 2010

PROLOGUE

September 14, 2003

I figured I had 20 minutes left to live. That's all. Then I'd have my peace.

Minutes before, I'd gotten out of bed for the first time in days and walked into the bathroom where I'd grabbed a full bottle of sleeping pills. There were 50 pills in the bottle. *That should be enough,* I thought as I headed for the kitchen. At the sink, I filled up a glass of water, and for what seemed like hours I stared at that bottle of pills, my thoughts racing.

Is this real? Am I dreaming? Am I really going to do this, and if I do, what will happen? Where will I go? Will any part of me — my consciousness, my mind, spirit or soul — continue to exist?

"Just do it," I said aloud. Slowly, I brought the bottle to my mouth, my hands shaking as much from nerves as from the weakness and fatigue of lying in bed for two months. I tilted the bottle up, but my subconscious made me stop. My tongue had involuntarily blocked the pills from rushing out of the bottle, and I put it back down. I got mad at myself. "You puss, do it!" I said. I tried again, and again, but my subconscious seemed to disagree.

It didn't matter. I was hell-bent on ending the pain. I had to focus on the present. I had to focus on my freedom.

The radio in the kitchen blared one of my favorite songs, "Amazing," by Aerosmith. As Steven Tyler sang about living a lie and wishing to die, I felt like Aerosmith was singing that song just for me. I blocked out all thought and focused on swallowing the pills. Soon, I'd be free of the suffering. The pills tumbled out of the bottle and down my throat.

I was buoyed by a sudden rush of energy and excitement. I had done it. Years of suffering were about to end. The ultimate question of what it was like to die was about to be answered. It was exhilarating and powerful.

Oddly, I wasn't afraid. Not because I'm incredibly brave, but because although I'd been raised Catholic, over the years I had become very agnostic. Because I didn't really have a belief, I had no expectations, good or bad, of what was next. But to think I was about to know the answer to the most important of questions was incredible.

I went back into my bedroom, and lay back down on the bed. It'd be about 20 more minutes until the pills began to work and for the first time in years, I felt like I'd escaped. I was free from this serious, debilitating depression, and I would have peace.

I knew it was a serious act, but what I had done was the culmination of two months of the worst depression a person can have. You are completely unmotivated, pessimistic and without energy. You feel like you can't tell anyone the truth and you're boxed into a corner. You're confused about who you are and who you want to be. You don't know what else to do. I thought it was the only escape from the horror I was living in.

The most alone I'd ever been, I fell into a conversation with myself. I thought about how some people say when you try to kill yourself and you're not successful, you're looking for attention. Well, believe me, I wasn't. I truly wanted to end it all. I started to think of other ways I could've done it. Maybe I should've jumped off the roof of the building. That would've done the trick. But jumping off the roof was no good. *With your wrestling training, you'd land perfectly right,* my inner voice said. *You'd distribute your weight perfectly and you wouldn't die.*

Yeah, too risky that I might survive. So what else could I have tried? I thought maybe I should've slit my wrists. That would be easy. Boy, it's obvious you're not thinking straight when you're trying to killing yourself, right? This is morbid, crazy shit. My thoughts wandered back 15 years to the summer of 1988, to Long Beach, New York. I was with a bunch of friends eating lunch on a beautiful Sunday afternoon at a beachfront restaurant and bar. I looked down at my friend T.J. Moran's hands and I saw two bad scars on his wrists.

"What's that T.J.?" I asked. I was innocent and naïve.

He was quick and honest with his answer. "I tried to kill myself," he said. "I was stupid. And now I have to live with these forever." He pointed to the reddened, jagged scars that streaked both wrists.

I had always liked T.J. I was impressed by his honesty and his confidence. Lying in bed, I smiled as I thought about him. He probably barely remembers me, if at all, and there I was, 15 years later, on my deathbed, thinking about him. Of all the thousands and thousands of people I'd met, thanks predominantly to my life as a professional wrestler and being on television, it was T.J. from the old neighborhood in Sunnyside who I thought about.

It's odd how the smallest thing can change a life. Or save one. It was almost unbelievable that those 30 seconds of interaction with T.J., 15 long years ago and 1,000 miles away, may have ultimately saved me. It was because of him I didn't slit my wrists right then and there.

Well, if they somehow find me, and they save me, I'll be walking around with those two constant reminders on my wrist, I thought. *Everybody's going to know what I did.* So instead of cutting my wrists, I took the pills. Cutting my wrists may have worked, if it wasn't for T.J. It made me think of the song "Name" by the Goo Goo Dolls, lyrics that lit up my own memories of scars and stardom until they were almost blinding. But the final darkness, a sweet relief from those spotlit memories, crept closer.

✱

You think some weird shit when you know you're going to die. The next thought that flittered into my brain was that I'd hid $3,000 in one of my socks. It was a seemingly insignificant thing to think of at such a moment. And that is one of the ironies of all of this: In that state of mind, I thought about how awful it would be if I died, and no one got that money. I saw tragedy in wasting $3,000, but totally missed the tragedy of wasting my life. I thought about getting the $3,000 out of the sock drawer and sitting it on the dresser. I wanted the police or paramedics to find the money when they found my body. Then maybe my brother or my parents would get it.

Oh shit. Oh God. My parents. My brother. I saw them crying over my coffin at my funeral. I saw my cousins and Aunt Pat and Uncle Johnny. Then my best friends: Dan, the Toms, Kidman, Hurricane and the rest. They were all crying, all hurting.

And it was all because of me.

But after two months of severe depression, I'd gotten pretty good at blocking thoughts out. I had to block out the thoughts of my family and friends suffering if I really wanted to die. I had to if I wanted to stop myself from putting my fingers down my throat and vomiting those pills back up. I had to. So I did. And poof: All thoughts of them were gone.

In bed, I waited for death. I don't know how long it would take for the sleeping pills to kick in, but I was trying to keep my mind off my parents and my family. "I gotta watch some TV," I said. I was lucky. It was a Sunday night, so I got to watch one of my favorite shows, *The Simpsons*. Homer, Bart, Marge and the rest of the gang allowed my thoughts to stop. And as I watched their antics, the colors of the characters and the background started to meld together. I felt myself fading away.

A peace came over me. I was finally escaping the despair that had been choking me for years. I slipped away into something—I'm not sure if it was a fantasy, a sleep or death. I have no recollection of the next three hours. There were no bright lights at the end of a tunnel, no out-of-body experiences or visions. I wish I could tell you stories of eternal bliss and peace and happiness, or that I saw my dog Ace, who had died years before. I wish I could tell you how I apologized to Ace for all the wrestling moves I'd practiced on him and that he forgave me and said "It's OK, I still love you." But I felt and saw nothing. I remember nothing.

But in the abyss something happened. In the middle of wherever my consciousness was, a feeling came over me, one I'd felt before. One I remembered from long ago, from nights of parties and drinking. One that rises inside of you, warning you, telling you it's time.

I had to throw up.

Somewhere deep inside of me, I was trying to save my own life. *Get to the bathroom*, my body said. *Get to the commode. Now!* I tried to get up from the bed, but in the three hours since I'd taken the pills they'd begun to take effect. My body was partially paralyzed and I fell to the floor, face first, busting open my nose. The blood started flowing immediately like dirty rain water in a gutter. My only thought was to get to the bathroom.

I started crawling across the floor, streaks of crimson streaming down my face and onto the carpet. The pill-induced haze was smothering me. I peed and shit on myself. And the vomit was coming too.

What a picture I was, this big, supposedly happy, successful pro wrestler. My dark eyes ringed with black circles and my goatee and long black hair covered in blood, I crawled like a baby through my own piss, shit, blood and vomit. It was pathetic. I was pathetic. But I finally made it to the bathroom and what a sight it must have been: a six-four, 250-pound athlete curling up as small as he could around the toilet. In short, violent spurts, the pills were coming out of me. I threw up all the food and bile from my stomach, and I dry-heaved for about 20 minutes more. I finally pulled back from the commode and I leaned back on the wall, just across from a mirrored closet door.

I saw what I looked like in that mirror: sad and pathetic, certainly no champion. Certainly no role model. As I literally faced myself, I realized I was not a good son, brother, uncle, friend or person. I was a beaten, selfish, sick loser. I saw what I'd become, and I was not proud.

I uttered the words — the words I would never forget — staring down this broken-down person: "How did you let yourself get to this point?" I asked. "What the hell have you done to yourself?"

I

THE RISE OF KANYON

"It's all about having confidence in yourself.
I don't fear that man standing across from me."
KEN SHAMROCK, WRESTLER AND MMA FIGHTER

(1)

GROWING UP IN SUNNYSIDE

I was shocked.

I didn't remember my dad ever doing things like this, and my six-year-old mind couldn't comprehend it. I was in my room, the one I shared with my eight-and-a-half-year-old brother in our apartment in Sunnyside, Queens. I spent a lot of time there, playing with my toys. On my own a lot, I knew how to occupy myself. Dad came home that day after working as an accountant in Manhattan. I left my cramped room, one of two bedrooms in the apartment, and met my older brother and mother at the dinner table.

We sat down, and immediately, Dad turned to us boys.

"I've got a surprise for you," he said.

I looked to my brother with wide eyes.

Dad produced three tickets from his pocket.

"They're for tonight," he said in his thick Queens accent. "At the Gardens."

They were wrestling tickets. Wrestling. Here, in my town. It never occurred to me that the same kind of wrestling I watched with my dad every Saturday night was being performed on a regular basis just four blocks from my house at the Sunnyside Gardens. And the concept that we were *going* was almost more than I could fathom.

After dinner, the three of us left the apartment and walked out into the cool evening air. We passed Tornsey Park, just across the street from the apartment complex, and the convenience store where, when we were older, all of us kids in the neighborhood would get beer from the Korean owner. But I wasn't focused on any of that.

We were going to see wrestling.

Dad had said something about how wrestling was regulating a lot of matches, not allowing young kids to see them in person because of the violence. I was just worried about getting in. But I knew Dad would find a way. He was going to sneak us into the Gardens.

✶

The Sunnyside Gardens was an old building that served as a flea market during the day. But at night, it was transformed into a wrestling venue. It seemed like hundreds of people were waiting in line when we stepped up to the door. The man at the gate was busy taking tickets from the crowd, and when we were close to the door, my dad pulled some trickery.

He gave the man our three tickets, but he kept my brother and me hidden behind him. As the crowd kept moving forward, Dad leaned close to the usher.

"I think you may want to check that man's ticket," Dad said, pointing to the guy in front of us.

"Yeah?" the usher said.

"Yeah. I think he may have bought it outside from a scalper," Dad said. "I hope he didn't get ripped off. It may be fake."

The usher focused his attention on the man who'd just walked in. He called him over and checked his ticket to make sure it was the real thing. As they talked, we kids became lost in the faces, and Dad led us inside. As we walked past, I heard the usher say the other man's ticket was fine, and he let them go. More important to me, we were in.

What I saw in there, I'll never forget.

We sat far away, so far that it was difficult to see the wrestlers. And the cigarette smoke—I know it sounds cliché—was thick everywhere throughout the arena. That night, the tag team of Billy White Wolf and Chief Jay Strongbow took on the Executioners for the tag-team titles. Billy and the Chief used a gimmick that they were Native Americans, even though, unbeknownst to us at the time, Billy was Iraqi and Jay was really Italian. The two were favorites of mine and my brother's, and we loved when the Chief would do his war dance in the ring. The Executioners wore black masks and acted as cutthroat as their name.

Even at that age, I was always ready to go out on my own, to explore the arena. After we found our seats I walked around a bit — not too far, not out of sight of my dad — but far enough to see what this world was like. I saw grown men shouting in anger or elation. I saw the bright lights of the arena and the athletes preparing for their matches. But it was the wrestling that really got my attention. It was so different than on television. It looked and smelled and sounded so much more real, the moves amplified by streaming sweat and the smacks of man hitting man and crashing hard to the mat. I was amazed. I had tunnel vision, exploring my little area of the Gardens. I think some part of me knew that this was something special — that it meant more to me than others, even my dad and my brother. This meant more to me because someday, I would be the one in the ring.

Someday, little kids would be out in the crowd, watching me.

✶

In the summer of 1976, Sunnyside, Queens, was exactly the opposite of what everyone thought of New York City.

Split between the elevated 7 subway and the honks and shouting on Queens Boulevard, the neighborhood had an urban environment but a suburban lifestyle with green parks and trees, two-story townhouses and multi-family homes. All in all, it was a perfect mix for a kid growing up — a five-minute subway ride to Manhattan, yet it still had a small-town feel. The town was filled primarily with Italians and Irish, though it was a mix of all cultures and nationalities, like our family — we were part Austrian, German, Yugoslavian and Czech.

We lived in a multi-story apartment complex just across the street from Tornsey Park, the center for the neighborhood's young crowd. There, kids would break up into groups, depending on their age, and play softball, street hockey or football depending on the time of year. The centerfield wall of the baseball park was actually the wall of the old Robbins clothes factory, and it was the northernmost part of town.

Any farther north and you'd wind up in Astoria, Queens. For that reason, we called the centerfield wall "Canada," because it was a northern border of sorts, and that's where we'd have our keg parties in our teens. The time and the neighborhood were very liberal. We'd all go hang out in Canada and drink beers, and for the most part, the cops and our parents looked the other way.

But it was a little tougher for me. We lived on the second floor of the apartment building, and the windows faced north — overlooking the exact spots where me and my friends would hang out and sometimes get into trouble. Not only did I have to watch out for the cops, I had to hide behind trees and benches because there was always the chance my mother might be looking out that window.

My parents, Jack and Barbara Klucsarits, were both accountants, and they moved from Manhattan to Sunnyside before I was born to live closer to my mother's folks, who lived on the first floor. Our apartment, 1,500 square feet, was all we needed, but there were times when I wished I had more room.

In the bedroom my brother and I shared, there was only room for a regular bed and a foldout bed, and the foldout was put away until we slept. At night my father would unfold it (my mother normally worked nights for a department store) and then we would go to sleep. Aside from my parents' room, we also had a small kitchen and a long, relatively narrow living room, complete with plastic-covered couch.

That was my world, and I loved it, even if there was part of me that would never belong there.

*

That summer, I was already practicing my wrestling moves.

Even at the age of seven, my friends and I were imitating what we were seeing on television. I was already loving "High Chief" Peter Maivia, the head of the famous Samoan wrestling family. The High Chief was a mountain of a man, with tattoos all over his body. He set up a royal family of wrestling, and passed his talents on to, among others, his nephew Afa and his grandson Rocky, who would go on to star in movies and develop a superstar following as the Rock. I loved the Samoans who were always good guys in their matches. Then I watched a match that made me rethink things. I saw the High Chief turn bad. He had aligned himself with the clean-cut champion, Bob Backlund, but in a shocking development, the High Chief turned bad and faced off against Backlund for the world title. I was conflicted, but I liked the way the crowd reacted to the High Chief. Something about it all made me like it, even though I didn't want to.

In my room, or at my grandma's house, my brother and my cousins and I would create our own storylines and try the moves: the sleeper hold, the airplane spin, head locks, splashes off the bed onto the floor and, of course, the pile driver. Sometimes we would take turns being good guys and bad guys, which we would later learn were called babyfaces and heels.

We practiced the moves so much that we learned how not to get hurt — and none of us ever did. Little did I know, someday I'd make it to the top of the wrestling world, performing in front of millions. But by then I learned I'd be more likely to get hurt outside the ring than in it.

✱

"Come on, Ken!" my father yelled, encouraging my older brother as he walked up to the plate.

Even before the age of 10, my brother proved to be a top-notch athlete. He'd play hockey and basketball, but in the summer of 1976 he played baseball at the park, and we would go to watch him. My father seemed happy there. He was so proud of Ken; I wanted Dad to be proud of me too.

But I wasn't as concerned with that as I was with a young man from the neighborhood, whom I would rather not identify, so I will refer to him as "Mr. X." At nine years old, he was one of the best athletes in the neighborhood. I think we knew, even then, that he would go on to become a great athlete. He had blond hair and blue eyes, and even as a kid, he was so coordinated on the baseball field. I was fascinated with him, as were most of the kids in the neighborhood. But it was different for me, because he was one of my brother's best friends. He was always around. At that age, three years difference was an eternity, so I had no idea how to relate to Mr. X or how to communicate with him. Instead, I decided to always just give him hell.

I teased him, bugged him, threw rocks at him and tried to fight with him to get his attention. For the most part, he tolerated me, but my brother would tell me to quit it. I sat there in the park with my father as he came up to bat. The kid didn't move like a nine-year-old. He was sure of himself, so agile. He could do anything.

"Go home!" I screamed. "You can't hit!"

My father paid no attention to me, just like the players.

I tried louder, but no one cared.

On top of being a great athlete, he was just a great person. I admired him, the way everyone looked up to him. I thought about him a lot, and when he wasn't around, I wanted him to be.

Later that night, I was in my room, thinking about Mr. X and looking at the trophies that lined my brother's dresser. I wanted trophies like that, too. My thoughts were interrupted by my brother.

"Hey," Ken said, walking into the room.

"Hey," I said.

"What are you looking at?" he said as he sat on the bed and took off his cleats.

"Nothing," I said. "I wasn't looking at nothing."

"Really? Hey, let me ask you something."

"What?"

"Have we fought yet today?"

I couldn't speak. "What?" I finally managed.

"Have we fought yet today?"

My mind thought back through the last 12 hours. There was breakfast, playing in my room, going to the park with Dad to watch Ken's game (but really watching Mr. X), coming home. I shook my head no. "No, we haven't fought."

With no warning, Ken punched me in the face. Hard.

That was how my brother wanted to end the day.

✱

We never got along, my brother and I.

Maybe it was because every day, he beat me up. Not just once in a while — every single day. But that was our relationship, and it would not get better until years later.

Around the time I was eight, I started playing sports too — roller hockey, baseball and basketball, like my brother. We each had our own groups of friends, though sometimes the groups would intermingle in the park. And when we had time, my friends and I would go down to the swing sets, where some intelligent park person had placed large black mats so children would not get hurt if they fell off the swings.

We did not use them for that purpose. Instead, these mats became the place to perfect our wrestling moves. It was there me and my friends Tommy Clarke, Tommy Moran, Danny O'Sullivan and others would wrestle. We'd taken our matches from my room and my grandmother's house to the mats, where, after a few hours of headlocks and sleeper holds, we'd go back to our homes, covered in the black that had rubbed off on to us. Our mothers always knew where we'd been the second we opened the front door.

After one day where countless hours were spent on the mats, I walked home with my good friend Tommy Clarke. We had black smudges all over our faces and hands, elbows and legs. Something was on my mind.

"Tom, do you know of any other kid whose brother beats him up every day?" I asked. "Do you know any kid whose brother punches him in the face?"

Tom thought for a second. He shook his head. "I don't think so. Me and my brothers fight. But they're pretty even. I don't think you'd ever catch us punching each other in the face."

I nodded. I didn't think so either. I thought about that as we parted and I went back to the apartment.

✷

In the middle of the hot summer sun, I put on my helmet, grabbed the bat and trudged up to the plate.

"He's no hitter!" one kid called out.

"He's no good!" said another.

This must be what it was like when I teased Mr. X, I thought. But he always came through — it seemed like he always got a base hit.

My father sat in the stands. Now he was watching my games, as well as my brother's. By the time I was nine, I was ready to try my hand at baseball.

The pitcher, who was a year older than me, delivered a perfect strike down the middle. I didn't swing. Coach had told me to take the first pitch.

"He's not swinging!" a boy yelled from the opponent's dugout.

I got flustered. I wanted to hit. *Throw it again*, I thought.

The second pitch was, again, right down the middle. But I was late.

"Strike two!" the umpire called.

I felt like I was letting everyone down. Everyone's eyes were on me and I couldn't do it. The spotlight was too bright. I didn't like it.

The kid on the mound smiled. He was bigger than me, and he could throw hard. His last pitch was too fast for me, and I was late with my swing again.

Three pitches. I was out. It was not a good way to start my athletic career.

(2)

WAITING FOR FIREWORKS

The best thing about being an altar boy was the annual trip. My family was Catholic, and I grew up as an altar boy, which meant I was doing just work in the eyes of God. But it also meant I would get to take the annual trip to the Great Adventure Six Flags Theme Park in New Jersey, which, at the time, seemed better than any heavenly reward.

While my family also took vacations, we had to schedule them around my brother and me going to summer camp. That summer, it was the Marist Brothers Camp, held in upstate New York. We took a bus up there for two weeks of track and field, swimming, movies, arts and crafts. My brother and I were split up into different age groups. In my group, 25 kids were packed into one cabin, and there was one community shower for all of us. I felt a little strange about that.

By the time the two weeks were over, I'd feel even worse.

✶

I was fascinated with one kid at the camp — Tommy. Even at nine years old, he was more mature than the rest of us. He was good-looking and even had some muscle definition in his arms. I didn't know what I was feeling, but I wanted his attention, in the same way I wanted Mr. X's attention.

I watched him as we ran around the track — Tommy could really run. After a long day of running events, we came back to the cabin, all of us in need of a shower. I was already nervous about that; I didn't want to shower in front of anyone else. But I wasn't necessarily afraid of being naked in front of others. I was scared because the thought of being in the shower with that boy made me nervous, but I was overwhelmingly excited in a way I didn't understand.

As everyone got undressed to go in, I hung back. I wanted to be the last one. I was scared, finally facing something I did not want to admit. If I didn't go in, I knew they would wonder why. I undressed and walked into the long hallway that led to the showers.

Knots formed in my stomach. Steam poured from the room.

I wanted to see Tommy. I walked in. No one was looking at anyone else. No one talked. The steam made things difficult to see, but a nervous energy filled the room. I think everyone wanted to get out as soon as possible.

Not me. I walked to the back of the room and took a corner shower, not far from Tommy. I faced the wall and turned on the shower, letting the hot water cover me. I desperately wanted to look at Tommy, but I knew it had to be subtle. I could not get caught.

I peeked over my shoulder and caught a glimpse of him. God, he was a great-looking kid. I swear he had muscles, even though he was young. But I looked back, quickly. I knew I couldn't stare. I was scared enough as it was.

I'd seen enough. I was confused. I was dirty. I needed to wash and leave as soon as possible. But one thought kept running through my mind: I liked seeing Tommy naked.

Then, another thought. Worse: Was I gay?

✶

Man, I did not want to be gay.

Gay was something weak or different or feminine. Gay was uncool and wrong. Gay was a part of our lingo as children. If you were bad in baseball, you were gay. If you said something stupid, you were a fag. If you were in any way unlike the others, you were queer. And being gay had come up in church before, and through no uncertain terms I'd learned that being homosexual was wrong. It was something that should be kept hidden, and definitely not acted upon. Either way, if you were gay, you were going to Hell, and that's a tough lesson for a 10-year-old boy to understand. Jesus, that's a tough lesson for a 38-year-old man to understand. But for me at summer camp, it was devastating.

It was unnatural. It was a sin. But I knew that I'd never been fascinated with girls the way I was with Mr. X or Tommy. That scared me. *I need to be fixed*, I thought. I needed to do something, turn a switch or push a button, and I would be like everyone else. I'd read somewhere that sometimes young people experiment, that they will do things and feel things that seem strange. I learned those urges were just a phase, that they would pass, and eventually, you would move on to lead a normal life.

I prayed that's what would happen to me. But I could not shake the image of Tommy in the shower. I thought about all of that during the long bus ride back to Sunnyside.

The bus bumped up and down and I was alone in my head.

"Hey, you," it was a familiar voice. My brother left his friends and came over to my seat. "What are you doing? You're not talking to anybody."

"Just thinking," I said, not wanting to be bothered.

"Thinking?!" he said, laughing. "Look, everybody, my brother's a regular brain-o, sitting here thinking about stuff!"

"Stop it," I said.

Something in the tone of my voice told him I was serious, because he got quiet. He looked at me funny, and then the moment passed.

"Don't be gay," he said, and headed back to his seat.

✶

By the time I was 12 I'd been questioning my sexuality for three years. I'd had the same feeling about certain boys my age, and older boys, but I was convinced I just needed some fixing. When I watched movies, I was fixated on certain young actors. Anthony Michael Hall was one of them. But while these attractive men on the silver screen and on the baseball field kept an unshakeable grip on my brain, everywhere I went I was told that was wrong. That *I* was wrong.

But absolutely none of it mattered while I wrestled.

Out in the park, on those dirty black mats, everything went away. There was no stress or confusion — there was only competition and performance. As a wrestler, I was concerned with imitating the moves and beating my opponent. I never entertained thoughts of enjoying the wrestling with my friends in that way — there was nothing sexual to it. It was only sport, mixed with acting and performing. But when the wrestling was finished, I knew I was not the normal red-blooded American boy. I was having gay feelings, and I wanted them to stop.

✷

It was around that time my friends and I started going to see the wrestling matches at Madison Square Garden. We really got into it, and some said we were obsessed—especially Tom Clarke and me. When the wrestling magazines came out on Tuesday, we were there waiting in the convenience store for them. Sometimes we'd be wrestling there on the curb as we waited.

People like to point to Hulk Hogan as the leader of the wrestling resurgence, but to me and my friends, it was Jimmy Snuka and Bob Backlund that brought wrestling back. Snuka, a dark-skinned wrestler from Fiji, was one of the first to popularize jumping from the top ropes. But his most legendary moment came in a 1983 match against Backlund, who was then the WWF champion. Snuka challenged him for the title, and in Madison Square Garden, the two faced off inside a 15-foot-tall steel cage. We were there to watch as Snuka did the unthinkable—he climbed to the top of the cage and tried what was, at the time, an amazing stunt. He jumped from the top, planning to land on Backlund, leave him for dead, escape the cage and win the title. Instead, Backlund moved, and Snuka missed, crashing into the ring mat like a car crash test dummy. Backlund kept the title, but the match was the best thing we—and most of the rest of the wrestling world—had ever seen.

Completely enthralled, our group would go watch wrestling once a month (usually on Monday nights at Madison Square Garden), although we had three major coliseums in New York where wrestling was going on, and we'd follow the best cards. It was then I started following the bad guys. There was something everybody loved about Snuka, even though he was bad. I liked him, and I liked how he was able to pull in everyone as fans.

Why did I like the villains so much? Was it because I already felt like the heel in my own story?

✷

"Chris, stand in the back," my teacher told me.

It was picture day, and by the time I was 12, I was already about six feet tall, towering over my classmates. I'd always be in the back for the class picture. But being tall meant I was starting to perform well in our street hockey matches. By that time, I'd decided to focus on hockey and wrestling, the activities I enjoyed the most.

When school was out, I would go home, put on my skates and roll around the neighborhood. I was always on my skates. But sometimes I'd get caught up in certain television shows after school, and it was a summer afternoon when I was watching *The Brady Bunch* that I figured out what I needed to feel normal.

In one episode Peter Brady was going out with a girl. He'd never kissed a girl before, so he was nervous. But of course, during the episode he ended up alone with his girlfriend, and she leaned in. So he leaned in.

And they kissed. When they did, there were fireworks. Actual fireworks in their heads. When I saw it, it made sense. I knew then that I had to kiss a girl, and that when I did, I would be better. I would like the girl, and I would be normal. Now I just had to find a girl.

In our neighborhood, kids were not dating or finding boyfriends and girlfriends. It just wasn't that way. Where I lived, boys and girls stuck with their own friends. If there was any dating, it was very infrequent. Ultimately, that would make it a good neighborhood for me to lose myself in.

I didn't think it would be difficult to find myself a girl. I was popular, because I'd established the reputation of being a bit of a class clown that year. Once I left a thumbtack on the teacher's chair. She came into class and sat right on it.

Her face did not flinch. "Who did this?" she said, not moving.

No one in the class spoke. Only when she threatened the whole class did I admit it was me, and I was sent to the principal's office. But deep down, I enjoyed the attention I got for those kinds of pranks. Even then, I was a performer.

Later in the school year, I had my chance to kiss a girl for the first time. When the opportunity arose, I took it, thinking all my troubles would be over.

Oh, how wrong I was.

(3)

THE LONG SKATE HOME

"Eileen likes you," the girl said.

Apparently, my popularity was increasing. Eileen, also 12 years old, was a girl in my class whom I'd known for a while. Through her best friend, she made it known she was interested in me.

"Tell her to meet me at the convenience store after school," I said. Was I attracted to Eileen? Honestly, no. But she was a girl others thought was pretty attractive. She was slim, with long, straight brown hair somewhere between the Marcia and Jan Brady mold. She had a pretty face, and she was always chewing gum, kind of like a Valley Girl. When I heard she liked me, I didn't think about wanting a girlfriend. I only had one thought: This was my chance to get a kiss and be converted.

Later in the day after school, I put on my skates and met my friends over at the convenience store. All of my crew were there with me, looking at the wrestling magazines and playing video games. That's when Eileen walked in.

She wore a long pink coat because it was just getting cool outside, and her brown hair drizzled down her back. Of course she was chewing gum. I left the group and skated over to the door, where she was waiting.

"Let's take a walk," I said. I was already more than a foot taller than her. We left the store and walked/skated to the park, where a lot of other friends were hanging out.

I got to the point. "Do you want to go out with me?"

She looked up at me. "Yes."

I was thrilled. I even had a plan for the kiss. It couldn't be too soon—it had to be just right. We held hands as we walked back to the convenience store, and I was smooth. Quickly, I grabbed her wrist because I wanted to measure it with my hand. It didn't go as well as I had planned. When I grabbed, I grabbed her wrist too hard, and immediately Eileen pulled away. She waited a second, then grabbed my hand again and it was over.

Yeah, I was real smooth.

✶

I asked Eileen out on a Tuesday. Wednesday, I bought her a bracelet, which is why I needed to know the approximate size of her wrist. I thought the bracelet would be the key to the kiss. Even then, I knew Eileen was nothing more than an experiment. I went to the Hallmark on Greenpoint Avenue and bought the bracelet, and I gave it to her that day.

"It's beautiful," she said. And it fit perfectly. I don't think she was expecting that kind of thing from me. I knew I'd surprised her. My plan was working perfectly.

The next part was tricky, because on Thursday, I blew her off on purpose. It was all leading up to Friday.

After school Friday, we hung out at the park with our friends. We really didn't spend that much time together. Everyone was supposed to be home around 11 p.m., and when it got dark, everyone started going home.

Eileen came over to me. "I have to go," she said.

"Well, I'll skate you home," I said.

She lived five blocks from the park, and she had to pull her pink jacket around her to keep out the chilly night air. We talked about school on the way, and when we got in front of her building, we stopped. I think she knew the next part of the plan.

We were standing on the curb, so I stepped off to give us less of a height difference. She looked up at me, and I stared back with wonder and a little bit of confusion. We were holding hands, and I knew what I had to do.

This is it, I thought.

I took one hand and put it behind her neck. Gently, I pulled her to me and our lips touched in an awkward way. She closed her eyes and we explored each other's mouths a little. I never closed my eyes. I watched her face and felt what she was doing and I waited. She pulled away after about 20 seconds and smiled.

I pulled away too, still waiting.

Moments passed without us saying anything.

"Have a good night," she said.

With that, Eileen turned and walked into her building. Slowly, I turned back toward the park and skated away.

There were no fireworks.

✱

As I skated back through the cool night, I couldn't get over what I wasn't feeling.

I felt nothing. No fireworks. No sexual excitement.

It was nothing like what I felt for Mr. X or Tommy. When I reached the park everyone had gone home. I made sure the light was off in our apartment window and I sat down on a bench.

How could this be? I thought. I kissed a girl and I felt nothing. Did I do it right? How else could you do it? I must have. She smiled when we were finished. She liked it.

I did not like it.

Tears started to roll down my face, and I couldn't stop them. I couldn't have my family see me like this. Through my tears, I realized that my life was going to be harder than most. It was a difficult bit of reality for a 12-year-old to have to face.

I knew it then, and it was something I'd have to handle the rest of my life. No matter what I did, I'd have to keep this secret. My friends could not know. My parents could not know. No one could know what I knew.

I was gay.

✱

As I matured, being gay became something I had no time for. That's how a teenager deals with a situation like this.

The following week after I kissed Eileen, I paid no attention to her. I was selfish; I was not a boyfriend. I only used her for the experiment. When I knew the result, I had no need for her anymore. After a few days of ignoring her, Eileen approached me. She was still wearing her bracelet.

"What's wrong with you?" she asked.

"I'm not ready for this," I said. "I'm sorry."

It was all I could say. Could I tell her the truth? No. Could I tell anyone? Of course not. I wished her well, but Eileen and I hardly talked after that day.

Instead of girls, I — like most people in my neighborhood — filled my life with other things: school, wrestling, hockey and friends. Every Monday and Friday my friends and I worked on perfecting our wrestling moves at the local rec center. Saturdays were filled with hockey against other YMCA teams.

On Sundays we went to church. But those times were a far cry from my altar boy days when I was still in God's good graces. What priests had said about being gay was always front of mind, and coupled with the uninspired dullness of the Mass, I was not interested in church. It became useful only as a meeting place for my friends before we set out for the day.

But religion hadn't lost its hold on me completely, and I tried to follow what the church said. I felt that as long as I didn't act on being gay, I was okay. I would not act on my feelings.

(4)

CULTURE SHOCK

Archbishop Molloy High School was an all-boys Catholic school two train rides from my home in Sunnyside.

After visiting about five different schools, only one felt right, and I decided on Molloy, which was known for two things: its academic reputation, and its reputation for sports, namely baseball and basketball. Future college and professional basketball star Kenny Anderson was one year behind me at Molloy. But I wasn't necessarily interested in sports at the school.

They didn't have hockey, which I would have played. They didn't have football, which my body shape was probably best suited for. They didn't have wrestling, which I was becoming more and more obsessed with.

But I was having more problems than that. I learned early on I don't handle change very well, and high school was a culture shock for me. I'd never been on a train by myself, much less had to connect trains to go to a new school. I'd never been in classes where I didn't know the majority of students. And most importantly, I'd never had to deal with the fact that I was gay while going through all of these changes. And being gay in an all-boys school was a whole new ball game. I knew we were going to have a gym class, and I knew we were going to be expected to take showers. I didn't want to do that. I was afraid I may get caught looking at some of the other guys. I got a break early on when I realized we weren't required to take showers, but it was at our own peril. I stunk a lot, and I always seemed to get my gym class scheduled for early in the day. That means I stunk all day.

Throw in the usual school pressures like homework and fitting in, and the pressure was building. I was freaking out — and I was ready to explode.

✷

In math class, I'd never had as much trouble as I had that freshman year. After one particularly difficult test, I was told I failed. Failed? That just wasn't something I did. I was angry with myself, and I was angry about my situation. After class I walked the narrow halls of Molloy feeling the kids everywhere and the world closing in on me. Ahead of me, I saw my math teacher, who just happened to be the principal of the school. I walked past him and I filled with anger. High school was terrible. Being gay was terrible. Math was terrible.

I passed the math teacher/principal, and as I did, I couldn't contain myself. Without turning around, I spoke clearly.

"You motherfucker," I said.

It wasn't loud. It certainly wasn't loud enough to be heard by anyone behind me, like my math teacher/principal. Unfortunately, it was heard by the man directly in front of me — the assistant principal and dean of discipline, Brother Roy.

He looked at me. They all wore the same flowing black robes, like a judge.

"Let's go," he said.

I thought the day could not have gotten any worse. I was wrong. Brother Roy would be the first person to hear me bare my soul.

✷

In Brother Roy's office, I sat down in an uncomfortable chair. I tried to lie my way out of the situation.

"Brother Roy, I don't know what you thought you heard but . . ."

"There's a lot of people who want to be in this school." He told me. "If certain people act like they do not want to be in this school, they will not be in this school. Others will take their place."

I nodded. "I understand."

"Now what seems to be the problem?"

I took a deep breath.

"I'm overwhelmed," I said. "I'm not adjusting." I told him about my anxieties. Well, I left out the big one.

"A lot of people go through these same feelings," Brother Roy said. "You aren't the only one, and people get over these fears. You too need to get over these fears."

He doesn't know what I'm going through, I thought. *How could he know?*

"It's harder for me," I said, not thinking.

"Why?" he asked.

Another deep breath. Was I going to do this?

"Because I'm gay."

There. It was out. I did it.

Brother Roy didn't flinch.

"Well, yes, that can be difficult," he said.

Yes it can, I thought. He had no idea. He twiddled his thumbs and I could tell he was looking for something else to say. Instead, we just sat there, quiet, confused.

✱

It felt good to tell someone my secret. By this time I'd kept it for four years. People say sometimes it feels like the weight of the world is off your shoulders. I don't know if it felt like that, because I still had to deal with it, but it did feel a bit lighter. Brother Roy decided I was more than he could handle, so he sent me to Father George Zahorian. Again, I was faced with a priest talking to me about being gay. It did not go well.

Father George sat in his office in his collar and looked terribly confused when I confessed that I was gay.

"Now, Chris," he said, "just don't act on these temptations. All of us are tempted by Satan. We cannot give in."

I nodded.

"I believe you can change yourself with the power of prayer," he said. "Pray to the Lord every night to help your soul. Pray to Him that you can overcome these temptations and continue to lead an honorable life by walking in His footsteps."

That was all I needed to hear. It was a catch-22. Of course I wanted to change. But in my mind I'd already tried that — it didn't work. I needed to accept who I was.

Fuck you, I thought. *Fuck you for trying to change me.* If I could trace this back to the feelings I had for Mr. X at the age of six, I had to assume I was born this way, or at least born with tendencies toward being gay. Who knows how or why this happened? No one — not scientists, not priests, not even gay people know how or why they are gay. *So maybe*, I thought, *the Higher Being made me this way, and if He/She/It didn't want me to be gay, why did He plant the seeds of these feelings in me, then put me somewhere where they'd grow like weeds?*

I was supposed to go back to see Father George. I didn't. Instead I met Brother Bernard, a charismatic counselor at the school. He was easy to talk to, a wonderful listener and someone who genuinely wanted to help students. I told him — the total of people who knew my secret was now three — and he wanted to help me.

We talked about what I was feeling, and he gave me some of the best advice of my life.

"I think about what it means to gay," I told him. "No matter what, my life is going to be hard. My parents want me to get married and have kids. I won't be doing that, will I? Everything will be hard."

"Wrong," Brother Bernard said. "You're looking at life the wrong way. Think of an ice cream cone."

He drew an ice cream cone on a sheet paper.

"There is a wide, open end, and there is a small, closed end," he said. "You are looking at life, and seeing it drip down into one inevitable point."

He paused.

"You need to flip the cone," he said, turning the paper. "Your life has endless possibilities. You will start from this end point, and you will flow out, into the open. You will do everything you want — because you can."

I met with Brother Bernard five or six times my freshman year, and because of him, I was able to get through being a freshman. It was the first time in a long time that any one affiliated with the church had given me peace or sanctuary.

✱

Through the rest of my freshman year, I coped. I kept to myself. My typical day involved coming to school, working and going home, where I would do homework and meet up with friends to play hockey and wrestle.

Such was life. With no pressure to date, it was easy to cover up my secret in the neighborhood. But other than the three men at school, I told no one else I was gay.

Before the end of my freshman year I attended field day at Molloy. Really, it was a chance for all the high school coaches to get a chance to recruit from the student body. I participated in some track and field events, including shot put, which I fared surprisingly well at.

I did so well, the coach wanted to have me on the team.

I told him no.

It was something I thought long and hard about, but ultimately it was something I knew I didn't want to do. I knew that if I committed to the coach, I would be staying after school, practicing, and I only wanted to escape home.

It wasn't that difficult of a decision to make. But years later, it would be one of my biggest regrets. Maybe if I'd decided to join the team, I would've fit in in some way.

(5)

IT'S SO FAKE

"You know it's all fake don't you?"

I didn't respond. My uncle Johnny didn't like wrestling. He never did.

But, because my father never got a driver's license — in New York he never needed one — Johnny ended up driving me, Tommy Clarke, my cousin John and my father to the Meadowlands in New Jersey to see a great card featuring the legendary Ric Flair and Steamboat, among others.

"I mean, it's so fake," Johnny said. "You can tell."

None of us said anything.

We'd scored some great seats — fourth row, and I was excited.

But I realized early on that sitting so close meant you lost some of the magic. I'd heard the rumors that wrestling was fake ever since I was a kid, and deep down I knew the matches were scripted, just as I assumed everyone knew. But I still didn't want to be reminded of it. Unfortunately, from the fourth row, you could see some tricks.

In one bout, we saw Jake the Snake — a lanky wrestler who, later in his career, brought snakes into the ring and found tremendous success in the WWF — pull out a razorblade and cut himself.

"Phonies!" my uncle shouted. He looked at us. "I can't believe you like this crap."

In a way, he was right.

It was tough seeing that there were tricks involved — I, like most fans, wanted to be kept in the dark. It's like watching a great movie, with great actors: You're caught up in the story, and you love it and you want to see what happens. That was good wrestling. But sometimes — like when we saw Jake the Snake pull his blade — it was like seeing the cables holding up Superman.

But when wrestlers gave those flawless, heart-pounding performances, when the whole crowd was riveted to their every move, razorblades and scripts faded into the back of my mind. Only a few months before, Tommy, his uncle and I went to Madison Square Garden to see Hulk Hogan beat the Iranian-born Iron Sheik for the title. The crowd roared as Hogan won his first title, and like Hogan, I ripped off my undershirt to celebrate his victory. Luckily, I had a sweatshirt to wear home.

The crowd's energy that night made an impression. I knew then I wanted to make a crowd roar like that. I knew I could do it.

But that night in the Meadowlands, I had a different feeling. Some, like my uncle, could not enjoy something like this. I wondered if there was anything that could turn him around.

Then Flair and Steamboat came out in an explosion of lights and music.

Flair, also known as the Nature Boy, was a six-foot, 242-pound wrestling machine, the perfect mix of a technically impressive wrestler and an outstanding showman, evident by the $15,000 robes he liked to wear in the ring. Steamboat, whose mother was Japanese, could unleash moves like Bruce Lee, mixing wrestling moves with a karate-like gimmick. Even to this day, his ability to make his opponents' moves look devastating as well as his ability to act hurt is legendary.

It was a 29-minute match, very physical, much closer to an actual athletic contest than anything else on the card. None of their stuff looked phony. Their suplexes were always amazing. Their holds were tight. Their intensity never flagged. And when the match was over, and Flair had won, the crowd cheered, with a fervor that reminded me of Hogan's victory at the Garden.

It was an amazing performance by two knowledgeable, incredibly seasoned wrestlers. You could tell they knew how to work the crowd. And even though you knew it was scripted, you still appreciated the effort. I looked down to my uncle, who was also clapping. That surprised me.

"You know what?" he said, pointing to the ring. "Those guys are entertaining."

Wow, I thought.

They won over Uncle Johnny, not an easy thing to do.

It was at that moment, after seeing those two professionals put on a perfect match, that I officially decided I would one day become a professional wrestler. But I didn't want to only make it as a pro—I wanted to do it right, the way Flair did. No—I was *going* to do it the way Flair and Steamboat did, the way Hogan did.

I was going to convert people like my uncle. I was going to be good.

✶

By high school, my friends and I already knew the importance of wrestlers being big. You had to be large, and in many ways, you had to be larger than life. In short, you had to be big to make it big.

My cousin Brian developed a fitness regimen and I adopted it. It was a multi-day routine, covering all body parts. Part of it had us putting a hockey stick through the backs of a couple of dining room chairs. We would use it to do pull-ups behind our necks, working our back and neck muscles, as well as to do pushups and chin ups from an inclined position. Later, my friend Danny O. and I would lie about our ages (you had to be 18) to join a gym and formally work on our bodies more, but even as young teenagers, we knew what had to be done. Bigger was always better, even if I'd never be big enough.

✶

By the time I was a junior, high school was a routine for me, and it was easier to get by. I made more friends, but my social life still centered around the neighborhood. My grades were good all through those years, and I was even starting to earn some money on my own. When I was a junior, things were as stable in my world as they could get.

By this time, I'd come to terms with the fact I was gay, and the best and easiest way to cope was to live with it, which to me meant ignoring it. I needed to focus on school, studying, hanging with friends, work, earning and saving money and working out. But more than anything else, my love of wrestling was becoming an obsession, possibly because I was looking for things to help distract me from thinking about being gay. My friends were just that—

friends. I did not lust after them. I did not openly want to be with them in a sexual way. So it was not difficult for me to practice wrestling moves with them, to be on the ground with them, and have it mean nothing more than wrestling. These were my friends, and they were straight. I knew that. And there was no way I was going to jeopardize my secret by revealing in any way that I was gay.

There was no sexual gratification when I was wrestling. It was about the sport, the performance, the moves, the competition. It was not something sexual. It didn't enter my mind.

After school and work one Friday, I walked to the rec center, where I'd become a regular. Just two blocks from my house, the rec center was no bigger than a high school basketball court. With Ping-Pong, billiard tables, a jukebox and most importantly, the mats, there were always kids milling about, and the facilitators there were very lenient with me and my wrestling buddies.

Tommy Clarke and I would get into our usual routine. There was no ring, only an area covered with wafer-thin blue mats. Four columns marked the corners of our imaginary ring, and chairs and tables lined the perimeter. Some of our friends filmed the matches, while others served as commentators. Those who didn't know us thought we were stupid or crazy, immature kids. But some came to watch and thought it was pretty cool.

Tommy and I knew each other's moves like dancers know their partners. We'd been doing this for a few years now, and we were very good at performing. We didn't talk, because there was no need. And we didn't script anything because we were so good at improvising the match. Climbing on top of a table was a signal that it was the other person's turn to dominate. When I jumped off, Tommy would roll away in the nick of time and then he would take control, or vice versa.

We'd start with a typical lock-up, and we'd alternate twisting arms, raking eyes, stomping and punching each other. Taking turns on the offensive, one of us would suplex the other or lay down a chair hit. We'd try sleeper holds, figure-four leglocks, body slams, pile drivers and sometimes the Boston Crab—a move where you get your opponent down on his belly, hold his legs up and sit on his lower back. Sometimes we'd throw each other into one of the columns or into imaginary ropes, bouncing off and flying back as if the ropes were really there. Not wanting to miss out on a pro move, we even stole little finger pricks from one of our biology classes, using them to scrape our foreheads to bleed.

Years later, I would learn we were doing it all wrong.

But right then, we were the kings of the rec center. We had live audiences and videos of our matches. We were wrestlers. We were actually pretty good. We were on our way.

(6)

REDEMPTION

"So, you been working out?"

My brother, who was going to college at St. John's University, was home, and we were once again crammed together in the little room in the apartment. This arrangement hadn't exactly rekindled our brotherly love: He had decided to bust my balls.

"Yeah," I said.

"So you think you're some big tough guy now, huh?"

"Not really."

"You think you can take your big brother now, huh?"

He hit me in the face.

As a junior in high school, I had grown to nearly six-four, three inches taller than my brother. Working out with Danny everyday hadn't hurt, either, and I was showing some cut in my biceps. I could handle myself.

"You think you can take me, now?" he challenged, hitting me again.

"Yeah, I think I can," I said.

He tried to hit me again. He was a lefty, so you had to be ready for him. I ducked and responded. Hard. It was time to fight back. When my fist hit his chin I could see the look of shock on his face. He was completely caught off guard, stunned as much psychologically as physically. I guess he never thought I would try to beat him.

Then I hit him again. And again. He couldn't beat me up anymore. I was too big. As I raised my fist to land another blow, something in Ken's eyes stopped me. He looked vulnerable, maybe even afraid. I stopped, knowing it was over, and he left the room. I don't know how he felt. Maybe he was in shock. Or maybe part of him felt like it was mission accomplished, that he finally "toughened me up." I'm not sure what he was thinking or what that day meant to him, but it meant a lot to me.

It was an initiation, a rite of passage. Our relationship changed that day. My brother was never a bad person, just wild. We'd never hung out together or talked much, and we didn't talk much or hang out while we were in college. Not until years later would we start really talking. But when we did, we formed a strong friendship, and I think it all started that day. Ken would come to mean a lot to me, and ultimately, he would even save my life.

*

Around that time, I wrote to every wrestling school I could think of. Most of the addresses were found in the wrestling newsletters and magazines I bought every week. When I found a new place, I would make sure to write down the address. There were only a few schools across the country, so I sent them all of my information and requested some from them.

Two schools sent me a return letter. One was from a school for the old World Class Championship Wrestling promotion out of Dallas, Texas, which was run by one of my childhood favorites, Chris Adams. The other was from a legendary promoter out of Portland, Oregon.

The Dallas school was touting a student in the pamphlet as the next big star. He had just started to appear on TV for the Dallas promotion, and his name was Steve Williams. He would later change his name, since there was already another American wrestler had made it big as "Dr. Death" Steve Williams. This supposed future superstar's new name? Steve Austin, as in "Stone Cold" Steve Austin, one of the biggest stars in wrestling history.

The Dallas pamphlet looked professional, and when I saw that one of their students was already on TV, I was really excited. But the other response was from a promotion that was known as a great starting ground for wrestlers including Scotty "The Body," (who later went on to become a friend of mine called "Raven,") Billy Jack Haynes and one of my favorite wrestlers, Rowdy Roddy Piper.

Before I opened the letter, I knew I was getting an invite. What would I tell my parents? If a wrestling school in Oregon came calling, I would have to go. And they would have to understand. I opened up the letter and saw the same handwritten note I'd sent off a few weeks earlier.

What the hell? I thought.

I went back to my room, sat on my bed and turned the letter over. There, I saw more writing, in a different hand. At the bottom was the signature of Don Owens, owner of the wrestling school in Portland. *Here we go,* I thought. *Here's my offer.*

I started to read. There weren't many words.

"Dear Chris," it said, "if my own kids wanted to get into this dirty, filthy business, I'd pull out a gun and shoot them."

What?

"Do yourself a favor and get a college education and never think about this again," Owens wrote. That was the end of the letter.

Holy shit.

It was like that kid in *A Christmas Story* who wants a BB gun, but his parents, his teacher and even Santa Claus tell him he shouldn't have it because he'll shoot his eye out. That was me. I wanted this, but everybody was telling me no.

Fuck it, I thought. *I'm doing it anyway.*

(7)

ROMAN CANDLES

Every Thursday, I played racquetball at an outdoor court on 47th Street with a group of friends. The games were set up by one of our former grammar school teachers, a good-natured loner of a guy named Bob. He enjoyed keeping up with his former students, and we enjoyed the six-packs of beer he would buy for us.

On this particular night, when he offered me a beer, I accepted — six times. It was more than my share. Feeling buzzed, I said my goodbyes and began my walk home. The beer left me restless. When I arrived home at around 11 p.m., I headed back out to walk Ace, the family dog we had named after KISS guitarist Ace Frehley. I strolled past the Real People Pub, that gay bar just five blocks from our house, strutting my stuff a little more than usual. I wasn't looking for action, but I also wasn't about to discourage it. I was horny.

Ace had always been my excuse to walk by the gay bar and casually ogle passersby and patrons. If my friends saw me walking by the bar, maybe loitering a bit more than necessary, I could always just blame the dog. I had never spoken to anyone outside the club though, just as I had never tried to hit on anyone at school. And I sure as hell had never been inside the club. But with the alcohol fueling my courage, I decided I wouldn't shy away tonight.

As my stroll slowed to a crawl in front of the club, I noticed a guy walking along the sidewalk across the street. From a distance, he looked fit with dark skin, maybe a bit older than me, probably in his early twenties. As he passed me, I paused for a couple of beats and turned around to check him out. He had the same idea apparently, as our eyes met. I fumbled with the dog's leash for a moment before ducking around the corner into an alley, out of his sight. I pressed myself against the wall, heart pounding, trying to disappear into the bricks behind me. After a minute or so, I walked back around to the front of the bar. I didn't expect him to still be there, but I wanted him to be. And he was.

This time I didn't glance at him, and instead walked with my head down at a good pace toward my house. I sensed that he was following me, but I didn't steal a look. Back at my house, I went inside and let Ace off the leash. With the window shade partially drawn, I glanced outside the building. The stranger was standing across the street searching the windows for me. Our eyes met again, and this time he motioned for me for join him. I restocked on courage with a couple swigs of vodka from my parents' liquor cabinet and headed downstairs.

He was gone.

"Damn it," I whispered.

Then I caught a glimpse of a man 40 yards away, across the street in the park. The figure stood under a tree that cast a wide shadow over the ground, not far from the monkey bars that had often been the drinking spot for me and my friends. *Fuck it*, I thought as I walked over.

He was even better looking up close.

"What's your name?" he asked.

I told him and asked the same question.

"Matt."

He told me he was staying with an aunt who lived nearby for the summer.

"Do you live there?" he asked me, pointing toward my building.

"Yes," I said, purposefully keeping my answers as short as possible. I was sure that I wanted this—whatever was coming next—but I couldn't shake the feeling that I was doing something dirty. And I was paranoid that one of my friends would jump out of the shadows and bust me. Even as desire overwhelmed me, I clung to a way out, thinking of an exit strategy.

Without warning, he kissed me. Stunned, I took a second to adjust, then gave in to the moment. It was my first real kiss. Where fireworks had been strangely missing from my first kiss with Eileen, there was now a pyrotechnic bonanza going off in my chest to rival the borough's Fourth of July display.

Our lips stayed locked for a minute. Then two. He was gentle; everything about the moment felt right. My hesitance vanished, and I filled with a sense of calm that was entirely unfamiliar to me.

Then a noise: a rustling, the sound of footsteps on grass nearing closer. I broke free, my head snapping around to the right. Someone was coming. I tugged on Matt's arm, begging him to squat down next to me.

It was one of my brother's friends, a kid named Joseph. I couldn't risk him identifying me, starting up a conversation, and later mentioning something casually to my brother. I didn't want to explain myself, not now or ever. Leading Matt by the arm, I hustled to the fence that outlined the park. The fence led down a hill and ended near the loading dock of a brick warehouse. We ran down the hill, ducking low and out of the way of the lone nearby light. I was breathing heavily as I crouched beside Matt, out of the sightline of my brother's friend. I wasn't sure if he had seen us take off, so we remained still and silent for a minute. When I could no longer hear Joseph, I relaxed, falling back into the grass.

Matt grabbed my arm and pulled me toward him, trying to nuzzle my neck.

"That was close," he muttered.

"I'm sorry, that scared me too much," I said, pushing him off me. I still wanted to be with him, but the thrill of the moment was gone, replaced by fear. "This is not worth me getting caught."

We walked back up the hill toward the monkey bars. Sensing, his disappointment I began to explain myself.

"Look, this is a tight-knit group," I told him. "Everyone here knows everybody else. And they all know everyone else's business. If people see us here together, they're going to wonder who you are, and why you're with me. They're going to keep asking questions until we run out of lies."

"I understand," Matt said, his voice sounding deflated.

"Look," I continued, "I don't know how much longer you're going to be staying here, but if you're here at the park and you see me with my friends, you can't look at me. Okay?"

Matt stared ahead, speechless.

"I mean it—you *can't* look at me!" I added with emphasis. "You can't talk to me. You can't communicate with me in any way. Okay? That's just the way it has to be, because people here will talk about it. They will wonder who you are and why we're talking."

Finally he responded, "Okay."

I felt awkward, clumsy, foolish. I turned toward my house.

"I've got to go," I told him.

That night, I lie in bed struggling to process everything that had just happened to me. Despite the exhilaration, the fireworks, the release of doing what I wanted for once, fear still trumped everything, and I hoped I wouldn't see Matt again.

✷

The next morning I awoke feeling dirty. Matt was still on my mind. There was no doubt I had hurt his feelings, but I wasn't feeling too sympathetic. I was only thinking about me and what I'd done. The words of priests and their countless, damning sermons were like a terrible voice-over to the memories of the previous night. I was a sinner. I was going to Hell.

I spent the day in a funk, feeling guilty and still restless, but determined not to repeat the previous night's affair. I took six showers that day and I still felt dirty. After a long day at my summer job—working a ticket window for the Port Authority—I ate dinner with my parents and headed back to the park to hang out with some friends. As we joked around, my mind began to wander to the events of the previous night.

Without warning, a familiar voice called out my name. I turned, and there was Matt, smiling. I didn't know if he was testing me or trying to out me in front of my friends. But I wasn't about to find out. I grabbed him by the shoulders and shoved him away from the group.

"You stupid motherfucker," I whispered. "What the fuck did I tell you?"

He didn't answer. The smile was gone from his face. His eyes widened.

"Dude, if you ever fucking say a word to me again, I will fucking kill you," I told him loud enough so my friends could plainly hear. I pulled him closer and lowered my voice. "I'm not just saying that. I will fucking kill you. Now get the fuck out of here."

I shoved him hard toward the entrance of the park. He gathered himself, then looked at me, clearly shaken up. I didn't care. I wanted him out of my sight. He turned to leave, his feet pounding the path that led out of the park. Still huffing, I held my ground for a minute to be certain he wasn't coming back.

"Who was that?" Danny asked while my back was still to the group. "And what was that all about?"

"I saw that guy in the park a couple of days ago," I responded, turning back to face my friends. "He was asking me for drugs."

Danny just nodded. That answer seemed to satisfy them. And me.

After that day, I never saw Matt again. But I thought about him from time to time, and I always wished I'd been man enough to treat him better.

✱

In 1985 the wrestling world took a hit — and my world did too.

Pro wrestler Eddy Mansfield exposed the world of wrestling to John Stossel of *20/20*. With all the rumors swirling around about wrestling being fake, Mansfield showed Stossel everything from cutting to how the matches were scripted. The not-so-secret secret of the pro wrestling world was out. But what people didn't know was that even though the matches were scripted, it took so much practice and effort to make the performance look real and good. Like my uncle Johnny learned that night in the Meadowlands, when pro wrestling is done well, it looks amazing — and the effect it has on the crowd is equally amazing. Wrestling *is* real, just maybe not in the way that people think.

Like when Tommy and I wrestled, I would let him get me in a sleeper hold, but once he did, I was actually in a sleeper hold. And many times, he would apply, or maybe more accurately, I would allow him to apply enough pressure to actually put me out. It was a strange mix of reality and illusion.

The *20/20* report still had a big effect on me, though. It was intense. Seeing a man show us how the moves were done was a bit like seeing KISS without their makeup on. It was just weird. But it didn't stop my passion for wrestling.

In fact, it may have increased it, because I was motivated to show the world how good wrestling could be. It was then I decided to come up with new moves, to do more than what was already being done. I knew wrestling took skill and talent. I wanted others who didn't believe — just like my uncle in the past — to realize it too.

Of course, if I was going to do that, I would have to keep a very big secret of my own. I'd never heard of a legitimate, openly gay wrestler before. Then again, I didn't really care, either. Nothing was going to stop me.

Not even the locked doors of the Trump Plaza.

(8)

THE TURNBUCKLE OF MY DREAMS

During my senior year of high school, my friends and I headed down to Atlantic City for *WrestleMania IV*. Because of a dispute over the 1998 world championship title involving a giant, a braggadocios millionaire, Hulk Hogan and an evil twin referee (only in pro wrestling, right?), they held a tournament in Atlantic City to determine who would be champion. Along with friends Mike Passariello (Pass), Mike Cannarozzi, Joe Gravina, Charles Croce, Cousin John and Danny, I took a bus down to Trump Plaza in New Jersey.

Pass's cousin Tom, of Tom's River, New Jersey, worked as a chef in the hotel next door, so we were hooked up with a suite and all the food we could eat. We lived it up. But the real story came after the match.

We watched as wrestlers like Andre the Giant, Hogan and Greg Valentine worked through the tournament. The final match of the tournament, and the main event of the show to determine the new champ, pitted "The Million Dollar Man" Ted DiBiase against Randy Savage, a crazy, wild-eyed fan favorite known as "The Macho Man." In the end, Savage made the Million Dollar Man pay, climbing to the top turnbuckle to deliver his signature flying elbow drop and win the world heavyweight title, with the crowd celebrating like crazy.

The show took about four hours, and by that time, we were tired and we knew we had dinner waiting for us at the hotel. We decided to head back. Full from the food, excitement and the day of drinking, the group fell asleep quickly.

I awoke at 2 a.m. with a vision in my head. I thought about the movie *Rocky*, and how he walked out into the empty arena alone the night before his big fight. I wondered if I too could get into the empty arena. As the others slept, I left our room, walked out onto the Boardwalk and up to the doors of the arena. I yanked on the doors. They were locked.

Shit. How could I get in?

I walked around the corner and saw a parking garage. Could it be another way in? I walked down into the garage, looking for an entrance. I turned toward the Plaza, and sure enough, there was a set of glass doors. I took a deep breath. I grabbed the handle on the door. I closed my eyes and pulled.

It opened.

I was in.

I worked my way through a labyrinth of underground hallways and I realized I was backstage at the Plaza. I desperately searched for any kind of entranceway to the arena, but I was lost. And then, out of nowhere, a loud, shocking voice called, "Hey, who are you?"

It was a janitor, looking at me like he knew I had no business being there.

Just look professional, I thought. *Look like you belong.*

"Hey, Charlie," I said, smiling. I kept walking.

I think the man was so befuddled, he didn't know what to say. I also doubt his name was Charlie. But before he could say anything else, I disappeared around the next corner. I worked my way up another ramp and around a bend, which led me to the opening into the arena. My eyes locked on the empty ring where, just hours earlier, I'd seen Savage jump from the turnbuckle and win the heavyweight championship.

The seats, filled with roaring spectators only hours earlier, rose empty into the yawning silence. While earlier the arena felt more like a gladiatorial coliseum, now it felt like a cathedral.

And I was headed straight for the altar. Heart pounding, I worked my way behind the curtain where the wrestlers come out, pausing at the top of the ramp that led all the way down to the ring. I busted through the curtain and down the ramp, imitating Hogan, pulling at my T-shirt and pointing to the non-existent crowd. The fans were back in their seats, banishing the silence with deafening cheers. Cheers for me.

It felt so right.

I stepped through the ropes and into the ring, moving right to the center. I spun in circles, soaking in this amazing moment.

So amazing I decided I needed a souvenir.

I looked up at the massive *WrestleMania IV* banner hanging from the rafters. It had to be at least 35 feet wide and 100 feet long. I tried to visualize how large it would be rolled up — it would be impossible to take.

I looked around me, and my gaze finally settled on a turnbuckle. I walked over to the one Savage had jumped from. I took it, slipped it under my shirt, and made my way out of the Plaza. When I reached the entranceway to the arena, I looked back one last time, taking it all in.

Someday, I thought. *Someday.*

✶

When I returned to the hotel room, the others stirred, but no one woke up. I tried to tell them the news, but they only wanted to sleep. The next day, they rose slowly.

"Hey," Danny said, "I dreamt last night that you told me you broke in to the Plaza and stole the turnbuckle Savage jumped off of."

I smiled. "Man, that's a crazy dream."

As the others started to get up, I walked over to the closet. I reached into my bag and pulled out the turnbuckle.

"Oh my God!" Pass said. I handed him the turnbuckle, and he ran his hands over it in disbelief.

Danny couldn't believe it either. "It really happened!" he said.

We grabbed our video camera, and they fixed it on a close-up of my face.

"This is Chris Klucsarits," I said into the camera. "It is March 29, 1988. Last night, Randy Savage won the world heavyweight championship."

The camera started to pan out.

"Savage jumped off this turnbuckle."

The camera then showed me holding my prized possession. I had the biggest shit-eating grin on my face.

✶

When I graduated from high school, I just assumed all of my friends and I would move down to Texas or Florida and join one of the regional wrestling leagues.

There was never a question in my mind. But somehow, that's not the way it worked out. A few nights after I'd graduated, my family was having dinner together, discussing where I would go to college. I told them I had something important to say.

"Mom, Dad—I don't want to go to college," I said. "I want to become a professional wrestler."

They stopped eating and looked at me. My brother, who was also home, did the same.

"Don't be stupid, Chris," my dad said. "That's not a job. That's not even a sport! It's a hobby."

My mother agreed. "You need to go to school, to figure out what you want to do in life," she said.

Since my brother had gone to St. John's, it was assumed I would also go to college. To be honest, up until I was a sophomore in high school, I didn't even know college was optional. I thought it was like high school, where everyone was supposed to or expected to go.

"I know what I want to do in my life," I said. "I want to wrestle. I'm going to do it."

My father just shook his head. My brother looked from me to my parents, wondering what would happen next.

"Here's the deal," my mother said. "You can do what you want. You're 18 years old and can make your own decisions. But if you decide you're going to pursue professional wrestling, you'll do it on your own. You will be living on your own. You will move out of this house."

I listened to her. It was a fair deal. I had a decision to make. I thought about it for a few days, going over the scenarios in my head. I didn't assume school would end my wrestling dreams, just postpone them for four years. I also knew that at 18, I wasn't ready to live on my own. I didn't feel mature enough. The more I thought about it, college seemed like a good idea.

A year before that, Danny had left for college at the University of Buffalo, an eight-hour drive from Sunnyside. I missed him, and I thought that might be the best option for me. Plus, it would prepare me to live away from home, my family and the neighborhood. After talking with Danny and my parents, I told them I'd made a decision. I'd go to college. But when I graduated, I would go into professional wrestling.

That compromise was fine with them. But I got a sense they really didn't believe I would or could make it as a wrestler.

Four years, I thought. What could happen in four years?

(9)

MY COLLEGE EDUCATION

Danny O'Sullivan was the kind of guy who was always comfortable in any kind of situation. When he went to a party, he knew just what to bring. If someone was sick, he knew if you should send a card or flowers. He was tall and good-looking, and he held an easy confidence about him. Because of that, people loved him, and by the time I went to visit Buffalo's campus for an orientation that summer, I already had a group of 20 friends — all Dan's.

Dozens of kids interested in the school were shuttled up to the campus for a weekend to get a taste of the college experience. We were there to meet other prospective students and to make sure this was the place for us.

I'd be leaving Sunnyside for the first time, and while I didn't handle change well in my transition to high school, college would be different. I'd grown more mature, and with Dan there, the transition would be smooth. The only thing that concerned me was keeping my secret.

In Sunnyside, everyone knew your business. But because of the culture of the neighborhood, where there wasn't a lot of dating, it wasn't strange for me to never go out with girls. You hung around with your boys, your crew. I knew college would be different. In college, you were living with all of your friends. And these people expected you to be hooking up — a lot, I supposed. Danny had told me a little about what it was like in college. I didn't know if I was a good-looking guy or not, but I'd heard that some college girls could be pretty easy, so I thought it wouldn't make a difference.

At 18, I was still a virgin, and I knew that if I was going to keep my secret, I would have to hook up with a girl. So on this orientation trip, I wasn't planning to check out the school as much as I was checking out the girls, trying to gauge how difficult it would be to have sex with a girl. But I knew that finding a willing partner was only the first hurdle — physically getting the job done might be the biggest obstacle of all.

*

But despite my girl-focused goal, the first thing I noticed at orientation was the guys. There were good-looking guys everywhere. College was going to be great! But I tried not to get distracted. I wanted to find a girl.

The University of Buffalo was divided into two campuses — the North Campus and the South, or Main, Campus. There were thousands of students there. Some came for the seismology department that studied earthquakes, some came for the health sciences. Some came to party. On Thursday night, bars would have ridiculous drink specials for the partiers, and on-campus parties were normally held in any of the coed dorms for the underage crowd.

My first party at Buffalo was orientation weekend. We went out to an island on a nearby lake, and everyone was drinking. I found out early it wasn't difficult to get a girl.

We were on the beach of the island when I noticed a girl looking at me. I thought she may be it. I needed some advice. Jeff Manly, another prospective student, was nearby.

"Hey, that girl's looking at me," I said. "Should I go over to her?"

"Yeah, man," he encouraged, pushing me away.

I went over to her — a pretty, petite blond named Gina. I asked her to go for a walk, and I thought she was into me. Later we sat down on the beach, not far from the party. The waves crashed on the shore, the stars shone bright above us — it seemed straight out of a romance novel and I knew this was my chance. I asked if I could kiss her, and she nodded. Something about making out in public reminded me of Matt, and I knew I wasn't going to have a problem faking it with Gina.

Each moment was more exciting because I was pushing what she would let me do. Would she let me touch her chest? Yes. Would she let me unbutton her shirt? Yes. Would she let me unbutton her pants? Yes. Each step we took made it exciting for me, even though I did not want to be with her. What I really wanted was to show my new friends that I was just like them, that I liked girls and wanted nothing more than to score.

But Gina wasn't that kind of girl. She didn't want to go all the way. But it didn't really matter, because for the rest of the orientation I could brag about how I got to third base with Gina. She served her purpose. But Gina wanted more. She wanted a relationship. Even two years later, she would still come chasing after me, wondering why we never went out.

I avoided her as much as I could.

✱

I moved up to Buffalo for school, and for those four years in college, my wrestling career was put on hold. I only wrestled when I came home from school for breaks and during the summers. A lot of times I missed it, and I decorated my dorm room in dozens of wrestling posters. Because we didn't get cable on campus, we'd have to go to friends' houses off campus to watch wrestling. A friend of mine back in Sunnyside also taped the pay-per-view matches and sent the tapes up to me. Of course, that meant I had to avoid finding out who'd won the recent matches.

Wrestling even played a role in deciding my major. I knew from tests in high school that my interests led more to social work or physical therapy. While social workers made no money, I liked the thought of helping people. When a friend of mine who was a physical therapy major explained some of the classes in his program, it sounded interesting. It was the wrestling angle that helped make the decision. If I couldn't initially make it as a wrestler, I thought I could become a physical therapist for wrestlers and get my foot in the door.

So while my college years might have meant setting aside wrestling for the present, I was determined that wrestling, and only wrestling, would be my future.

✱

After making out with Gina, I was more confident than ever. I knew I could survive in college because I could keep my secret. But if I was really going to sell myself as the typical heterosexual male, I was certain I would have to go all the way.

My first three weeks did not go very well. I brought girls back to my room each Friday night, and each time was a comedy of errors.

The first time I came too soon. Like, before my pants were even off. The second, I put the condom on wrong, rolling it out like a sock. The girl laughed and left the room.

The third Friday I thought I was ready. I brought Cathy back to my room. She was tall and unattractive. As we fooled around on my bed, I again successfully became excited, although I was still thinking about having sex with men. After making out for a few minutes, I reached for a condom.

"What are you doing?" Cathy asked, eyes wide.

"I'm getting a condom," I said. "I thought we were going to have sex."

She laughed. "I'm not having sex with you."

Three strikes. I was out. Just like in baseball.

✶

By that time, word was spreading about my inability to get laid. It was perfect. No one suspected I was gay. On the fourth Friday, a friend of mine told me she knew a girl at another school who was "really easy." It was just what I was looking for.

The easy girl's name was Christine, and it did not matter to me what she looked like. Christine went to Cornell, and that weekend, she came up to Buffalo with a group of her friends. They knew I wanted to have sex for the first time, and Christine was willing, so the friends set us up.

She was not attractive at all—short, pudgy and her face wasn't pretty. But as I said, she was willing. During that week's party, we went back to my room, and this time, I did everything right. Got excited. Didn't come in my pants. Put the condom on right.

"There ya go," she said.

Being inside a woman felt strange—warm and wet and not altogether unpleasant. As Christine directed me, I took it slow and we swayed back and forth on top of the bed. She smiled and looked up at me as my body shivered. When I finished, she hugged me. It only took a few minutes, and it was over.

I'd done it. Everyone knew I'd lost my virginity. The next day I called my father and brother just to tell them. When they asked me what she looked like, I was honest.

"Well, she looks like the kind of girl that gives you crabs," I joked.

Sadly, it was no joke.

✱

Later that day, I started to itch. Upon further inspection, I discovered Christine did, in fact, give me crabs. My first time and I got crabs! I didn't even *like* girls and I got crabs from a girl!

"Son of a bitch," I said.

When my roommates asked me what was wrong, I showed them. Later, we would refer to them as my "Little Friends." As in, "So, Chris, how are your Little Friends doing? They gone yet?" Luckily, Christine went to Cornell and I never saw her again. At least I didn't have to deal with another woman wanting a relationship with a gay man.

(10)

CHASING MY DREAM

Danny and I still worked out every day.

Our average day at college went something like this: We got up, still groggy from the party the night before, and we went to class — we were religious about going to class because we figured if our parents were paying for it, we needed to go — then we worked out, did some studying and partied. It was a great time. But every day I missed not being able to wrestle. And every day I was faced with the temptation of meeting really good-looking guys.

Sometimes, a group of our Sunnyside friends would come up by the busload — like 20 of them. Many of them didn't go to college, or if they did, they went to St. John's and lived at home, so the whole concept of going away to college was foreign to them. We would have them up when the Jets played the Bills, and we would always get into fights at the games. It's one thing to cheer for your team, but it's another thing to cheer against another team. But we did it anyway.

Those were good times, and like a lot of people say about college, probably the best times of my life. Nevertheless, I would take a risk, one that would ruin everything about those good times if I got caught. I could not overcome my curiosity, and after 12 years of pent up gay aggression, I needed to let it out.

I knew just where to go.

✱

It was called the Gay and Lesbian Alliance. It was the college's official gay group. Afraid of being seen, I would never go in a place like that. But I would stand outside the building and watch others who went in. It was the spring of my freshman year, and I would make it a point to watch those people walking in and out of the Alliance, just as I'd watched people go in and out of the gay bar in my neighborhood.

I never knew what it would lead to, but secretly, I wanted something to happen.

On a warm spring day, I was walking by the Alliance, alone, when I saw another student come out of the building. He was dark-skinned, Polynesian, and I could tell he really took care of his body.

I looked at him. He looked back. Even though I was a relative novice in meeting other gay men, there is a sixth sense, a way you know when someone else is gay and interested in you. I knew it immediately with this student. When our eyes met, it was as if we had found a similar yearning within ourselves.

I walked into the men's room in a nearby building and he followed. I went back outside and he followed again. I sat on a bench and he walked over.

"Hi," I said.

"Hey, how are you?"

I'd seen him around campus before. "Good. How you doing?"

"I'm good," he said.

When I kissed Matt in high school, the one thing I didn't like was the game, that chase where I had to follow him and he followed me. It was like a drawn-out foreplay. I liked this college kid. I didn't want to beat around the bush.

"Are you gay?" I asked, knowing the answer.

"Yeah. You?"

I nodded. "What are you doing tonight?"

He said he was free. "Is there someplace we can go?" he asked.

I thought about it. I knew what might happen. It had to be a place where we could be alone, where we could enjoy each other without the chance of someone catching us.

"I know a place," I said. "It's private. Meet me tonight."

I didn't get his name, but we agreed to meet at 9 that night in a secluded underground back entranceway to an academic building on campus. I knew it could be a little strange because it was technically outdoors, but we would be under an overhang, so it would give the feeling of being indoors.

As the night approached, I got increasingly nervous. I'd played out the scenario a lot in my head, but I never knew I'd be this scared. What if someone saw us? But it was more than that. I felt dirty after kissing Matt, and I didn't want that feeling again.

In the end, my lust overcame my nerves. When I showed up at the academic building, he was there. We descended the stairs to the underground entranceway. The doors were locked, and we knew there was hardly any chance anyone would be coming by. Still, we were both nervous.

He undressed, and I took in the sight and smell of his body.

"You know that after this, you can no longer talk to me, or even look at me when we pass on campus," I said.

He nodded. Unlike Matt, this guy understood.

"I have roommates," he said. "They don't know."

"Me too."

His body was toned, from his arms to his abs. He was more experienced than me, and I let him take control. We kissed, savoring the warmth of our bodies against one another. He was gentle and I could tell he'd done this before. He was smaller than me, so he stood up on a step.

And just like all those years before, when Eileen stepped up on the curb to kiss me, I'd come full circle. He took my shirt off, then the rest of my clothes.

I made love to a man for the first time.

✷

I knew what I was, and I was now comfortable with it.

I was gay. I was acting on my gay feelings with other gay men. And it didn't feel dirty. I never got the name of the student, and we were able to meet up again.

Even though I'd risked my carefully constructed image to be with him, it felt liberating. I was finally able to be myself. But I did wish I could have taken that step somewhere other than the entranceway to an academic building.

Other than that, my sex life in college was limited. Obviously I wanted to do it more, but it was just too risky. Other than a few encounters with a friend later in college, I just couldn't risk acting on my urges. There were times I felt I had to fool around with women to keep the secret, so I did.

Because secrets always came first.

✱

As a sophomore, Danny and another friend, Terry, told me about the rugby team. They explained to me they needed big guys to help in the scrums (when a group of players pushes ahead to allow backs to run ahead with the ball). I knew I needed something to help me keep in shape during the school year. Although I was lifting and working out every day, this would help with my cardiovascular training. I thought back to high school, when I didn't join the track team. I regretted that.

"It's good for the exercise, and it's good for something else," Terry said. "It'll give you some school spirit."

He was right. It was something I didn't have much of.

"Plus," he said, "we have great parties."

I decided to do it, and it would be one of the best decisions I ever made. We had two seasons, one per semester, and our college hosted other college teams. In rugby, we played 80-minute games and eight games per season. The sport requires no equipment, and it's all about strength and stamina. As Terry promised, it was good for my cardio and my school spirit, but it also provided me with some of the best friends I'd ever make—friends who would hear of my dream to be a wrestler. They would also mistakenly hear my biggest secret.

✱

I was 20 years old, and by that time I'd had sex with a man and a woman. I'd experienced the best of college, but I was away from home and my natural comfort zone. I was trying to be comfortable with hiding my sexuality, but that was impossible when I was still living in fear that someone would find out. To top it off, I was away from wrestling, what I really loved to do.

That kind of confusion, stress and fear does strange things to people. One night after a match, the rugby players had gathered at a local bar to celebrate. We were good, and we knew it. We drank and congratulated each other. But I didn't want to stay out all night. I had studying to do.

"Whaddaya mean you have to study?" asked Stumpy, another player who talked a big game.

"I'm heading out," I said.

"Well, I don't think you are," Stumpy said, reaching under his chair and producing my school books — all of them. He knew I wanted to study that night, and before we went out to celebrate, he'd gone into the house and stolen my books.

"Fuck you," I snarled.

I didn't like to be told what to do, and I didn't like people taking my things. Stumpy had done both. As I have during various times in my life, I snapped, and I ran out of the bar, toward Stumpy's house. I crossed the street when I noticed Terry running after me.

"Wait!" he called. "It's just Stumpy! He's only trying to get at you!"

I stopped and turned around. The alcohol was swimming through my system. My head wasn't clear.

"Fuck you," I replied, shoving Terry out of the way.

I ran toward Stumpy's house, my only objective was to get him back. I was going to make him pay for taking my things. As I ran, I knew what I needed to do. I'd take his computer. When I got to his house, I looked in his window.

Stumpy had beaten me back. He sat there, looking out at me. He was smiling. I pounded my fist on the window and screamed.

What now? My alcohol-filled mind wasn't working correctly, so I can't explain why I did what I did. But in that moment, I only had one thought.

Fuck school. Two years of this, and I wanted to leave. I wanted to leave these college people and follow my dream to wrestling school. This school, this major, everything was wrong. I had to go. Looking back, maybe I was just trying to run away from myself, but I was feeling too much, and I had to do something.

I heard Terry running behind me, chasing me, but I didn't care. I ran to the ATM — at that time, the only one on campus — because I had a plan. One, I needed to empty my checking account. Whatever money my parents had given me, I would take it. Two, I would take a cab to the airport, where I would hop a flight to Atlanta. Yes, Atlanta was where I needed to be. There, I would get a job at the WCW and start my wrestling career.

That was the plan.

"C.K.!"

I heard Terry calling my nickname, but I kept running. Ahead, a fence stood between me and the student center, the location of the ATM. At full speed, I jumped on the fence, which was probably 12 feet high. I started to climb, thinking there was no chance Terry could catch me.

I was wrong. He caught me halfway up the fence, and pulled me back down by my belt. I fell to the ground, gasping for air.

"What the hell are you doing?" he screamed at me.

I looked at him. I know I had fury in my eyes.

"I'm chasing my dream!" I screamed.

Terry shook his head. "What?"

"I'm chasing my dream," I said, quieter this time, my chest heaving.

"What's your dream?" he said.

I looked up at him. "I want to be a professional wrestler," I said.

Terry nodded. "Okay," he said. "Be a professional wrestler."

He helped me up.

"But you don't have to be one today," he said.

We walked back toward the bar. My mind was racing on pure adrenaline.

"There's something else," I said, stopping.

He turned. "What?"

"I'm gay."

He looked at me, studying my eyes. I could tell he didn't know if I was telling the truth.

"You know what?" he said, "It doesn't change anything."

Terry turned around and led the way back to the bar.

(11)

SECRETS AND STEVEN TYLER

My secrets were out. No one really knew until then that I planned on pursuing a wrestling career. Some people thought I was crazy. Some thought I would never do it. Even years later, people would refer to the night I snapped and "Chased my dream." But Terry and I never spoke of my other confession. As far as I know, he never told anyone, and it was never an issue between us. It was the first time I told one of my friends I was gay, and there were no repercussions.

To this day, I don't know why I had to unburden my soul. It was like being away from wrestling and keeping my own secret was strangling me.

*

While I couldn't wrestle in college, I could feed my wrestling addiction by attending the big wrestling matches that came to the area. My junior year in college, a week to the day after my 21st birthday on January 11, 1991, a group of us went to see Ric Flair take on Sting in the Meadowlands. At six-three and 250 pounds, his face covered in white paint, Sting cut an impressive figure. He was enormously popular and because of that, he was receiving an amazing push—meaning the promoters were scripting him to win, feeding his popularity.

Our seats were seven rows back on the floor. With lesser wrestlers, seats that close might have ruined some of the fantasy, but these two were the reason it's called *pro* wrestling. Going in, we all had a feeling that Flair was going to win the belt. We'd all been reading the newsletters and magazines, and the prediction was that Flair would take the title.

While we were as excited as ever, that was a dark period for wcw. The President was Jim Herd, known as the "Pizza Man" because it was said he once owned a string of pizza joints. It was also said he knew more about pizza than he did about wrestling.

My friends and I were all drinking that night, and when I was out of beer, I left my seat to go get more. The beer was being sold on the main level, so I had to go up a flight of steps. At the top I noticed a heavyset guy with white hair sitting at a table alone. I did a double take. Was it Jim Herd?

After I ordered my beer, I took another look. "Mr. Herd?"

He turned around. "Yes?"

"Mind if I sit for a minute?"

He seemed shocked a fan would ask to sit with him. "No — sit, sit," he said. "You look like a big fan, do you mind if I ask you a question?"

Now I was shocked. "Not at all," I said.

"What do you think of Ric's hair?"

They'd just told Flair to cut his hair really short. They wanted to make him look like a gladiator and get that theme going, but I thought it made him look stupid. I hated it. Still, I didn't want to do anything to hurt Ric.

"It's great," I said. "It really makes him look younger."

"What do you think of the Steiners?" he asked, talking about a young group of tag-team brothers. "We're thinking of splitting them up and making Scott the champ."

"Bad idea," I said. "Ric should be your champion. He's going to win the title, right?"

"Just watch," he said.

"What? He's going to win, isn't he?"

"Just watch," he repeated. "So you don't think we need to break up the Steiners, eh?"

"No," I said. "You don't have many great tag teams out there, and they're really, really good. You don't need anyone else to be the champ. Ric Flair should be the champ."

With that, Flair's entrance music came on.

"Hey, I'd love to keep talking to you," I said, "but I've got to go — we've got great seats."

"Nice talking with you," he said.

I got up to leave, but I turned around again. "Mr. Herd?"

"Yeah?"

"I'm going to work for this company one day."

He smiled. "Okay, kid."

"I mean it," I said. "I'm going to be here."

He waved goodbye, and I went back to my seat. There, we watched Flair win the title, which he would keep for a while. Later, I wondered if I had any input in that storyline. Was Herd listening to the opinions of a 21-year-old drunk?

I wouldn't put it past the Pizza Man.

✶

After a trip to *WrestleMania* VI at the SkyDome in Toronto, we went to our fourth straight *WrestleMania* in 1991 at the Los Angeles Memorial Sports Arena. In Toronto, I again tried to work some magic backstage, but when I returned to the arena, the ring was already taken down. Dammit. For *WrestleMania* VII, I had a plan.

Danny's buddy was a lighting technician who sometimes did work for the WWF when they were on the east coast. His buddy gave him an official jumpsuit, which Danny later passed on to me.

My plan was to wear the jumpsuit under my normal clothes, and when the match was over, I would jump over the railing and blend in with the crowd, going backstage with my camera. I'd snap some pictures, then make my way back out to the ring to grab my coveted apron.

I flew down to L.A. with Danny, Tommy and my friends Joe and Mike. On our drive to the arena, we were all pumped up for the big show.

"Turn it up, man!" Mike said. Aerosmith, his favorite band, was on the radio. "Steven Tyler is the fucking man!" Mike was always talking about Steven Tyler and Aerosmith. Then again, I guess I was always talking about Ric Flair and Hogan.

"This is going to be huge, man," Danny said. "We're going to see Piper and Virgil. We're going to see Hogan. This could be the best *WrestleMania* yet."

"It will be when I get backstage," I said.

Danny was right. The matches were great. The massive six-five, 300-pound Undertaker defeated Snuka. Randy Savage and his wife, Elizabeth, reunited.

And when Hogan won the championship by dropping Sgt. Slaughter—an army drill sergeant-type—it was time for me to go.

"Give me half an hour," I told Danny. I really didn't think it would take any longer. When I got up, it was no problem to walk down to the floor, hop the fence and join the group. Ticker tape fell from the ceiling and a mass of people headed for the backstage area. Just like all those years ago, when my father secretly ushered us into the Sunnyside Gardens, I blended with the crowd and, camera in hand, I got ready to take pictures. I made sure to turn off the flash. I figured I didn't want to draw any more attention to myself than necessary. Plus, why would someone official—as I was trying to look—be taking pictures, anyway?

The first thing I saw backstage was the party. Wrestlers were eating food, people were laughing. It looked like a good time.

But someone was not happy.

"Fuck that bastard! What the fuck did he think he was doing?!"

It was Roddy Piper, aptly nicknamed Rowdy because of his boorish behavior. Piper used a Scottish gimmick and was known to come out in a kilt as bagpipe music played. When I walked in, Piper was screaming at Sensational Sherri, a curvy brunette whom Vince McMahon had groomed in the World Wrestling Federation. Apparently, Piper was angry at Virgil, a muscular black wrestler known for starting feuds. Something unforeseen had happened that night, and Piper was conveying it to Sherri in his typically aggressive way.

"That Goddamn son of a bitch should be more careful! I swear to God..."

Piper was one of the guys I wanted to get a picture with. Should I interrupt this tirade? Why not?

"Mr. Piper?"

He stopped, immediately, mid-sentence, and turned to me.

"Yes, how can I help you?" he asked, using manners I didn't know he had, his flushed skin cooling with his temper.

"I, um, I wanted to get a picture with you."

"Of course." He smiled.

Sherri took the picture. Then he took a picture of me with her.

"Thanks very much," I said. As I turned to walk away, I heard him again, back to his old form.

Across the room, I saw Savage leaving for his trailer. I wanted to get a picture with him bad. That night, he'd lost to the long-haired, war-painted Ultimate Warrior. But afterward, things got better for Savage when his wife,

Elizabeth, ran back into his arms after they had been separated.

"Mr. Poffo!" I called.

He turned immediately after I called him by his real name. He stepped toward me. Behind him, I noticed Elizabeth.

"I've got to tell you," I said, "when you and Elizabeth got back together, I almost cried."

"Thanks, man," he said. I was shocked to hear he talked just like he did in the ring—loud, shouting like he was talking at a New York construction site.

After getting a picture with him, I continued to wander pretty much unnoticed. Then I remembered the ring apron. I rushed back to the arena, where several officials were in the middle of taking down the ring. I approached the apron, which was tied on with a cable. I knew I could get it off. It looked beautiful, with the *WrestleMania* logo on it, and I knew it'd look even better in my room. I bent down to unhook the cable, when I was interrupted.

"You! Who are you?! What are you doing?"

I looked up to see a man running my way. It was Danny Davis, the official.

"My name's Chris, I was hired today from the temp agency," I said. "I was just taking the aprons off the ring."

"Those cables are under tension," Davis said, pulling me away from the ring. "You can't do that."

"Oh, I'm so sorry," I said. I was serious. And I was convinced I was going to get arrested.

"Who'd you say hired you?" Davis said.

"What?"

Davis stepped toward me. "Who hired you?"

I was at a loss. What could I say? How could I answer this man?

I said the only name that came to mind. The only name I'd been hearing the whole trip.

"Steve Tyler."

"Who?"

"Steve Tyler."

Davis stared at me.

"Steve Tyler hired you?"

I hesitated. "Yes."

Davis pulled a walkie-talkie out of his pocket. "Steve? Yeah, can you come down to the ring?"

I couldn't believe it. There actually *was* a Steve Tyler — and he was coming this way. I saw a man walking toward us. It had to be Tyler. As he approached, I caught his eye. He looked at me, and I stared back.

"What do you need, Danny?" he asked.

"This guy here says you hired him this morning," he said, gesturing toward me. "Did you hire him?"

Tyler looked me up and down. "Yeah, I did," he said, smiling.

I smiled back. Tyler was a good guy. I got the idea he just liked fucking with Davis. Tyler turned around to walk away, and as he did, wrestling official Howard Finkel ran up to us.

"Danny! Danny!" he was screaming, and he held a belt over his shoulder. "They broke the fucking belt again!"

I looked and saw the one million dollar belt, and I knew why Piper was angry. Virgil broke the belt — something he'd done before.

"We've gotta get it fixed by tomorrow night!" Finkel said.

Danny looked at Howard. Then he looked at me. He shrugged and left with Howard, leaving me alone. The luck! I couldn't get the apron, but I had a story much better than any souvenir.

✱

I made my way backstage again, where I mingled with other wrestlers. I noticed I'd been getting pages on my beeper, and when I looked at my watch, I realized my friends must have been calling me. I'd been gone for about two hours. Oh well. When Sgt. Slaughter walked by, I stopped to get a picture with him too.

I pulled out my camera, and after the picture was taken, a maintenance man who'd been working nearby stopped me.

"Are you using a flash?" he asked.

"Well, I turned it off," I said.

He shook his head. "You may want to use a flash back here."

I took his advice and turned it on just as the Ultimate Warrior walked by. After getting a picture with the Warrior, I looked up to see my friend Joe, walking around like he owned the joint.

"What are you doing here?" I said.

"I just walked in to look for you," he said. "We've been calling you — what the hell happened?"

"Joe, look," I said. "I've gotten all these pictures with Savage and Piper and Slaughter."

I told him the Steve Tyler story and he agreed the time was well spent.

"Just wait until these pictures are developed," I said. "It was definitely worth it."

Of course, it wasn't. The next day, when the pictures were developed, the only one that came out was the photo of me and the Warrior—the only picture where I used the flash.

(12)

PETE AND THE LOWER EAST SIDE WRESTLING GYM

I wasn't able to go to the Hoosier Dome's *WrestleMania* in 1992. It broke my streak of four in a row. But on the very same night as *WrestleMania* VIII, I was making my wrestling debut as Chris Morgan.

But we're getting ahead of ourselves.

In 1991, I was home for Christmas break during my senior year in college. I had gotten an internship in physical therapy at the Rusk Institute at New York University, and I thought I was going to be busy in the coming months on what would otherwise be called a vacation. I had no idea how busy I would be.

During my college career, the sports newspaper the *National* began its circulation. As a daily national sports newspaper, it featured a wrestling column every Friday, written by Dave Meltzer. Meltzer also advertised his wrestling newsletter, which I ordered through the mail. The newsletter provided information on all of the regional and independent leagues throughout the country, and my friends and I ate up all the information we could get. Another source of information for us was the John Arezzi radio show. Broadcast from Long Island, Arezzi talked wrestling from 10 a.m. to noon on Sundays and we couldn't get enough of that either.

Just a few days before Christmas, my cousin Brian O'Hagan called with news. "This is going to ruin your Christmas present," he said, "but it's worth it."

Brian was one of the cousins I'd wrestled with growing up. He was interested in it as much as I was, but at 25, he was already a police officer and he lived on the east side of Long Island. But Brian knew how much I loved wrestling, so he'd ordered me some autographed pictures through John Arezzi's radio show. The catch was we had to go to the radio show to pick them up, and he wanted to know if I'd like to go too. Hell yes, I wanted to go.

Brian and I walked into the waiting room of the studio to pick up the autographed pictures. But sitting in the lobby was a kid — someone around my age — and I recognized him from one of my newsletters. He was being sued by wrestling promoters because he'd been making allegedly illegal videotapes of wrestling matches. Brian and I sat down and made small talk with the kid, who was scheduled to be on the radio show.

Out of nowhere, my cousin changed the topic of conversation. "Hey, do you know where I could buy a wrestling ring?" he said.

I was surprised — he'd never expressed this interest to me.

"Yeah, I think I know somebody," the kid replied.

By the time we left the studio, we had a lead on where we could get a ring of our own.

✶

When I did anything wrestling-related, I didn't tell my parents. They wanted me focused on my education, even though I was getting further and further away from it. The kid at the radio station had told us about the Gladiator Gym in Manhattan, where they told me to go to an address on the lower east side — the corner of Houston Street and FDR Drive. "Look for Pete McKay," they told me.

Pete McKay? That area of town was primarily Hispanic, and McKay didn't sound Hispanic at all. I thought the building was going to be another gym, but it wasn't. The directions led me to a six-story apartment building and I was told to go to the back door. The structure looked run-down, and it all felt a little shady. I thought I was about to get jumped.

I knocked on the back door, and a man who looked like a hefty Gomez Adams answered.

"Are you here for the ring?" he asked.

"Yeah. Are you Pete McKay?"

He nodded.

I walked in to what I thought would be a dingy apartment, but instead I found a spotless space, the walls lined with wrestling memorabilia and leading back to a modified gym. As Pete walked back to the gym, I noticed he looked to be in his mid-fifties, and he had an odd twitch in his neck. Sometimes his neck jutted out involuntarily. It was obvious he had no control over it.

I learned the place was called the Lower East Side Wrestling Gym. It was a wrestling school. I couldn't believe it. We walked back through a wide hallway to the gym, where he showed me the ring. I couldn't take my eyes off of it.

He saw me looking.

"Well, there it is," he said, putting a hand on the ropes.

"How much?" I barely got it out.

"Three thousand," he said.

My eyes never left it.

"Look," he said, "do you want to get in?"

"Me? Do I want to get in the ring?"

"Yes. Do you want to?"

I didn't answer. I just got in. My only previous experience in a ring was at *WrestleMania*, when I stole the turnbuckle. There, I hadn't had the guts to try any maneuvers. Now I wanted to try everything. I ran to one side, bouncing off the ring and landing on my back.

Oh my God. The wind knocked out of me, I struggled to get up. This was all wrong. When I was growing up, all the time I thought the mat would be like a trampoline. But it wasn't like that at all: It was rock hard.

As I struggled to get to my feet, I heard laughing from the other end of the gym.

It was Pete. I got to my knees and held my chest, gasping for breath, not sharing his amusement.

"You really want to do this, don't you?" he asked.

I nodded my head yes.

"Come back on Saturday," Pete said. "There's a bunch of guys who will be here."

✶

That's where my formal education began. I came back the following Saturday, and began to practice with several other aspiring wrestlers. After initial workouts with some of the other guys, Pete invited me back whenever I wanted. He never mentioned anything about money, though I knew most of the normal wrestling schools charged about $3,000 for tutoring.

For eight weeks, I worked my internship at Rusk during the day, and at 4:30 p.m. I headed to the ring, where I worked on my moves. When my parents asked where I was, I explained I was studying at the medical library, preparing for a presentation I would have to give at the end of the internship. The only problem? The Lower East Side Wrestling Gym was only a few blocks from where my father worked, and the time I arrived at the gym was around the same time he would start his trek home. With no explanation ready for why I wasn't at the medical hospital, I was always worried we would pass each other on our way.

At the gym, I picked things up quickly. By my third Saturday, I noticed others whispering and pointing at me. I had really taken to Pete's teachings, soaking up knowledge. But apparently, I was too good.

"Come here!" Pete shouted.

Everyone else in the gym gathered around.

"I know who you are," he said, walking to me. "And I know what you're doing."

I was confused. "I don't know what you're talking about, Pete."

He grabbed me. "Tell me you're not working for Johnny Rodz!" he said.

"What?! Who's Johnny Rodz?"

He looked at me for a long time. His neck twitched its awful twitch.

"Johnny Rodz runs a school across town," he said. "And we're convinced you work for him. We're convinced you're here to spy on us and tell him what we're doing."

"Why? Why do you think that?" I was scared Pete was going to ask me to leave.

"Because," he said, "there's no way you're just learning this stuff."

He pushed me away. "You're too good," he said.

✶

I knew nothing before I met Pete. Every day I would work at my internship, which was basically nothing more than fetching coffee and supplies, and I would wait for 4:30 when I could hit the gym. Every night I was either lifting weights, working out or learning how to be a pro wrestler.

Pete taught me the tricks — hiding and using a razor blade, taking aspirin before a match to make the blood flow quicker and clot faster. But his most important lesson was learning to protect yourself. Pete was also preaching safety first, so he taught me how to fall correctly, how to throw a punch and make it look real and how to take the weight of another wrestler body slamming you.

After a few weeks there, I went into the ring to wrestle some of the others at the gym. That's when I met the Power Twins — and they beat the shit out of me in the ring. They did not pull their punches. They found their mark. And at that time, I had no idea how to defend myself. When I fell, I landed straight on my back. When they jumped on me, they landed full force. When it was over, the two brothers laughed and walked out of the building.

I was pissed. Sore and angry, I pulled my battered body over and sat next to Pete.

"Did you see what they did to me?" I asked.

He nodded his head yes.

"I want to go outside and beat the hell out of them," I said. "What was that fucking shit? They tried to kill me."

"I don't think they tried to do that," Pete said, patting my leg. Even that hurt.

"Obviously, you weren't paying attention," I said.

"At least they were still safe with you," he said. "You aren't hurt."

He twitched.

"Sometimes wrestlers who have been around a while will test a new one," Pete said. "It's called paying your dues. They'll beat you up a bit, but it's good for you. It teaches you to be tough, it makes you aware. There are some people in the world, in the ring and out of it, who will do bad things to you, maybe because they're jealous. They may try to hurt you on purpose. And because of that, this experience was good for you. We can teach you to protect yourself, just like we can teach you to be a wrestler."

I tried to understand what he was saying.

"Sometimes you may not know the people you're fighting," he said. "And those people may not be good people. You need to learn to be safe."

His neck twitched again, and he stood up.

"Let me tell you a story," he said. He walked over to the wall, covered with pictures and memorabilia. "That's me," he said, pointing to a black and white picture of a younger version of himself. He wore tights and boots and looked ready to rumble.

"I was in my twenties there," Pete said. "That was before everything—before this," he pointed to his neck. "Back then, wrestling was very much based on your nationality. A wrestler named Pedro represented the Hispanics. Hogan was for the Irish. When you were breaking in, it helped if you were a certain nationality who could appeal to others."

He smiled.

"When I was a young wrestler, there were enough Hispanics around," he said. "But they needed some Scots. That's why I changed my name. Originally, my last name was Gonzalez, but I knew I wouldn't get any matches with that name. Overnight, I became Pete McKay, and sometimes my name alone got me jobs."

"Nice to meet you, Pete Gonzalez," I said, shaking his hand.

"Likewise," Pete said. "When I was coming up, it was a tough world. Some guys would hurt you just so they could get a better chance to move up in the ranks. Some guys would do it because it was like initiation."

He twitched again.

"And that's how this happened to me," he said, pointing to his neck again. "In one of my first matches, I took a hard body slam, right down on my back."

He walked back to the chair and sat.

"After that I was never the same," he said. "I just started twitching like this. I can't stop it."

"Do you hurt?" I asked.

"Not really," he said. "But it could have been a lot worse."

We sat in silence for a moment.

"It's good you're in college," he told me. "You can't do this kind of stuff forever. If someday, you can't do this anymore, you'll have a degree. No one wants to get hurt."

✶

I remembered everything Pete told me, and I kept lying to my parents about where I was. I spent less and less time in the neighborhood, and more time in the gym. Pete was like a dad to me, and I wanted to make him proud. He would set up brooms for me, leaning them against the ropes with the bristles pointing toward the ceiling. That was how I learned to pull a punch—I had to make contact with the broom without knocking it over. It's also how I learned to drop-kick.

But the safety tips were the best. Pete told me that when an opponent jumped on you, you raise your back a bit off the mat so your arms take the impact. When you're jumping off the top rope, land with your left leg straight and your right slightly bent. If you don't, you're likely to rack yourself.

Every day, I left sore. I invited my cousin Brian to come and wrestle, and when he did, I could tell he was nervous. By this time he'd gotten married and had a kid. Wrestling wasn't a career option anymore, but I still hadn't realized it. I wanted him to come and give it a try.

"Sure, man. I'll come when I can," he said.

I thought he would be more excited about it. But after a few weeks, he came to the gym he'd helped me find. We both got in the ring, and for a moment, it was like we were kids again, playing on the black mats in the park or jumping off the couches in his parents' house in Long Island. Then I suplexed him, and on the way down, Brian threw his elbows behind him to break his fall. Unfortunately, it's one of the worst things you can do. You're supposed to break the fall with your back, and spread the impact. Instead, Brian's elbow grew to the size of a softball. It was so bad he even had to take off of work. I felt terrible about that. Before the injury, Brian was starting to walk away from wrestling. Afterward — there was no decision to be made. Wrestling was over for him. And there were no more thoughts of buying a ring.

I also had to face the fact that my friends — Tommy and Danny, among them — were probably not going to want to do this anymore. They were growing up, getting serious girlfriends, and down the road they were going to have families. Something occurred to me in those eight weeks with Pete, something that both thrilled and scared me at the same time: I was going to be the only crazy bastard of the group to try to earn a living in professional wrestling.

Good, I thought. I didn't need anyone to hold me back. I knew I was going to make it.

✯

Pete wasn't the only teacher at the school. We were also coached by Ismael Gerena and Bobby Bold Eagle, who taught me some of my first innovative moves. Bobby was an amazing wrestler, and he taught me things he'd picked up while wrestling all over the world, like the reverse crab — a hold where you actually get all of your opponent's limbs and neck in one hold. It's nearly impossible to break. Both Ismael and Bobby were old-school wrestlers, and Bobby was a master at building rings. He actually wrestled as the Black Tiger in the WWF, so he had a lot more to teach than moves. It was then I started to learn about the real world of professional wrestling.

✷

At the end of the break, I finished my internship by presenting my research on how the brain is affected by strokes. The brain's inner workings have always intrigued me, and I found time for the research even while practicing my wrestling. But even though I was fascinated by the work I was doing, nothing could compete with working with Pete.

Even with all the time I spent at the gym, Pete never charged me a dime. I knew from reading some of those newsletters that he could have charged me a few thousand dollars, but Pete never talked about it — and I certainly never brought the subject up. I thought he probably knew I was going to make something of myself, and he just liked me and wanted to help me out. The day I left to go back to school, I stopped by the gym to tell Pete I'd be back.

"I know you will," he said, smiling that Gomez-like smile. He hugged me.

"Thanks . . . for everything," I said.

"It's a good thing you're in college. I told you that, right?"

"Yeah, you did," I replied.

"Good. You have to get your education."

He was right. It was time to go back and finish college. Once again, I would have to leave wrestling behind. Or so I thought.

(13)

THE DEBUT OF CHRIS MORGAN

During that last semester of my senior year, I scored another internship, working at a local hospital on campus. On breaks from school, I'd been going to see Pete because I wanted to keep in touch. I guess I shouldn't have been surprised when Pete called me around that time and asked if I wanted to wrestle professionally for the first time.

"I got a gig, and I want to know if you'll be my tag partner," he said.

"We'd be tag partners?" I asked. I couldn't believe it — my first match and I'd be wrestling with Pete!

"Yep, I know the guy putting this on, and I told him you were pretty good," he said.

I said I would think about it and let him know. Of course, there were problems.

I was working out every day, but I would have to start training harder. That wouldn't be difficult. But growing up in New York, I'd never had to drive before, so I'd never learned. I still hadn't told my parents or my brother about my continued interest in wrestling, so I couldn't go home. And — the biggest issue — I'd have to take a day off from my internship, something that was seen as a big no-no in the internship world. I told Danny about this, and said I was concerned about it affecting my job prospects at a hospital in the future.

"This is a big deal," Danny said. "If you don't do it, you'll regret it. Besides, you love wrestling, and you should do what you love."

Just like Danny. He always knew what to say. I called Pete back and told him I would do it. Thanks to him, I was going to wrestle my first match.

✶

With Pete helping promote the small-time match, I had a shot at winning. But I also knew that we wouldn't know for sure until we talked with the other wrestlers beforehand. But that was just one of my worries. I had no idea what to wear or what the venue would be like. To make matters worse, we were going up against *WrestleMania VIII* in Indianapolis. I'm pretty sure folks were more excited about that than our little card.

I had another worry, something other wrestlers did not have to ever think about. What if I got physically excited in the ring? I didn't think it would happen, but what if it did? What if I was attracted to another wrestler? Back in grade school, it had never happened. Then again, it was all about fun in those days. The stakes were much higher now. I decided to be proactive. I called a doctor in the city.

"Yes, my name is Paul, and I'm a dancer," I said. "I'm having a problem with my dance partner. Actually, it's not a problem. I like her — very much — and it's obvious when I'm dancing, if you know what I mean."

"You mean you're getting an erection when you're dancing?" the doctor replied.

"Um, yes. What can I do about that?"

He told me about saltpeter, a food additive that when mixed with water is supposed to help suppress erections. I tried it. Then I tried to get an erection. Let me put it this way — the saltpeter stuff didn't work. Then I experimented with different kinds of underwear. I discovered that the smaller the pair of underwear I wore, the more snug they fit, and the less likely I was to get excited, because I just didn't have the room. I figured that would probably work.

The day before the fight I took a bus down to Pete's, where I spent the night. Pete's wife treated us to some food and beers, and we had a great time hanging out, talking about the next day.

"So, what are you going to wear?" he asked, neck twitching.

I didn't know. I had nothing to wear.

"What do you think?" I said.

"I think you need some of my old trunks."

He went back into his bedroom and reappeared with a pair of old red and blue wrestling trunks. I loved them.

"Now, you don't have boots, but you won't need them for this fight," he said. "You can just go barefoot."

I nodded, and took a drink from my bottle.

"Lastly, what do we call you?" he asked.

I shook my head. I'd never thought about it before. My friends in college called me "C.K.," because it was so much easier than saying my last name.

"I'd like to keep my first name, and the K," I said. "That makes it feel more like me."

"OK, we can do that. How about Chris Kutter or Chris Killer or something like that?"

"Doesn't really sound right."

Pete thought some more. "How about Chris Kanyon?"

Chris Kanyon. Kanyon.

"I like the sound of that," I said. I kept saying the name in my head, trying to hear it pronounced over a loudspeaker.

"There you go," Pete said. "Chris Kanyon."

In a day, I'd be wrestling as Chris Kanyon for the first time. Of course, that's not exactly the way it worked out.

*

The match took place at Long Island Junior High School in Levittown, and there were only 300 people there in the gym to watch. Still, I'd never wrestled in front of 300 people before. I'd told my friends and my cousins about it, so they were there, and that added to my being nervous. I had on my trunks, and multiple pairs of small underwear to keep me in the trunks, and I was already talking to myself.

Stay calm, I thought. *Remember your moves. React and put on a good show.*

My cousin Brian saw me in the crowd and came down from the bleachers to talk to me. By this time, his arm was healed and he was back to normal.

"Hey, man. Good luck, OK?" he said.

"Thanks, man," I replied. "Hey — it means a lot for you guys to be here."

"We wouldn't want to be anywhere else."

"Yeah, right. You wouldn't want to be in Indianapolis for *WrestleMania VIII* right now?" I smiled.

"Well . . . maybe there."

"You know what? They've got 62,000 people in the Hoosier Dome for *WrestleMania* right now," I said. "Hogan's there. Ric Flair's there. Randy Savage and Sid Vicious. Nobody there is as nervous as I am right now."

Brian smiled. "You're going to do great." Brian went back to his seat as Pete came up to meet me.

"This is a Hispanic-themed show," Pete said. "So we've got a problem. You won't be able to understand anything these guys say. You won't be able to talk with them beforehand, so just follow my lead."

"Who's supposed to win?" I said. I thought we'd know a lot more about the match before we started.

"Just follow my lead."

The ring announcer introduced the teams, and when Pete told him who we were, he didn't hear my name correctly.

"And in this corner, the challengers, Pete McKay and Chris Morgan!" he said.

Chris Morgan? Great.

The match had already gotten off to a great start. Forevermore, my first match would be under the name of Chris Morgan. Pete was also wearing his red and blue trunks, and he was barefoot too. Watching him in the ring was something to see, kind of like watching your dad hop into the ring. I couldn't believe I was having my first real match. But I also couldn't believe it was so unorganized. I had no idea what to do or who was going to win. And I realized that in all of this excitement, I never needed to worry about getting an erection. There was no way I could try to concentrate on what I was doing and think about sex too.

Ours was a tag-team elimination style match, and in just a few minutes, Pete eliminated one of their guys. He just lay down on this Latino guy, and he was out. Then Pete was eliminated by the Latino's smaller teammate, who used a snap mare, grabbing Pete's head and rolling on his front to lay on top of him and pin him. *Here I go,* I thought. I came in versus the smaller guy, probably five-seven and 150 pounds. *Oh my God,* I thought, *what were we thinking? This disparity is laughable.* With a smaller fighter going against me, I had no idea how to make this match look real, so I did all I knew how to—I wrestled.

To his credit, the smaller man was really friendly and very eager to make our match look good. Because we couldn't talk to each other, and we had no set plan, my first match was the closest thing to real wrestling. The two of us were wondering what the other would do next. We were nearing the 11-minute mark when I decided to really show the guy what I could do. I hit a body slam, then dropped an elbow and pulled his leg.

"One," the referee shouted, looking at us.

"Two," he showed us both his two fingers.

Then he paused. Like us, he didn't know how this was supposed to turn out, either. Finally, he sensed we were ready to quit.

"Three!" he called, waving his arms and declaring me the winner.

I, Chris Morgan, had won my first fight.

✶

That match led to a second one later in the spring, one that didn't require a day off work. Whereas my first matches in Long Island were unpredictable and unorganized, Pete had more of a hand in running this one — a street match out on the streets of Manhattan.

On Avenue A, in the lower east side, I arrived to see an unconventional crowd — thousands of people were everywhere, on the street, hanging outside their windows screaming. All of them were into it. It was a primarily Hispanic area rich in culture and excitement.

Pete had set me up against Billy Firehawk, a young but experienced wrestler known for his physical style. Since Pete had set up the match, we knew I was going to win, which was special against a veteran like Firehawk. This time I felt less nervous before the match, as I looked out into the crowd and saw my friends and cousins. Even Danny and Tom were there to share in the moment.

I hadn't expected them to come. But they did anyway, and they brought the video camera. I'm glad they did. Firehawk was a big brute of a guy, just under six feet tall but weighing in at about 250 pounds. He was not someone you wanted to fight on the street. In the ring, our match was tough and physical. Later I would realize I didn't yet know the psychology of matches that well. As the crowd was screaming for us, just going crazy, I didn't know how to play up to it. But I knew I could learn.

Firehawk was a pro. He was firm and stiff, and he knew how to make a match look great. He was the kind of fighter I worked well with, and at the end of our 11-minute match, when I won, I shook his hand.

"It was a real pleasure doing this," I said.

"You're good," he said. "I think I may have something else for you in the future, if you want it."

I said I'd love to wrestle with him again.

(14)

MY "FAGGY" WRESTLING COSTUME

When I graduated from college, my parents came up to Buffalo to see the ceremony. My life was on track, in their eyes. I'd applied for a job as a traveling physical therapist in Columbia, South Carolina. I would sign three-month contracts and have the freedom to move around the country if I wanted. On top of that, the company paid twice what regular therapists made—about $70,000 a year—and they paid for my housing and utilities. I told my parents it was a sweet deal, and that I needed to leave for South Carolina by the end of the summer.

While the job was promising, it wasn't the real reason I was headed to South Carolina. In fact, I'd chosen that state as the place I wanted to go—I just hadn't told my parents that. From reading the wrestling newsletters, I knew South Carolina was in the middle of the independent wrestling scene. Not far from Tennessee, Atlanta and North Carolina, I knew I could officially start my dream there, and if I needed to move, I would just go to another wrestling hotspot like Oregon, Texas or Florida.

In June, Billy Firehawk called Pete. He wanted to wrestle me in a match at the old ECW Elks Lodge, just 20 blocks from my parents' apartment. Though the match was so close to home, I didn't tell my parents about it. In any case, the lodge seated 500 people and about 100 of them ended up being friends of mine. The place was going nuts.

Most of it was thanks to my brother Ken, who'd organized a large portion of the crowd. I hardly talked with my brother throughout my entire college career, but he had since moved out of my parents' house to a place a few blocks down the street from theirs, and I think he missed his little brother. In the days leading up to the match, we talked for the first times in years. "I'm proud of you, man," Ken told me the day before the match.

I reflected on those words backstage as I listened to the roar of the crowd.

"Man, that sounds like a lot of people," I told Pete.

"Yeah, and you know a lot of them," he said.

Then we heard the chanting. It started slow, like a thunderstorm, far off in the distance. It was still a little inaudible from our position backstage. But you knew it was going to get louder — and soon.

"What are they saying?" I asked.

Pete shook his head.

I went around to the edge of the curtain and looked out. I couldn't believe my ears.

The people I knew in the crowd were chanting my name — my new name.

"They're saying 'Kan-yon!'" I screamed.

"Well then, you better be good," Pete said. "Now, about your trunks," he gestured to a bag on the floor.

"Yeah?"

"They didn't turn out quite the way you wanted them to."

"What do you mean?" I'd asked Ismael Gerena's wife, a seamstress, to sew me some new trunks in blue and orange — the colors of my beloved New York Mets.

"Take a look," Pete pointed to the bag.

I opened the bag, and pulled out my new trunks. The colors were off — way off. Instead of dark blue and orange, they were baby blue and pink. Baby blue and pink?

"Oh no," I said. "These look, I don't know, they look — *faggy*."

"Yes," Pete said. "Yes they do. But what can you do about it now, right? The crowd is chanting your name."

Outside, I could still hear them. They'd been chanting for me during all of the undercard matches, and they were working themselves into a frenzy. I had to use the trunks. I put them on over my usual tight underwear. They were hideous.

✢

When I was introduced as the challenger to Firehawk, the crowd was still chanting Kan-yon, and the energy was electric. My friends had goaded most of the others in the crowd to chant my name too, even though they probably had no idea who I was. So, when the curtain came up, many of the 500 were chanting in unison.

Then they saw my trunks, and all at once, they stopped. In fact, it seemed as if all 500 gasped at once at the bulky wrestler wearing the pink and baby blue drawers.

The only thing I could do was perform. I knew that when I lost, the crowd would be disappointed. But this was Firehawk's show, and he was going to win. During our 15-minute match, we put on a great show, and it was a learning experience just to be out there with him. In the end, he pinned me, and the crowd — which had been unbelievable all during the match — got angry and frustrated. After the pin, Firehawk got up and played to the crowd, asking them to keep cheering, but then he congratulated me on another fun match and walked out of the ring.

I waited a second, then, with the crowd still shouting, I stood for dramatic effect, and once again they began cheering and chanting my name. I knew a couple of things after that fight — we'd put on a good show, and I loved the sound of the crowd chanting my name. The only thing missing was my parents cheering me on, faggy costume and all.

✢

My brother had moved in with his girlfriend, who would soon become his wife, and I noticed immediately that he had changed. Gone was Ken's aggressive nature, his animosity and his tendency to self-destruct. It was replaced by something resembling peace. I think he was just happy.

"So what do you want to do?" I asked as we shared beers.

"With my life? I don't know," Ken said. "I'm thinking about going into accounting, like Mom and Dad."

"That sounds like a good thing," I said.

"Yeah. Hey, Chris?"

"Yeah?"

"Let's keep in touch when you go down to South Carolina, OK?"

"I think that sounds nice."

"Me too."

And as we sat drinking our beers, we enjoyed the presence of one another's company. That was a new feeling for me, and I liked it.

*

I only had one other match that summer, a time-limit draw set up by the promoters of the first fight at Long Island High School. But midway through the fight, one of the other promoters skipped out with the money, and we never saw him again. It was my first taste of what the business was really like.

As the summer dwindled, the realization that I would be leaving home set in.

I went over to the Lower East Side gym once more, to thank Pete and tell him I'd see him on my break.

"You do good down there," Pete said. "Have fun and get better."

I told him I would. After saying goodbye to Danny and Tommy and my other friends, I came back home and found my parents waiting for me at the dinner table.

"We're proud of you, son," my dad said.

My mother came and hugged me. "Are you all packed up?" she said.

"Yeah, I think so. It was tight, but I got everything in the car."

"How about your wrestling gear?" my dad asked. He looked me straight in the eye. "You didn't forget that, did you?"

"Oh boy." I put my head in my hands.

"Look, son, you're not in any trouble," Dad said. "We don't think you should've hidden this from us, but you're not in trouble."

"What you're doing is fine, Chris," Mom added. "We think you're a great person, and we're proud of you."

"Why didn't you tell us about the wrestling?" Dad asked.

I looked at the both of them. "The last time I told you about this, you told me I was stupid," I said. "You were paying for college, and I didn't want you to think that was going to waste. I want to do this, so I was going to do it, even if you didn't like it."

I told them about Pete, and how I found the gym. I told them about the matches, and the last one at the Elks Lodge.

"Well, five hundred people is a lot of people," my dad said. "I think I would've liked to have seen that."

"I'm sorry I didn't tell you." I felt horrible.

My mom smiled. "Make sure and tell us the next time hundreds of people will be shouting your name," she said.

I told them I hoped to continue my training in South Carolina, though I wasn't completely honest with them. I did not tell them it was the sole reason I had decided to work there.

"Well, if it makes you happy, do it," Dad said. "I'm glad you're going to be working too."

My parents didn't think wrestling was a career. I knew it would be. The next day, I grabbed the keys to my Taurus and left Sunnyside. Though my car was bursting with all my worldly possessions, the most important thing I had was in my pocket: a list of contacts that would be the key to my future.

(15)

THE LAND OF TRAILERS AND FREAKS

That summer I'd collected a lot of information from my wrestling newsletters — I'd even seen my own name a few times from my small matches in New York. When someone from Columbia, South Carolina, was mentioned, even in the letters section of one of the newsletters, I wrote down the name. The list was getting long, but I knew these were the people who I would get to know when I was on my own in a new state. That was how I'd learned to deal with new things: You prepare, and you make the situation better for yourself. That's how I survived.

Columbia, the state capital of South Carolina, was the typical college town — home of the University of South Carolina Gamecocks. There were lots of young kids, lots of urban professionals and lots of bars. It was the perfect hangout for a young guy, just out of school. Luckily for me, there was also a strip known for its gay bars. My employer had put me up in some nice apartments, five miles from the hospital, with a view of the community pool. There was a gym so I could work out. The whole place had a relaxed feel to it, and it made it easy to call it home.

As I drove into town my first day there, I flipped through the stations on the radio. I landed on a station where a booming voice was saying something I couldn't believe.

"Everybody here loves the COCKS!" the man screamed. Immediately, I wondered where the hell I was. Coming from New York, I was a sports fan — or so I thought. I liked the Mets and I liked to watch hockey. But I didn't have a clue about college football, and in Columbia, it's all about college football — the Gamecocks, or as the college set calls them, the Cocks.

In a few days, I'd be leaving to work as a physical therapist at Columbia Baptist Medical Center. There, I would help patients rehabilitate from things like strokes or car wrecks. After I'd unpacked my apartment, I knew what I had to do next. The next week, the NWA was doing a show in Atlanta. I wanted to go, but I wanted someone to go with me.

I pulled out the list of names, taken from the wrestling newsletters. First on the list: Jeff Wilson. I figured there were going to be a lot of Wilsons in the phone book. I was right. There were hundreds.

"Hello?" the voice on the other end of the phone sounded tired.

"Yes, is this Jeff Wilson?" I asked.

"Yeah, who is this?" the voice was more agitated now.

"Jeff Wilson, who wrote a letter to the Dave Meltzer wrestling newsletter?"

"Yeah, now who the hell is this?"

Bingo. I struck gold on my first try.

"This is Chris Kanyon. I'm a wrestling fan, and I've even wrestled a little, and I wanted to go to the NWA match next week at the Omni. I was wondering if you wanted to go."

A pause. "Man, how'd you get this number?" He was yelling now. "How do you know me? What the fuck?"

I told him how I'd moved from New York and that I'd gotten his name from the newsletter. He calmed down.

"Man, I don't think I want to go," he asked. "I hope that's OK. But I do have someone I want you to meet."

He told me about a friend who had set up some wrestling matches in the area. "Why don't we come over and take a look at your tapes?" he asked. "Maybe we can get you a match."

Holy shit, I thought. I really did strike gold on my first call. I already knew someone with connections. We made an agreement that instead of going to the NWA match, Jeff and his friend would come over to my apartment and watch my tapes.

"Hey, do me a favor," Jeff said. "My friend likes to drink. Have something for us to drink, ok?"

I made sure to stock my fridge with beer.

✶

In my first week in South Carolina, it became obvious that I was juggling more alter egos than ever before. At work, I was doing a job that was emotionally and financially rewarding. It still was not what I wanted to do, but I pretended I was satisfied. At the hospital, I worked primarily with females, and I was a well-built man trying to pass myself off as heterosexual. At home, I was hanging out with a lot of young professionals like myself and still playing both of those roles.

Even though Dan wasn't there to guide me, it was easy to make friends. It was like living in the college dorm again. We spent our time grilling out, playing volleyball and lying by the pool. Many in that group were into drugs like cocaine. I declined, but I didn't mind hanging out with them. Sometimes on Friday or Saturday nights we would go to a club or a party, but most of the time I was content to chill. It was a good life, one that many people would have loved. But I wanted to be in the ring, learning more, making myself into a great wrestler.

And in my personal life, I was struggling. In the south in 1992, it wasn't easy to be gay. There was still a stigma, and I wasn't ready for anyone to know who I really was. In Columbia I rarely went to the gay bars because I was afraid my friends from work, or worse, that my wrestling friends would see me. I know that the chances were slim to none, but I still had the fear.

The next weekend, Jeff and his friend showed up at my apartment. When I opened the door, I saw two totally different characters. One looked like a hillbilly redneck with long greasy hair. He wore a T-shirt and grungy jeans. That was Jeff. The other was a striking figure—he looked like a younger, muscular Jack Nicholson, almost devilish, with a neat polo shirt tucked into designer jeans.

"Chris Kanyon," said Jeff, "this is my friend, Jim Mitchell."

I shook their hands, and I think they could tell I was nervous. Jeff kept talking a lot, while Jim never spoke.

"Can I get you guys some beers?" I asked.

"You bizzle your ass you can," Jeff said.

I looked at him. "I'm sorry?"

"Bizzle," Jim said, sitting down on my couch. "It's called 'carnie' talk around here. Everything ends in 'izzle.' So instead of saying, 'Bet your ass,' Jeff here said, 'Bizzle your ass.'"

Jim had a southern drawl that was alluring and creepy all at the same time. "Now, uh, Chris is it?" he asked.

I nodded.

"How about those beers?"

As I went to the fridge, I could hear Jeff's izzles flying all over the place. I didn't get it, and I wondered if I liked either one of them. Later, as they watched my tapes, I still didn't know what to think. Jim never said a word. He only nodded every now and then to emphasize something Jeff said. Jeff talked all night, never seeming to pay much attention to my tapes. But he did talk a lot about money, and about how we could make it.

"Jim here does some independent shows across the state," Jeff said. "We think we can probably get you into some, if you want."

"Yeah, man — of course," I said. "I'd love to."

"Good. Now we think —"

"Chris," Jim said, interrupting. "You think I could have another one?" He held up an empty beer bottle. I looked from Jeff to Jim and back.

"Sure," I said, and I walked to the fridge. In the kitchen, I could hear them whispering, then talking under their breath. I couldn't hear what they were saying.

When I returned, Jim took the beer (his eighth) and got up from the couch. "I'm afraid we'll have to be leaving," he said, and Jeff — who now sported an irritated glare — also rose from the couch. "We'll be in touch."

I shook each of their hands, dumbfounded. "Um, Jim?"

"Yes, Chris?"

"Am I going to be wrestling for you?"

"Oh yes, definitely," he said. "Especially if I can crash here at your apartment from time to time."

He laughed, and I did too. I thought at the time he was a little crazy. As I opened the door for them to go, Jeff stood there, quiet.

"Jim, where can I find a wrestling school?" I asked.

He laughed again—a guttural sound. "The legendary Moolah Wrestling School is about three miles away from here."

With that the two left, and as I watched them leave, I noticed them arguing again as they walked down my apartment steps. I didn't know what to think about those two, but I knew that, at the very least, they gave me good information. I had a wrestling school just three miles away. There were only a handful of wrestling schools in the nation.

This has to be destiny, I thought.

✶

Though I didn't love it the way I love being in the ring, my daytime work was something I enjoyed. There were moments in Columbia where I knew I was making a difference. And there was no time when I felt that as much as when I was working with Mr. Cipher, a man in his late sixties who could have easily passed for a younger, stronger Vincent Price. I was told by his family that he lived a wonderful life, and that he had always acted young for his age. He had been active, and he lived life to the fullest.

When I first saw him, he was in a vegetative state recovering from a stroke that partially paralyzed the left side of his body. I knew from my schooling and internships that a right-brain stroke would leave the left side of the body in this condition. It even affected the left eye, meaning that if people stood in Mr. Cipher's left eye line of vision, he wouldn't be able to see them. Possibly most interesting, it causes people to react and think in different ways. If you asked Mr. Cipher to draw a clock face, he would draw the right half of the circle. Then he would try to fit all the numbers in that right half. But I knew that with my help, with assistance and therapy, the mind could retrace its damaged pathways, and slowly, with repetition, Mr. Cipher could relearn to use that side of his body.

There are set methods for recovery. But I learned it's more than that—it's about connecting with people, and in a way, I could do that. I was personable at my job, and I did enjoy helping people. It was one of the few things in my life that was not an act.

When Mr. Cipher came into his room after surgery, you could tell his mental light bulb was dim. But you also knew he was at least a little bit aware of his situation. After surgery, people are generally filled with fear that they'll never get back what they lost, and the best way to get them to commit to rehabilitation is to help them through that fear. You relate to them, and comfort them. You convince them you're going to help make them better. Weeks into living in Columbia, I started to pick up a bit of the Southern twang, and people seemed to respond to that. They liked hearing me talk like them, so I would.

I knew right away Mr. Cipher was in trouble. There was virtually no response from his eyes. The good thing was he had a lot of family with him, to help with care and recovery.

"What can we do?" Mr. Cipher's daughter, Pamela, asked.

"Well, we can touch the left side of his body, just press all over, up and down," I said, showing her. "You guys can do this as much as you want to help him."

The next day, when I returned, I could detect an immediate difference. He was coming out of the stupor. His eyes were more alert, and he could watch me as I walked around the room. He could also respond to instructions, and move parts of his right side. Getting a patient to stand up is a major goal in surgical recovery, as it gets the blood circulated and clears the fluid from the lungs. With a lot of work, by the third day, Mr. Cipher was sitting up in bed and maintaining his position.

"This is good, Mr. Cipher," I told him, massaging his left side. "This is helping you get better. This is helping your blood circulate, so you can get the feeling back in your other side."

He nodded, trying to communicate, but all he could do was grunt.

"It's OK," I said, working on my twang. "You're getting there."

A major progression is getting the patient to move from their bed to a wheelchair, so they can go downstairs to a therapy room with parallel bars and other instruments. By the end of the week, Mr. Cipher was already downstairs.

"He's doing wonderful," I told Pamela. "He's had the fastest recovery I've seen here."

But it helped that Mr. Cipher loved life. He was very willing to listen to me, and to work on our exercises. Whenever I asked if he was tired, or if he wanted to quit, he would say no. He would always keep pushing. In school we were taught that recovery from strokes is possible. Many times the damaged brain is due to swelling near the stroke area, and with work, the swelling goes down, allowing the patient to utilize more of the brain power in the once-affected area. Mr. Cipher was a textbook case. But he also worked hard. He wanted to get better, and he wanted to live.

Witnessing his recovery was an inspiration to me. It was a prime example of how when you wanted something, you worked until you got it. By the second week, he was communicating with one-word responses, and by the third, he was talking, even though the left side of his face couldn't move. After months more of hard work, Mr. Cipher was even better. It was as if he'd beaten the stroke.

It was the most remarkable recovery I would ever see. And even then, I never thought about giving up wrestling to devote my life to this job. It was like getting an upgrade on a flight from New York to L.A. This job was definitely an improvement from my normal life, but I was still on a flight to a career in wrestling. Nothing was going to stop that.

Not even Moolah herself.

✱

"Let me tell you something about Jeff," said Jim, who had shown up at my apartment, unannounced, as he frequently did. Jim was drinking, as usual. I was already convinced he had a problem, but hey, we all have problems.

"Jeff is—in a word—a weasel," he said, stepping through my door and sitting on the couch. "Jeff had you pegged, my friend. Pegged."

"What do you mean?" I was confused.

"He was ready to rob you blind, son. Blind."

"What?"

"He was going to play you, play you for a mark. As soon as he talked with you on the phone, he called me up and said we had a real easy mark this time. He said he'd just found a guy we could scam out of a lot of money." Jim took a drink. "And he meant you."

"But I thought he wanted to promote me, I thought —"

"Welcome to the world of independent wrestling, my friend," he said, laughing. "This world is filled with weasels. And no one — not you, or me, or Ric friggin' Flair — is safe." He took another drink. "Well, maybe Flair is safe."

"Why are you telling me this?" I asked. I didn't know what to think.

"Because I watched your tape," he said. "I watched it, and you're good. You need a lot more time in the ring, but you're good. I knew you weren't a mark when I saw the tape."

"How do I know I can trust you, then?"

He looked me in the eye, and again, I thought he was a little creepy.

"You don't," he said. "And that's good — now you're in the right frame of mind. But I will tell you this. I can get you matches, and I can get you into wrestling school. Look at me — this is who I am. Sometimes I may need a place to sleep, or something to drink. That's me. I don't have much. But I'll take us as far as I can, I promise you that."

He held out his hand.

"Deal," I said, shaking it.

In just a few weeks in South Carolina, I already had a manager.

✱

Moolah's wrestling school was known as much for taking your money as it was for producing wrestlers. Jim had warned me about a few of the things they would try to do, like getting me to buy jackets with my name on them, or making me purchase tapes of my own performances.

Plus, there was the $3,000 class fee. But Jim said that if I was a wrestler with experience, they would waive the fee. Basically, I had to prove I was good enough.

That Saturday, I woke up early and got ready. I still didn't have much to make me look like a seasoned wrestler. I had my trunks and my old wrestling shoes, but that was it. I walked out into the muggy air and waited for Jim to pick me up. The sun hadn't completely risen yet, but I could feel the heat getting trapped already. It was never hot like this in New York. The cicadas in the trees offered a soft hum that seemed to spread throughout the land in the southern states.

The peaceful moment was interrupted with a loud crackling coming my way.

Far down the road, a dark blue Cadillac struggled to make it down the street. It had to be Jim. From the looks of it, the car had to be about 20 years old, but maybe that was just the wear and tear Jim had put on the vehicle. A light wisp of smoke trailed from the rear as it made its way toward me. I noticed the windows were rolled down. Great. No air conditioning.

Jim stuck his head out the driver's side window. "Come on now, boy, no time to wait!"

Again I wondered what I'd gotten myself into. I walked around the front of the car, and I noticed a few more tendrils of smoke coming from the hood.

"Are you sure this is going to make it three miles to Moolah's?" I asked.

Jim laughed. "Don't get smart, boy, it doesn't become you. Now get in. Your life is about to change."

When I got in I noticed Jim had a beer in his hand. He was taking swigs with one hand and driving with the other, a position that would become a common occurrence in our friendship. Jim was dressed like he was when I first met him. Not too dressy, just a polo and jeans, but neat enough for you to know he cared about what he looked like. A quick survey of the car revealed something entirely different: It was junk, and it was filled with junk. The front seats were at one time some kind of velvet, like the car had been owned by a pimp, but the material had been worn and covered with cigarette burns and tears. The back seat was worse. Papers, clothes, books and half-eaten fast food all festered back there, and if there were seats, I couldn't tell. Some of the clothes looked odd, but I couldn't tell why. It was as if the pants had holes in them or something. Not rips, but strategically placed holes.

"Those are my assless pants," Jim said. He looked to the back seat while continuing to steer the car, even though his eyes weren't on the road. "It's for foreplay, you see. Some people are into these kinds of things. You know, for sex."

I stared at him. I didn't know what to think.

On top of a pile of old papers, I saw two books that told me more about Jim. One was called *An Introduction to Sexual Deviancy*. The other was *The Satanic Bible*.

"Are those your books, Jim?" I asked.

"Oh yes," he said, again smiling his creepy smile. His hands had returned to the wheel, the car's engine sputtering away. "Those are two very important books. You've already realized I'm a bit of a sexual deviant, what with finding the assless pants and all. I don't have to explain that, do I, Chris? You know what it's like to be a sexual deviant, don't you?"

I stared ahead at the road. "I'm not sure I understand what you mean, Jim."

"Of course you do!" he said, slapping the wheel. "Everyone has these feelings inside, awkward feelings that make us all excited, right? Don't you, Chris? Haven't you ever had a sexual feeling that made you feel awkward, or even scared?"

I said nothing.

"Of course you have," he said. "It's nothing to feel strange about. I merely give in to my sexual urges."

He took another swig of beer.

"Now, it's common knowledge around here that I am a card-carrying member of the Church of Satan," he continued.

I was relieved he'd moved on to a new topic. "So you worship the Devil?" I asked.

Jim laughed again. "If there's anyone in the world — or outside this world — who I worship, it's probably Jack Nicholson. What is the Devil, anyway? According to the Church of Satan, the Devil is the spirit inside all of us, Chris. It's human instinct. We support a view of human beings as animals, and we reject those in society who wish to inhibit us. We're not demons." He smiled. "We only believe in what is natural and right. We want to do good by other creatures, but those who do not do good by us" — he drank the rest of his beer and crushed the can — "are punished. And without mercy."

He stopped the car in front of what looked like a trailer park.

"When you think about it, punishment, competition — it's all just like wrestling," Jim said. He looked in the rear view mirror at himself, checking to see if he had food in his teeth. "Get out of the car, son."

My head was swimming with all I'd learned about my new sexually adventurous, devil-worshipping friend. "Why should I get out of the car?"

He put a finger to his tongue, then swept his eyebrows back.

"Because we're here."

✱

It didn't just look like a trailer park. It was a trailer park.

"This is some of the land Moolah owns," Jim said, leading the way. "Actually, this street is called Moolah Drive. Some of her wrestlers live in these trailers. The ring is in the back here."

I followed Jim as we tiptoed through the high weeds of the park. Some of the trailers were rusted and seemed to be unused. Others were definitely inhabited, with clothes hanging out to dry on the line. A huge lake sat right in the middle of the park, and toward the back, there was an old garage. I'd never seen anything like this place before. It was like something out of *Deliverance*.

But I had seen Moolah on television before. She was a former wrestler, a real pioneer for women in the business, and now in her sixties. Picture Lucille Ball on steroids. Big red hair, big breasts, a lot of makeup and a sweet Southern accent. I knew what to expect from her at least.

Jim opened the door to the garage, and the smell of sweat enveloped us. Inside, wrestlers of all shapes, sizes and ages were working out in the ring, doing exercises and practicing moves. The garage was barely big enough to hold the ring, and the ropes touched some of the walls. And there was no flooring—only dirt. No air conditioning, either.

In the corner, Moolah sat with a small fan blowing cool air on her. Behind her, an older woman sat, combing the hair of what looked to be an elderly midget woman.

"Hi, Moolah," Jim said as he walked up to her. "This is my friend I told you about—Chris Kanyon. He'd like to work here if he could."

She gave Jim a kiss on the cheek and then she looked me up and down. She was just as I remembered from television.

"Thanks, honey," she said to Jim. She turned back to me. "Now, you want to come down and train?"

"Yes, ma'am," I said, trying to sound like I was at least a little Southern.

She adjusted the fan in front of her. "I see. Now what kind of experience do you have, honey?"

Jim jumped in for me. "He's been wrestling professionally now for about three years, ma'am," he said, smiling.

Her eyebrows raised. "Really?"

"Really," Jim said.

"Well, if you're that experienced, why don't you come back next week and show us some of your moves. OK, honey?"

I smiled. I was in. "Yes, ma'am."

We left the garage and went back out to the trailer park.

"This place is like an old carnie-show," Jim said. "A lot of these guys are just dirtball wrestlers who will never amount to anything. Those women are taking their money and the guys will never have anything to show for it. But that's how they make their business, son."

"Who were the other women?" I asked.

"Well, the older lady, that's Mae Young. She trained Moolah to wrestle back in the day," Jim said. "Some of the guys around here call her 'Mae Not-So-Young.' She must be in her late seventies by now."

"And the midget?"

"I told you it was carnie-like, didn't I?" Jim laughed. "That would be Miss Katie. Those three women live here, together, and sometimes I think Miss Katie is just like a little pet to Mae."

We got to the car, and I looked back.

"You're not in New York anymore, Chris!"

I was certain of that.

We got in and closed the doors. Jim tried to rev the engine of the Cadillac and eventually it came to life.

"But that's the beauty of this place," he said. "Sexual deviants, members of the Church of Satan, old wrestling broads, midgets—all are accepted here. We don't care what you are. If you're genuine, we'll like you."

I smiled. I liked the sound of that.

(16)

MISTAKES

It's always a big moment when a wrestler gets his first real boots. When Jesse Ventura retired, he took his first pair of boots and threw them in the river. When mine finally came in the mail later that week, I knew it was a big moment for me too. They were black, a shiny flossy black like the color of a new Lincoln Town car. I got goose bumps when I opened the box and took them out.

For fun, I put them on and looked at them in my full-length mirror.

Damn, I thought. I looked like the real thing.

Days later, Jim came by to see them. He approved.

"Looks like they were made for ya," he said.

That weekend, we drove back to Moolah's. Inside the dusty old garage, the same wrestlers were in the ring, working on their moves. Just by looking I knew I was further along than those guys. I knew I belonged. We just had to convince Moolah. When we came in, she motioned for us to walk over.

"Hey, honey," she said to Jim. Then she looked at me. "This is the boy you say has been wrestling for about three years, hmm?"

"Yes, ma'am," Jim replied.

Moolah got up from her chair and walked to me. I'd taken off my shirt so she could see me in my trunks and boots. She walked around me, in a complete circle, looking me up and down. When she came back, she was standing in front of me again, and our eyes met.

"Nice boots," she said.

I smiled. "Thanks." I was proud of the boots.

Moolah sat back down, and she settled her hands under her heavy breasts. She looked to Jim. "Three years, huh?"

Jim looked to me, then back to Moolah. "Yes, ma'am. Three years."

At that point, Jim knew Moolah had spied my new boots. He knew she'd figured out I had a little less experience than we were letting on. Of course, it would have been nice for Jim to have relayed this message to me. He didn't.

"So pull up a chair, um, Chris, was it?" Moolah said. "Pull up a chair, Chris, and tell me a little about yourself, OK?"

"OK," I said, and I drew up a chair next to Moolah. I got comfortable; this was going better than I thought.

"Chris, uh, maybe you might want to—" Jim started.

"No, no—don't interrupt the boy," Moolah said, and Jim got quiet. "Stretch out, stay a while."

I did as I was told. We were sitting next to the ring, where a couple of amateurs were trying their best to look professional. I even decided to put my feet up on the mat and stretch out like Moolah said. I put my boot up on the mat.

"So, you're from New York," Moolah said, admiring my boot.

"Yes, ma'am. Born and raised," I said.

"I see," she said. I noticed she was looking at my boot.

Then Jim stepped in. "Moolah, we need to be excused for a moment, I hope you understand," he said. He took me by the arm and led me out of the garage. Moolah watched us leave. She said nothing, only her smile letting me know she'd heard us at all.

"Scuff your boots," Jim said to me.

"What?" I said. They were my new boots. Why should I scuff them?

"Scuff them up. We told her you've been wrestling for three years but you came in with new boots."

It dawned on me. I understood.

"Do you think she knows?" I said, quickly rubbing my boots on the concrete outside.

"She knew when you walked in, jackass," Jim said. "She's not an idiot. Lucky for us, that goes both ways. She knows you're green. But if you're good, there's no way she'll turn you down. After all, she's not an idiot, right?"

We went back in, and I was allowed to take a turn with some of the guys in the ring. It was an easy tryout. I worked my normal routine, just like I was wrestling with Danny and my cousins back home in the park. During one break in the action, I saw Jim and Moolah talking. Moolah looked at me and nodded.

I was in.

✱

Jim told me about the normal scam. A kid would wander in to Moolah's with no contacts, and most of the time, no experience. He would ask to be trained as a wrestler, and to someone in the business, it would be easy to see the kid didn't have what it took. Maybe he wouldn't have the skill or the look or the charisma. But that's not what Moolah and her ladies would say. They would tell the kid he definitely had it, that all he had to do was wrestle with them and they could show him the way.

Then they'd start taking the kid's money.

They'd make the jacket for him, and the boots, and maybe they'd take pictures of him. Then they would have him buy all of it, because he would be told he needed it, or, like me, he would be proud and want to buy it. Then they would start taping his matches, and every good wrestler needs to keep his matches on tape, so they would sell him the tapes too. All of this was on top of the $3,000 fee for the wrestling classes. Moolah and Mae would then book gigs for the kid all over South Carolina. But unbeknownst to the kid, that's as far as he was ever going to go. Because he didn't have it, he wouldn't make it any further.

Luckily, I knew the game, and Jim was there to keep me on the right path. He was also there for me as a friend, even though it was an interesting relationship. Sometimes he would just show up at my apartment needing a place to stay. But he was always ready to help critique my matches and push our careers forward.

For me, wrestling with Moolah was all about exposure. We'd drive all over South Carolina, and we made no money. She wouldn't even pay for our gas. But the experience was invaluable. Sometimes even old Mae Young would come into the ring and kick us in the nuts or beat us up. But this is what we did, what we put up with to make it, to learn to get better.

Of course, Jim was also getting me matches, and through him I was learning to watch myself more on tape, to break down my mistakes and improve on everything from selling punches to selling my falls. Jim taught me to look at myself in a critical way.

"Don't look at what you did right," he told me. "What you did right was great. You know that, you don't need to see it. Look at what you did wrong. Be tough on yourself and figure out how to make those mistakes better."

It's something I'd take with me for the rest of my career.

At that time, Jim was trying to get us into Smoky Mountain Wrestling — one of the up-and-coming American venues for wrestlers just on the cusp of the big-time. On Saturday mornings, we'd read the newsletters and watch pay-per-views, dreaming of the time when we might get our shot.

I'd still been keeping up with others who read those newsletters too. From time to time I talked with a good friend of mine, Georgianne Cropolis of Estoria, Queens. Georgianne had been writing to the newsletters since I was in college, and she was as knowledgeable about wrestling as any fan I'd ever met. Sometimes I'd see her name, and others, in the pages of the magazines and newsletters, and when I did, I had to call and tell her hello.

But it was difficult to keep up with a lot of folks back home. I didn't call my parents or my old friends as much as I should have. And after some time in muggy South Carolina, one phone call would stop me cold.

✱

In the fall of 1993, I'd been wrestling matches with Moolah and Jim, keeping myself fit and working my job at the hospital. I was really wondering if I wanted to stay in Columbia, and on a lazy Saturday morning, Jim and I were watching a pay-per-view when the phone rang.

"Hello," I grumbled, irritated that someone had interrupted our video.

"Chris?"

That's all it took. I knew. It was Pete McKay's wife, and she sounded tired.

"What's happened?" I said. "What's wrong with Pete?"

"It's OK," she said calmly. "He's going to be OK."

Pete was no longer able to run the Lower East Side Gym, she said. He'd had a heart attack.

✱

Using my vacation time, I went up to see Pete. I had to. He was the one who really got me into the business. He was like another father.

I flew to New York and after making sure he was energetic enough to see me, I made my way to his apartment. There, his wife let me in the door and I walked in to see a different Pete than I remembered. He'd lost weight, and instead of standing to greet me when I walked in the room, he lifted a hand, and sat up in his soft recliner.

"Hey, Pete."

He smiled. "Hey, Chris — Chris Kanyon."

I had to smile to. "That's right. The name stuck with me."

"It's a good name." Pete twitched — he hadn't lost that familiar trait.

"How you doing?" I sat down next to him.

"God, I feel great," he said. "But you should've been here when I had the heart attack. That wasn't such a good time."

"You look good."

"Well," he sat up a bit straighter. "I don't know how good I look, but I know I'm feeling better."

"How's the gym doing?"

"Worse than me," he said. "You know how I've always needed that city funding to keep it open? I don't think it's going to keep coming. I think we may have to shut it down."

"Oh God, that's terrible," I said. "You're going to have to close down? I didn't know things were that bad." I immediately thought back to the $3,000 Pete never made me pay.

"Well, I'm going to fight — as much as I can."

"Pete," I brought my chair closer to his. "Why were you so good to me? You didn't have to help me. People in this business don't always help people out."

Pete smiled. "I don't know, Chris." He pointed to a picture on his nightstand. "You see that picture?"

I picked it up and gave it to him.

"This is my young son, Danny," he said. "Danny isn't a wrestler. And that's fine with me. If he ever wants to be, that's wonderful, but he knows he doesn't have to. He knows I'll be pleased with whatever he does in life."

He pointed at me, and he twitched. "But you, you're also like a son to me. You love wrestling so much that even though you went to college, even though you have an opportunity to do something more with your life, you still choose to bust your ass and become a professional wrestler. And it's something I know you'll do.

"I wanted to help you because I wanted to do for you what I hope someone will do for Danny if he ever wants to get into the business," he said. "Sometimes you need people to help you along the way."

He smiled.

"Plus, I like you," he said.

I took his hand. "I like you too, Pete."

I had to wipe a tear from my eye.

✱

I stayed on in South Carolina throughout the winter, and until Christmas, when I traveled back home to see my family and friends. At that time, Pete broke the news to me: He'd lost the gym, and it nearly broke my heart.

Secretly, I'd been wondering if I wanted to stay in Columbia any longer. The town was feeling increasingly small and boring to me, and I think I needed a change of scenery. The job was fine, and my co-workers were good people, but at certain times it was difficult to hide that I was gay. I would sometimes go out with them, and we would socialize, though I never had a girlfriend. No one seemed to wonder why, though sometimes, things got a little weird.

One of my co-workers, Melanie, was married, and always seemed to like being around me. A nurse, Mel had an easy laugh and was a good-looking girl: young, with a pretty face and dark hair. She took care of her body and I'm sure she was lusted after by some of my heterosexual co-workers. One day after work, the two of us were alone in the office.

"Chris, why don't you have a girl?" she asked, putting her hand on my arm.

"Um, I guess I haven't found the right one yet," I said, trying to come up with anything that could get me out of the situation.

"What are you doing tonight?" she asked, looking up at me.

"I don't have any plans." It was true. It was a Friday night and I hadn't planned on doing anything except watching wrestling tapes.

"Why don't we grab some dinner on the way home?" she said.

I said I thought that would be OK.

We met at a local restaurant and had some drinks and dinner, nothing intimate at all. Our conversation centered around work and gossip, but rarely went into intellectual waters.

"Where's your husband tonight?" I asked.

"Out with some friends," she replied. I thought I saw something else in her smile, but I couldn't put my finger on it.

She took another sip of her drink. "Chris?"

I was looking at something on the bar television. "Yeah?" I said, looking back at her.

She put her hand on mine and looked into my eyes. "I want you to take me back to your apartment and fuck my brains out."

I didn't know what to say. Maybe she could sense my confusion.

"It's OK," she said. "I know we work together, and I don't want it to be weird. No strings here. I've wanted you for a long time."

There were several of things I could've done. I could've made an excuse and left. I could've accepted the offer and fucked her. I could've told her I was gay.

"I'm gay," I said.

She pulled her hand away. "What?" She looked genuinely shocked.

"It's true. That's why I don't have a girlfriend," I said. "I'm gay."

✷

We went home and ultimately went our separate ways—Melanie back to her husband and me back to my empty apartment. I wondered what the people at work would think. I knew word would spread.

On Monday, I went into the hospital early, with a plan. I knew the people who tended to gossip the most, and one was a male nurse, Bobby. If I could get to Bobby before anyone else, I could diffuse what could be a troubling situation for me. When Bobby got to work a few minutes after me, I knew I was in good shape.

"Hey, man," I said to him when he walked in.

"Hey. What's up, Chris?"

"Dude, you'll never believe what happened Friday," I said. "Melanie asked me to fuck her."

"What?" Bobby couldn't believe it.

"I know, right? We were out to dinner and she just took my hand and told me to take her back to my place and—I quote—fuck her brains out."

"Holy shit, man. You've got to tell me what happened."

"Here's the deal," I said. "I wanted to, man. I mean, Mel is hot, you know? I mean, she's the most fuckable chick here."

"Totally."

"But she's married, dude, and I do not want to break up somebody's marriage," I said. "I couldn't do it. I didn't want to. She's hot, but she's not worth it."

"I don't know, man," Bobby said. "She's pretty hot. I think she's worth it. You're a better man than me."

"Well here's the thing," I said. I had to approach this gently. "I didn't know how to let her down, so I told her something — I told her a lie."

"What'd you say?"

I waited. "I told her I was gay."

Bobby laughed out loud. "You said you were gay? Really? Who would believe you're gay? You're the biggest, toughest guy here."

"Well, she believed it."

"Wow," Bobby said. "I can't believe she bought it. I mean, that's funny."

"Yeah, well, we have to make sure she thinks I'm gay, OK? Let everybody know that Mel has to think I am gay." I felt relieved. Bobby thought this was a good story, and he'd pass it along to the others.

"OK, man," Bobby said. "But we're going to have to do some convincing."

"Yeah," I said. "I'm sure we can do it if we try."

(17)

AWE AND DISGUST IN THE MIRROR

During that time, my cousin Brian came down with his family to visit us on vacation. Brian wanted to see me do some amateur wrestling, but he also wanted to meet Jim, since I talked about him all the time.

After a match Moolah had set up for us, I brought Brian backstage to meet Jim, who was dressed up like a mix between Dracula and Satan. He sported long fangs and a red cape, but he also had a tail. It was the perfect scene for Brian.

"Jim, this is my cousin Brian," I said.

"Pleased to meet you, sir," Jim replied, grinning and revealing that he had a red substance resembling blood in his mouth. "Any friend or relative of Chris Kanyon is a friend — or relative — of mine."

"Uh, hi," Brian said. "Nice costume."

"Costume? Oh, this," Jim said, gesturing to his outfit. "This is what I'm wearing out tonight. I have a date."

"A date?" Brian couldn't comprehend it.

"Yes, an energetic young lady named Juanita who claims she's a witch," Jim said. "I think I may get lucky tonight."

Brian's mouth dropped open.

"Well, there you have it," I said. "That's Jim."

We walked out into the chilly night and Brian still hadn't spoken. We got into the car to make the trek back to my apartment. When he finally broke the silence, I thought it would be about the spectacle we'd just seen, but Brian surprised me.

"You're really close," he said.

"What?" I put the car in gear.

"You're going to make it," he said. "All those times when we were wrestling in the backyard, you always said you were going to be a pro. I don't know if I ever believed you, even up until now. I don't think I did." He paused. "But you're going to do it. I'm going to be watching you on television."

I nodded. "Well, I always believed it. You're right — I am close. Give me some more time. I'll do it."

He smiled, and slapped me on the shoulder. "Don't forget about us when you're wrestling in Madison Square Garden, ок?" he said. "I want tickets."

"Don't worry," I said. "I'll get you tickets."

✱

My experiences with other gay men were dwindling. For one, I was always afraid Jim or one of my co-workers would drop by, and there I would be, with a date. Only it would be a man, and I would be discovered. I was certain that the headway I'd made in my wrestling career would disappear.

Still, I could only wait so long. I had needs.

On a cool night, I went to one of the few gay bars and struck up a conversation with a well-built Italian named Damian. Damian and I became fast friends, and we decided to go back to my place.

It was late, and I knew this would be a good time to bring someone home. No one would be watching, and I felt safe that I wouldn't be discovered. When we got to my place, I asked if he wanted a drink.

"I'll have a beer," he said.

"A man after my own heart," I replied.

Not wasting any time, we quickly made it to my bedroom, and as we kissed, I caught a glimpse of myself in a full-length mirror. There, I was, kissing another man. Having my shirt unbuttoned. Having my neck kissed. I was filled with a sense of awe, and something else, like disgust. There's something about old taboos, and even as a gay man, I was not ready for the sight of me kissing another man.

"I, I'm sorry," I said, pushing him away.

"What's wrong?" he asked.

"I wish I could explain it," I said. "But I have some issues with all of this. I'm sorry."

Damian didn't understand. I didn't think he would.

I went to bed alone that night.

✷

Being on the road with Jim and the other wrestlers was always an adventure, not to mention an education — in wrestling and in life.

On the road one night, we'd set up a match at a real backwoods place in South Carolina. Jim had told me and another guy named Johnzee, who always brought a long chain with him to the ring, that we were dealing with a real sleazy promoter. But he told us going in to be prepared, so we knew what to expect — or so we thought.

In the locker room before the match, we sat off on our own, quiet like. It was part of an old wrestling rule to keep to yourself, to not talk unless you are spoken to. So we stayed quiet and changed into our gear. Johnzee was getting his chain ready, and Jim was smoking a cigarette when the promoter, a big guy named Johnny, came into the locker room.

"Hey, no smoking in here," Johnny yelled to Jim.

"Oh, OK," Jim replied, taking another drag.

Johnny saw Jim take another drag, and immediately and jumped on him, knocking Jim to the ground. He grabbed Jim's cigarette and flipped it over, pointing the burning side toward Jim's face, urging the hot ash toward Jim's eye.

"I said, 'No smoking,'" Johnny repeated.

It happened so quickly, I didn't have time to react.

Johnzee, on the other hand, had seen a few things in his time. He slammed his thick chain on the metal locker room chairs, the air ringing with a loud CLANG!

Johnny looked up, and Jim used that moment to get up on his feet. After that, everyone went about their business like nothing had happened. I was wide-eyed.

Later, the two explained that was nothing like what they'd seen before.

"Bring something with you," Johnzee said. "At every match, no matter where you are, have something to defend yourself, because you're never sure of what's going to happen."

"And," Jim said, "always be skeptical of those shady promoters."

✱

In the winter, the hospital asked me to stay. They wanted to hire me on full-time and that seemed to be the nail in the coffin. It was time for me to go. If I were hired on full-time, I'd be giving up a lot of benefits and taking a huge cut in pay. It made more sense to ask my company to relocate me so I could move on and keep the same deal.

After working in the ring with Moolah and with Jim for several months, I wanted to move to a place close to Columbia. The agency offered me a place in Florence, South Carolina, about 70 miles west of Columbia. That sounded like as good a place as any to me.

But once again I was saying goodbye to friends — all the people at the hospital, all those at Moolah's and, even more important, Jim.

Jim turned out to be my best friend down in South Carolina. In a way, he kept me in the wrestling business and I kept him fed and under a roof. He brought me to Moolah's where, believe it or not, I did learn some things. I Americanized my wrestling at Moolah's. Pete had taught me to wrestle in a way that was reminiscent of Mexican wrestlers, where I would work primarily over the right arm and right leg. With Jim and Moolah's help, I learned to switch, and work as American wrestlers do, over the left arm and left leg. It was an adjustment, but one important for my future career.

It was also the time when I started trying new moves. Sometimes I would imitate a move I'd seen someone else do incorrectly, but I never developed anything really good during my time in Columbia. Nothing seemed to work, so I just kept trying to think creatively. It was a time of great experimentation, even though nothing concrete came of it.

On our last night in Columbia, Jim took me out to a local movie theater, a small house that showed independent films.

"There's a movie I want you to see," he said. And of course, he brought the beer.

The movie was Quentin Tarantino's *Reservoir Dogs*, a movie about violence, trust, loyalty and the uncanny relationships among seemingly different people. I couldn't help but see the symbolism for Jim and me.

"This theater is great because you can buy beer and hot dogs here," Jim told me as we sat down. After we finished our first round, Jim, already drunk off the six-pack he'd had before we entered, offered to buy more. I let him.

He got up, and blocked the view of the few others in the small theater.

"Sit down you drunk!" one patron yelled.

Jim stumbled to the concession area, and returned with hot dogs and two cans of beer. "Here ya go," he said to me, but we fumbled the exchange and the can crashed on the tile floor. As the movie entered a particularly stressful scene, all the viewers heard was our beer can rolling down each aisle as it made its way to the front row. When it settled, Jim could not control his laughter.

And by the end of the movie, he had passed out.

We went home and I got him on the couch, where he slept until the morning. When we woke up the next day, it was time for me to leave. Jim woke up with his usual hangover headache.

"Good movie, huh?" he smiled.

"Yeah, I liked it a lot."

Jim looked away. "I tell you with a tear in my eye, I am going to miss you."

I gave him a hug. "You know what, dude?" I asked. "This isn't the end of us."

And I was right.

(18)

SMOKY MOUNTAIN HIGH

For months, Jim had been working behind the scenes, talking with Jim Cornette, a leading booker with SMW (Smoky Mountain Wrestling) based in Knoxville. Smoky Mountain, which produced a weekly television show and sent its wrestlers out to locations all over the South, was the up and coming production in wrestling. Compared to what Jim and I were doing with Moolah, going to Smoky Mountain would be like playing beer league softball and suddenly finding yourself in Double-A ball for the Mets. It was the number three promotion in America and drew more than 2,000 fans at every show.

It was big time.

With the motto "Wrestling the way it used to be — and the way we like it," it attracted fans with its small-town feel and by producing storylines weekly for episodic TV. By 1993, people across the South were using their huge satellite dishes to reach out and grab Smoky Mountain's shows because they loved the characters and the stories.

Jim had known Cornette for a while, since we became friends in Columbia, and Jim was always pushing Cornette to bring him up to Smoky Mountain to be part of the show. He would send Cornette tapes of our fights with Jim acting like a promoter and sometimes getting in the ring. Jim was always a good talker, and he knew that he could be a great promoter if he could get on TV. He could twist words and phrases, and he could really play to the cameras. Plus,

Jim had his whole Devil persona, which he loved to play up too. Cornette must have seen that quality in Jim too, because three weeks after I left Columbia, I got a phone call. It was Jim.

"Sonny boy," Jim said in his Southern drawl, "how'd you like to come with me to Smoky Mountain Wrestling?"

I couldn't believe it. Jim had talked his way into Double-A ball, a legitimate, high-profile gig.

I committed on the spot. I wasn't sure how it would work with my new job, but I didn't care. After just three weeks apart, Jim and I were back together. And this time, we were going to be in Smoky Mountain.

✹

Cornette was a guy who was originally a photographer but ended up talking his way into being a major booker for Smoky Mountain. Maybe that's why he liked Jim so much — both of them had the gift of gab. But where Jim could be social, could talk about pop culture and be charming, Cornette had a short fuse. He would fight you in a second, and some people were convinced he'd rather shout at you than be civil.

Cornette had been getting pressure from his backer — record producer Rick Rubin, who provided the money for the shows — to develop a new character. Rubin, best known as producer of the Beastie Boys, Run-DMC and other music legends, wanted an Egyptian Mummy character to be introduced into the Smoky Mountain scene. Honestly, no one knew why Rubin wanted the Mummy, but he wanted it, so it went into development. The Mummy was going to be big and scary, but unfortunately, it also wouldn't be able to talk. Cornette needed someone to act as a promoter for the Mummy, someone who could talk well and play up the character, but someone who also had a dark side — someone the audience would believe would actually hang out with a Mummy.

Cornette thought of one man: Jim Mitchell.

"Cornette told me to wear a fez," Jim told me in a visit to my place in Florence. "They said they needed someone who looked like part of the occult. I told them I was their man."

"Do you think it'll work?" I asked.

Jim smiled. "Who cares? The important thing is, I asked them if I could bring you along, and they said OK. So no matter what, we're there."

Secretly though, we had our doubts about the Mummy character. One of the beautiful things about Smoky Mountain was the old-time feel of the wrestling. The things that attracted fans were the acts and the stories, and this just didn't feel like a great story. But, like Jim said, who cared? We'd made it inside the Mountain.

✶

From 9 a.m. to 5 p.m. I worked at my job at the Florence hospital. At the time, I'd joined a 24-hour gym, where I could always go to work out. I'd also started tanning to make myself look better in the ring. I'd go to the gym after work, then get home around 9 p.m. I'd watch TV, have dinner and go to bed. On Tuesdays, I would usually take a half-day of work and make an eight or nine-hour drive with Jim to the site of our next match — sometimes it was in Knoxville, Tennessee, sometimes it was in Lenoir, North Carolina.

It was a tough schedule to keep, but we were excited, so we'd do it.

Jim and I arrived at our first Smoky Mountain match ready to go. It was a taping in Knoxville in front of a live crowd, and I remembered one of the most important rules of wrestling: always bring your gear. I didn't know what I would do or if I would be involved at all, but I brought my trunks and my boots. I was ready if they needed me. Turns out, they would.

Apparently, something had gone wrong with the production.

Walking up, we spotted Cornette, practically frothing at the mouth over whatever had gone wrong. I could see why some people called him "Mama's Boy." He was a nerdy-looking dude, someone who dressed like a redneck trying to look like a rich guy. He wore a loud red suit, with a bright red tie, and his glasses made him look even younger than he was.

"What the fuck happened?!" he screamed to no one in particular. His face was growing as red as his tie. "The audio went out on the interview! The fucking audio went out on the interview!"

Jim looked over to me. "Apparently," he said with a smile, "the audio went out on the interview."

I couldn't help but smile back.

Cornette was on the rampage. He was wearing a microphone and headphones and looking around like he was a warden and there'd been a jailbreak. "Who is responsible for this fucking bullshit?"

We watched as a younger man, someone straight out of *Revenge of the Nerds*, walked sheepishly up to Cornette. All the kid needed was a pocket protector.

"This was you? You were responsible?" Cornette asked.

The kid nodded.

"Well, let me tell you what has happened," he said, putting his arm around the kid and leading him toward the ring. "We just staged a fight in the post-match interview, OK? It was a fight. A fucking fight. We made it look like it was real, OK? It looked good, like it was on the spur of the fucking moment." He pointed to his headset. "But the audio went out during the interview. Do you see what this means? Because the audio went out, we can't just go back and do it again. Do you know why?"

The kid didn't say anything.

"I'll tell you why. Because if we do it again, everyone here will know it is fucking fake! See, we like to do what we can to make sure people think this is real—not fake."

The kid looked like he might cry.

"Now go on and get your stuff," Cornette said. "You're fucking fired."

Jim looked to me again. "That's the Cornette we know and love."

Cornette finally noticed us, and walked over. He shook Jim's hand.

"Can you believe that fucking cocksucker?" Cornette said. "He could've ruined our operation here."

"Well, I guess it's a good thing you got rid of him, then," Jim said.

"Damn right," Cornette agreed.

"Jim Cornette, meet Chris Kanyon," Jim said. I extended a hand and Cornette shook it.

"God damn this one's tall," Cornette said. "Did you bring your gear?"

"Yes, sir," I said.

"Get ready—we're going to use you tonight."

✶

I was known as a "Job Guy." My goal was to make the champs look good, and the better I did at making them look good, the more jobs I got. Cornette paid $125 per fight, and if you could get a few of those, you were on your way.

That first night, Cornette liked me because I was tall, and he thought I could match up well against his tag team, the Heavenly Bodies, who held the Smoky Mountain Wrestling Tag Team Championship. I didn't know the Heavenly Bodies well, but I knew the two guys—both good-looking, by the way—had been around a while and had earned a lot of respect for being good guys.

I also knew, especially after watching how Cornette dealt with that production kid — that I did not want to fuck this up. I needed to do well if I wanted to come back. Even though I hadn't quite mastered some of the moves I would use later in my career, I knew there was one thing I could do to stand out. I just hoped I would get the chance.

I needed to get one of the Heavenly Bodies to DDT me, meaning I needed one of them to fall down and drive my head into the mat. Most job guys would take a hit like that by landing on their belly or their back. That was fine. But I had developed a new way to do it, where I would actually balance on my head for a moment, then, with my body stiff, fall like a tree, which would elicit more of a reaction from the crowd.

And it would also make my opponent look better, thereby making me look better. If I could get them to do that to me, then I could impress some people.

Before the match, I tried to talk to both members of the Heavenly Bodies, but I found out they didn't talk too much. They just said it would be a normal match, and to be ready to take over, then let them take over when they said so.

The match went well, and we did a lot of normal stuff, pretty elementary, really. But when the time came, they boys told me to take over. For a few minutes I was in charge, and I just happened to be in the right place when I let them take control again. I said, "Gimme a DDT."

And they did. When I went down for the DDT, I could do it differently, because my long hair covered up forearms. I used my forearms to brace the impact instead of my head, but with the hair covering them up, you couldn't tell. All the crowd saw was me seemingly land on my head, balance for a moment, and then fall back, all at once. When I landed, someone in the crowd screamed, "Oh my God, that guy just died!"

Of course, I was fine. But I took a lot of joy in knowing that I sold the move.

The Heavenly Bodies then pinned me for the win. But they let me know I'd done well.

When we came off, Cornette came backstage. He was smiling when he turned to me. "You my friend, just earned your money," he said.

✶

I ended up fighting with the Heavenly Bodies a lot. They knew I could do well, and I had a good time with them. But things were different in Smoky Mountain. That was the first time I started to notice the difference between wrestlers in the locker room. Some of them looked unnaturally big, and only then was it obvious some guys were getting less than legal help to keep themselves muscular.

"That, my friend, is the evidence of steroids," Jim said.

I also learned about in-ring protocol. During a Battle Royale match, I went against Pistol Pez Whatley, a huge black wrestler who'd been around for a while. He was the babyface, while I was the heel. But during the match I was unsure how to stop Whatley; I tried something called a "ball shot," where I dropped to my knees and threw a forearm at his crotch.

Whately blocked it, and immediately I knew I'd screwed up. If it was OK, Pez would've kept it going, kept the illusion. Before I threw it I had no idea it was a faux pas, but as soon as I done it, one utterance from Whately drove home the lesson: "Not from a green boy just out of wrestling school."

My blood ran cold. So the nut shot was off-limits. Now, out of respect, I'd have to let him beat my ass. That was the way things were done in wrestling. It's about paying your dues, and respecting those who'd come before you.

Pez pulled my hair. "Take a big bump," he said.

Uh-oh, I thought. Here it comes.

Pez head-butted me, but hit his own thumb to stop the impact. I was stunned. He wasn't going to beat my ass after all. "Rake my eyes, stupid," he said. So I did. When the match was over, and we were back in the locker room, I apologized.

"I didn't know," I said. "Thanks for being cool."

Pez just looked at me. "Shut the fuck up, you fucking green boy," he said.

The others in the locker room just laughed, and I knew he'd acted that way for show—Pez was a good guy. He could've beaten my ass, but out of kindness—or maybe feeling sorry for me—he decided not to.

I was lucky.

✶

As I worked as a jobber, Jim was making appearances on the show and throughout the Smoky Mountain circuit as the promoter for the Mummy. He would do the interviews and tell everyone how the Mummy, named Prince Kharis, was going to kick everyone's ass, and the buildup was becoming pretty exciting. Jim called himself Daryl Van Horne, and he was identified as a collector of human oddities who had discovered the supposed 4,000-year-old Prince.

114 WRESTLING REALITY

Jim was good at what he was doing, and he could really sell an act, even if it wasn't the best gimmick.

And sometimes, he'd do things that even surprised himself.

While trying to start a feud with some other wrestlers during a taping one night, Jim was insulting them, trying to say anything he could that would get on television.

"Really?" he said to one particularly large black wrestler. "Well, I heard you felched the family dog."

When the scene was over, Jim practically ran my way. "Did you hear what I said? Did you? I can't believe they didn't get mad at me for that one."

I didn't know what he meant. "What did you say?" I asked.

"I said he FELCHED the family dog!"

"What's felching?"

Jim's smiled faded. "Felching is when you shoot a load into someone's ass and then you suck it back out." He blinked. "You didn't know that?"

No, I told him. I did not, in fact, know that.

"Well," he said, "the world needs to catch up with the new sexual fetishes of the time."

When it was time to debut the Mummy, Jim was ready, and so were the Smoky Mountain fans. The monster was to come out to a house show crowd in Lenoir, North Carolina, and guess who drew the job of fighting the big son of a bitch?

Me.

The guy playing the Mummy was six-eight and 280 pounds, and because babyfaces and heels were kept in separate locker rooms, I couldn't talk to him beforehand. The only thing I knew was his finishing move — the Mummy was supposed to pick me up by the neck and throw me on my back for the pin.

I walked out into the ring, waiting amid the restless crowd's cheers as they waited for the monster. Jim came out too, calling for the Mummy. Apparently, the Mummy only answered to Jim talking in tongues, because Jim was speaking this odd mix of carnie and other languages.

"Come on ouzzle, my monstizzle," Jim said.

The lights were lowered, and all of us wanted to see what this thing looked like. As creepy violin music played over the intercom, the lights started to come on as the Mummy walked out. And it was hilarious.

We watched as this big guy wrapped in toilet paper from head to foot staggered out to the ring. It looked like they had tried to do something about the whiteness of the toilet paper, like maybe they tried to make it more dirty, so they rubbed real dirt all over him. It was a dirty, toilet paper–covered Mummy. And it was obviously hard to walk because the dude was wrapped in toilet paper.

When the monster stepped out into a spotlight, the crowd didn't react with awe or horror. Instead, they laughed.

And I laughed, too. And so did Jim. And so did the referee.

Pretty much everyone watching the show laughed a lot.

The laughter was hard to stop when the Mummy made his way to the ring. He had no moves. The Mummy couldn't wrestle. And because the toilet paper was wrapped tightly around his mouth, the Mummy also could not speak, so I had no idea what to do with him. I decided to do whatever I could.

I walked up to the Mummy and said "Shoulder block." I went into the rope and swung back to the monster. When I hit him, I fell on my back and landed hard. When I did, the dirt from his bandages shook off on to me, and fell in my eyes. Now, I couldn't see, and what was a mess to begin with descended into something far more comical.

The ref just couldn't stop laughing at this comedy of errors. It was the craziest thing I'd ever been a part of. I couldn't see a thing, so I stood up and whispered one final request to the Mummy. "Let's just end this," I said.

So the Mummy lifted me up by my neck and threw me down, pinning me.

Mercifully, it was over.

(19)

SCREWED BUT MOVING ON

"Jesus Christ," Jim said, looking around the room. We'd been traveling to some shows where we had to spend the night, so we packed a bag. Or, in my case, packed three. "You pack like a damn woman, son."

I looked around and saw my pile of luggage, ridiculous compared to Jim's single bag.

"Why the hell did you bring so much stuff, anyway?" he said.

I didn't know what to say. I sat on the bed and put my hands in my head.

"I'm not sure," I said. "I guess I always just have to be ready for anything."

"Is all of this just clothes?" Jim asked, sorting through the bags. Then he looked up. "You didn't bring any drugs did you? Please say you did."

"I didn't. It's just clothes."

He stood up. "Hmm. Well, I guess if I run out of underwear, I came with the right guy, then," he said.

As he laughed, I couldn't shake the weird feeling I had. I brought three bags for an overnight stay. Why did I do that?

✶

During the few months the Mummy continued its run, I was having an amazing time as a jobber, really proving myself as a wrestler who could make others look good. At just 23, I was close to getting a real shot at making my mark in

Smoky Mountain Wrestling, which everyone knew was a training ground. The next step? The kingdom of the wrestling world—the World Wrestling Federation. Everything seemed to be going as planned. By this time, I was appearing on TV, even if only on satellite, and I was really learning about the business. I thought I was ready, and apparently, Cornette did too.

"I'm going to give you a shot," he told me after a match one night.

I nodded. I was ready for this conversation. I felt I'd proven I was good enough.

"I know you make those other motherfuckers look good," he said. "You can take a beating and make it look real. But can you put together a series of moves? Can you fire up the crowd? Can you become what they want to see every night?"

I thought about it. "I think so," I said.

"Then get ready," he told me.

Cornette later told me he wanted to see me fight Gorgeous George Jr., a wrestler with a perfectly kept head of blond hair who came into the ring with a purple feather boa. This was going to be my big shot. The match would be live for the crowd, but not for TV.

That night, I sat with Jim in the Knoxville locker room, almost shaking because I was so nervous.

"Look, you're going to do fine," Jim said. "Don't worry about it. Just go out and do your thing, son. Do your thing."

My big move was going to be a cross-body block. I climb to the top rope, jump and land perpendicular on George's chest. It's an aerial move I'd done before, and I was confident it would work.

I was wrong.

In some rings, the ropes are just that—ropes, tightly woven and held together, very sturdy. In other rings, the "ropes" are actually cables, with garden hose around them that spins on the cables, making them extremely unstable. When I went to the top rope, I stood and raised my arms, ready to jump on George. But the ropes were of the cable variety, and my feet spun.

I landed on my shins, and George saved the realism of the match by quickly landing on me and pinning me.

As I walked off, I looked to Cornette, who'd been watching from the control room. He said nothing. He knew he didn't have to.

The car ride home from Knoxville to Florence was brutal. All I did was bitch about how I'd blown my big shot. Jim, stretched out in the passenger seat of the Taurus, didn't want to hear it anymore.

"Look," he said, "you screwed up. Big deal. Now you know to check the damn ropes beforehand. Big deal. If I'd seen them, I could have told you and you would have been alright, but it didn't happen. Oh well. You're 23 years old — if you make it next year, you could still have a 20-year career and retire at 44. Sounds pretty good, don't it?"

I hadn't thought of it that way. I looked out at the dark open road in front of us. "I guess."

"Chris, are you ready for all of this?"

"Yeah, of course I am."

"No, think about it," he said. "What if you went out there tonight and wowed them all. Are you ready? Do you know how to do interviews?"

"No."

"Do you know how to carry a feud?"

"No."

"Look, if you'd gotten a spot, all the attention would be on you," he said. "And you may not be ready. But look, you can learn. You can be ready when the next time comes. You can work on all of that shit. And I can help."

That sounded good. "Alright."

"OK then," he said. "Now, let me tell you what I've been thinking right now, something I've learned that's helping me out."

"What's that?"

"When you get any gig, even this dumb Mummy bullshit, you make it last," he said, lighting a cigarette and taking a drag. "You know what I mean? You never know when the next storyline comes along, so you work that shit until it's stale. I'm going over in my head right now who we can feud with or start something with to keep this going. I don't know how long I can do it, but I'm going to try."

I liked the way Jim thought, and I liked that he'd made me feel better already. We still had a future, and I was fulfilling my goals pretty quickly. We had all the time in the world.

Then it all fell apart. And I would start behaving in a way that — later on — I would realize was very abnormal. It was the first sign of the trouble to come.

✷

Even a great mind like Jim's couldn't keep the Mummy gimmick going. It just didn't catch on with fans, and it wasn't something that would ever catch on with them. After just a few months, the Mummy gig was dumped, and Jim's relationship with Cornette soured too.

"You were fired?" I couldn't believe it, but Jim had called me to tell me the news.

"I said some things I shouldn't have," Jim said. "It escalated, and I criticized the show, and he told me to hit the road."

It wasn't hard to believe. I thought back to my first meeting with Cornette. I knew he had that temper, and to cross him meant you were gambling with your fate. Jim gambled and lost. But he wasn't only gambling with his future; he was gambling with mine. I knew that because he was out, I was out too.

"I'm sorry, Chris."

What could I say? I couldn't be mad, really — he had brought me to this point.

"We'll be back," I said. "We will."

"Yeah, well," he said. But he didn't finish. For the first time I heard something in his voice that led me to believe he was finished with wrestling. "Look, Chris, I can hook you up with some more matches, ok? I don't want you to feel like I'm quitting on you. I'm not. You can keep going."

I didn't know what to think, really. I'd always seen Jim and me making it big together, either with him as my promoter, or with him promoting an adversary of mine. Now he was thinking of quitting. What would I do without him?

It didn't help that I wasn't entirely enamored with Florence, South Carolina. It was unlike the other places I'd lived — totally rural. There weren't very many young people around for me to hang out with, so I had no friends. I was mainly living to work, and living to go out and make my mark in Smoky Mountain Wrestling. When even that was taken away, I didn't see much of a reason to stay in Florence.

Sure, I could go back to Moolah. I could start over. But I didn't want to. I wanted to keep going. This was my first major setback, and it wasn't really my fault. Still, I was out.

And something happened to me.

I went out to a bar that night, in part to drown my sorrows. And maybe I just wanted to talk. A woman at the bar looked my way and nodded.

"I've never seen you before," she said. "You come in here much?"

"No, never," I said. "This is my first time here."

The woman, a pretty blond in her mid-30s, took a seat beside me.

"Well, it looks like you could use a friend," she said.

"Yeah, I think I can."

"What do you do?"

When she asked, I stopped, and thought about it. What did I do? It was a good question. I was 23, and I realized I was a physical therapist holding on to a kid's dream. Yeah, I'd come close to being a professional wrestler, but I blew that chance. And in reality, I was just a physical therapist, a regular old Joe with a regular job. A regular old gay Joe, for that matter.

"I'm a physical therapist," I said. "That's what I am."

The woman said some other words, but they melded together and faded like so many beer bubbles.

"I'm sorry," I said. "Would you excuse me?"

I left without finishing my drink.

✱

In the following weeks, things took a slide. I'd felt lonely before, but now I was unmotivated, lonely, frustrated and fatigued—even though I never stepped out of bed on the weekends. I was stuck in my life, but something else was happening, something I couldn't even try to explain. Despite studying the brain and how it works, I couldn't fight the allure of the endless chasm of depression. It enveloped me, making me question everything about my life, but it didn't provide any answers.

I wasn't Chris Klucsarits or Chris Kanyon. I was nobody.

I needed to change something—at least I thought I did. And that made me realize I needed to go home—and, most surprising of all, I needed to quit wrestling and get on with my life. Surely then I would get back to feeling normal.

"I've thought a lot about it," I told Jim on the phone. "I think it's what I need to do."

"I can't argue with you, son," Jim said. "The wrestling world is a bad, bad place right now. I'm disgruntled, though."

"No, you're right," I said. "I think I need something new in my life. I need a change. I've talked with my company and they've got a place set up for me in Wallingford, Connecticut. It's two hours from New York."

"That sounds great," Jim said, though I could tell he was sad. "Hey, Chris?"

"Yeah?"

"I'm sorry I got you into this and let you down."

"Hey, man, I never would have gotten this far without you."

"Alright then," he said. "Hey—maybe I'll come up to visit. We can go out and find some Italian girls."

"Maybe," I said.

✶

It took a while for me to move to Wallingford, a middle-class town most known for producing TimeLife classics CDs. It seemed like most of the people who lived there commuted to bigger cities for jobs, and here I was, moving there to work.

But it took a few weeks for my job to get started, and in the meantime, while they set me up with another apartment, I stayed with my cousin Brian and his family. I didn't want to bother my family, and Brian was kind enough, after all I'd been through, to let me in. When I told him about my current situation, he was confused, like my friends and my brother, but he didn't judge.

I'd learned to live light as I moved from place to place, as most of the stuff I owned still fit in the Taurus. As we moved it all into Brian's place, he posed the question everyone was wondering.

"Why do you want to quit?" he asked, hauling boxes into the house. "You were close, right? I thought you wanted it."

I thought about it for a second. I didn't want to say any more than to answer what he had asked. He didn't need to hear about my personal problems or anything I told Jim.

"It was a kid's dream, man," I said. "You know what I mean? Yeah, I was close, and I had a shot, but I blew it, and it's over. I got lucky to be that close, and just as quick, I was done. That's all. Time to grow up."

"Sounds like your parents talking," Brian said. "If that's what you want, then fine. But I've never known you quit before, especially not at this."

I sat down on Brian's porch.

"There's something that feels good about earning a living, man," I said. "There's something that feels good about going to work, and coming home and living my life. You know that, right?"

"Yep. I sure do."

"And I like the fact that there's some normalcy there," I said. I knew Brian would relay this to my family too.

Brian dumped his box on the ground. "Alright, man," he said. "Then I'm happy for you. Surprised, but happy."

The box tipped, and my personal items fell out all over Brian's front yard: an alarm clock, some shoes — and a couple of gay porn magazines.

Brian bent over and started to pick it all up. He hadn't noticed anything yet.

"Well, now that you're not wrestling, we can hang out more," he said. "We could double-date or . . . "

He picked up the magazine.

"What the hell is this?" he said, showing it to me.

I looked at the magazine. What to do?

"Oh God," I said, feigning disgust. "What is that?"

Brian looked at me funny. I could tell he was suspicious. "That is a fag rag."

"What?"

"A gay porno magazine."

"Oh, I know what that is."

"You *do*?"

"Yeah."

I didn't say anymore. Brian's eyes asked his questions for him. Was it my magazine? Was I gay?

"That magazine belongs to Jim Mitchell," I said.

"*What?*"

"It was Jim's," I said. "Look, Jim wasn't a fag, OK? But he was definitely a sexual deviant. Remember when you met him backstage? Remember how he was?"

"Yeah," Brian said. But he kept looking at me with those accusing eyes. "Yeah, I remember."

Brian packed up the box and brought it up to the porch.

"That Jim was an interesting guy," he said, heading inside.

"Yep, he sure is," I said.

Brian didn't mention the magazine again.

✱

"I got a big favor to ask you," I said later on that day.

I was talking to Jim, who was half-listening to my story from the end of his phone in Columbia, South Carolina.

"What do you need, brother?" he asked. I could tell he'd been drinking.

"Get ready for a shock," I said. I took a deep breath. "Your old friend Kanyon . . . is a fag."

Jim didn't say anything.

"Jim?"

"Yeah, Chris. Sorry buddy, I didn't hear you. Can you say that again? I've got some friends over and we're having an, um, interesting time."

"I'm a fag."

A pause. "Really?"

"Yes, really."

Another pause. "Wow." And in the background, there were girls laughing. "You old bastard. Is this why I never saw you with girls?"

"Yes, Jim. That's why."

"Well, ain't that something. Congratulations on being a fag, buddy."

"Thanks, man. I've known for a long time now. I just never really told anybody. Oh, and I'm not telling anybody, ok?"

"Sure. But why are you telling me now?"

"My cousin found my gay porn stash. I had to blame someone."

"And you thought of me? I'm touched."

"Yeah."

"Look brother, I gotta go," Jim said. "But your secret's safe here."

"Thanks, man," I said. "And if you hear from my cousin, just remember to say you like gay porn, ok?"

"Will do."

✺

We were having breakfast one day when we got the phone call.

"Yeah, is this Brian?" It was Jim, calling for my cousin.

"Yes. Who is this?"

"Yeah, Brian? This is Jim Mitchell, Chris's friend. I believe we met once here in South Carolina. Well, I understand you accidentally found some of my magazines when Chris was moving his stuff into your place."

Brian was stunned. "Yes, um, yes we did."

"Well, I sure am sorry to have caused you or your fine family any grief," Jim said. "Please accept my apologies for being a fag."

"I—I accept."

✺

Moving back to Connecticut turned out to be a quick-fix for my mood.

I felt better . . . for a while.

The winter of 1994–95 was brutal, a dark and gloomy affair that regularly dumped inches and inches of snow on us at different times.

But living in Wallingford, Connecticut, was good for me. It was quiet, and I had money. Instead of working at one hospital, this time, I was shuffled between seven to eight nursing homes, which was a change for me, being that I still wasn't what I considered to be a skilled driver. The job provided less of a sense of accomplishment than my old job. While I was really helping people before, rehabilitating patients in the hospital, my new patients in the nursing home were already in poor states. They needed someone to help move their arms and legs to keep them flexible, and most weren't coherent.

An interesting job for someone who was already suffering from depression.

Outside of work, things I liked became things that had no interest to me. I did not wrestle. I stopped watching it on television. Socially, I stayed to myself. I didn't return messages often. I didn't want to. It wasn't despair so much as hopelessness, a feeling of being emotionally numb.

I didn't even frequent the one gay bar in Wallingford. I didn't really know what was wrong with me. I thought I was just going through a life change, giving up my dream and trying to become an adult.

At night I came home from work and watched my beloved New York Rangers play hockey. But I lived for Fridays. At the end of that workday, I drove home to New York. Danny and some other friends of mine had graduated from college and now lived in an apartment, not far from our old neighborhood. I visited them and my brother, who as always, was supportive. It was therapeutic to see the old gang and visit our old hangouts. It was enough to make me believe I was getting better.

My parents really had no reaction to my decision to stop wrestling. They always thought it was something I would eventually give up. And knowing this meant focusing on my career, they were comfortable with my decision.

Every week I would count down the days and hours until I could leave and return to New York, where my old friends waited for me. It was comfortable and inviting. It was safe.

But a funny thing always happened on those trips to and from New York. Driving on the interstate, I would always have to pass through Stamford, Connecticut, where I would see the big black sign of the WWF—the World Wrestling Federation headquarters.

Two times every weekend, I had a constant reminder of what I'd passed up.

✶

As my three-month stint in Wallingford neared its end, I kept thinking of the WWF building and what I'd given up. Was there a reason I had to pass that building every weekend? It felt like more than a coincidence. It almost seemed like destiny.

That week I'd watched a film alone, something Jim had recommended to me — *Glengarry Glen Ross*, based on the play by the great David Mamet. In it, Al Pacino's character reminds his co-workers of his philosophy on life: "When you die," he says, "you'll regret the things you didn't do."

I started wondering if I'd made a mistake. I started thinking I might need to try wrestling again. One thing was certain: The next Friday evening when I passed that WWF building, I had to stop and look around.

Call it curiosity or karma, but I felt like I needed to do it to survive. I got off the exit and pulled around to the front. It looked to be about eight or nine stories, made of black glass, with the huge yellow WWF logo near the top. That's what caught your eye from the interstate. That WWF glowed to me, calling out like a siren.

It was too late then, and I could tell no one was around to let me in. It didn't matter. I stood there in the freezing cold for more than 15 minutes, looking at that building. I thought about those times when I was a kid, when I knew that I was going to be a professional wrestler. I thought about how I'd gotten so close, and how because I felt so strange, I decided to quit for good. That yellow sign stared back at me, unchanging, but I felt something stir within me.

Wrestling was calling me home.

✶

I had no plan, and I had no way of knowing what was in store for me. All I knew was that my current three-month deal was almost finished. I'd hibernated throughout the winter, and now I was ready to go back out into the world.

It was like someone had flipped a switch inside me. Chris Kanyon had come back to life, and he was bringing Chris Klucsarits with him.

After talking with my friends and employers, I knew I needed a change of scenery. I needed to work in a hospital again. I wanted to work in New York, but apparently, so did most everyone else in the world. There were no spots for me in the Big Apple. The best they could do for me was a hospital in Allentown, Pennsylvania — less than a two-hour drive west of New York.

No one knew my true intentions, though.

Pennsylvania was home to Eastern Championship Wrestling, another one of the country's major promotions. I'd been lucky enough to wrestle in Smoky Mountain, but now I was going to be close to another of wrestling's hot commodities. ECW was gaining momentum quickly, and I knew that I could get back into wrestling if I was somewhere around the action.

All I needed was an in.

I went back to my friend in Queens, Georgiann Makropoulos, an older woman with slightly graying hair and the build of a linebacker. Georgiann could talk tough and then go into the kitchen and bake you some cookies — just so long as you stayed on her good side. She tended to love me more than most of her wrestling friends. She knew I was dedicated to the sport, and she always said I'd be wrestling on TV one day.

I stopped by her house a few days before moving to Pennsylvania. I had one question.

"Chris Kanyon you son of a bitch!" she said when she saw me at the door. "Come on in! I'll make you something to eat."

"Thanks, Georgiann," I said, walking in. "How are you?"

"Wonderful now that you're here," she replied. She led me through her small home, which seemed to be covered in fur, due to her 10 cats. Small hints of her love of wrestling also came through the cat hair, though. On the bookshelf, she kept old tickets from matches she'd seen. On a far wall, she'd hung a picture of her favorite wrestler, Night Stalker, a young guy who was just breaking into the business.

"What can I do for you?" she asked, sitting down on an old couch.

"I can't say long, Georgiann, but I need a favor."

"Anything."

"I'm moving again, this time to Allentown, Pennsylvania."

"Well that's not too far away, is it?"

"Nope. But I need to know if there's a school anywhere near there, someplace where I can resume my training."

"Oh yes," she said, her eyes growing wide. "There is definitely a place for you."

(20)

SAY HELLO TO AFA

When I left Connecticut and settled in Allentown, I felt like my head was back in the right spot. I was filled with hope and joy at finding myself again, and I was ready to get back to work. But more importantly, I was ready to get back to wrestling.

And I had just the place to help me.

Georgiann told me that four miles from my apartment sat the Wild Samoan Training Center, owned by the legendary brothers Afa and Sika Anoa'i, who had become world champion tag team partners in the early 1980s before they toured the world. It helped that they were trained by their uncle, "High Chief" Peter Maivia.

At that time, there were probably only seven premiere training schools in the country, and it just so happened I had lived next to two of them — Moolah's and now the Wild Samoans. It was almost too freaky for words.

I had gotten my mind refocused, not only on wrestling, but on life. I knew I was just two hours from home, which meant I could go back any time I wanted. But I also knew that I had to go out and live if I wanted to feel better. My new job at the hospital provided more stability, along with younger people for me to hang out with. All in all, it was a good situation.

But if there was one area in my life that didn't return to normal, it was my personal life. Allentown was a surprisingly liberal place, with a few gay bars and a nice social scene, but I found myself too paranoid to go to any of those places — at first. The only thing I ever knew about Allentown was from the Billy Joel song of that name, when he talked about closing factories down and giving up dreams.

That wasn't what I saw. It was a nice place, very tolerant, and a place where I felt like I could be myself — if I wanted to be.

But first things first. After my first week of work, I knew I had to go to the Samoans' school.

It was a bright sunny day when I walked into the school tucked in a brick strip mall building in Whitehall, Pennsylvania. Aside from the name on the window, it would have been difficult to tell this was a wrestling school. But on the inside, it was unlike the other schools I'd seen before. Bright, with pictures lining the walls of their many famous graduates — like Bam Bam Bigelow — the Samoan school was nothing but professional. The place was immaculate, and when I walked in, I knew I was going to do well.

I'd come armed only with my wrestling tapes, but I knew I could meet with Afa based on my experience with Moolah and Smoky Mountain.

I entered a small gym with just one ring, but dozens of guys were working out.

"No! You work harder! Harder! That's it! Good, good."

The voice came from one corner of the ring. That's when I saw Afa for the first time. His head was huge, and black, curly hair sprouted from every angle. He was a wide man, thick in every limb and especially in his trunk and legs. At the time, he was probably in his mid-fifties, but he'd looked the same since I had seen him on TV years earlier.

I approached him and waited for the guys in the ring to take a break.

"Who are you?" he asked in a quiet voice after he'd noticed me.

"My name is Chris Kanyon," I said. "I'm from New York, but I come to you from the Fabulous Moolah and from Smoky Mountain Wrestling."

His black bushy eyebrows arched. I could tell he was impressed. For a man of his size — well over six feet tall and 240 pounds — Afa had soft features that revealed his humble and warm nature. "You come with good credentials," he said. "But we will see how you wrestle."

Afa called over one of his guys, another big Samoan with an unpronounceable name. I stripped down to my trunks and boots and got in the ring with the man. He seemed like a good guy and was willing to let me show what I could do.

I worked the guy pretty well, showing off my arsenal, which by that time included things like a figure-four leg lock, suplexes, drop-downs and hip tosses. As I completed one move, we went on to other, more complicated moves. After about 30 minutes, I came out of the ring, my chest heaving. It had been a while since I'd wrestled anyone.

But then I saw Afa, his face spread into a wide grin. It looked like Afa thought I'd be good for the Samoans' school, and I was pretty sure it would be good for me.

"You wrestle good," he said in broken English, but his smile said enough. "We like you to stay."

I told him I would. "Thanks, Afa."

"No, no," he said, shaking his head. "People here call me 'Pops.'"

I smiled, too. "OK, Pops."

When I left the school that day, I felt better than I had in weeks. Afa was going to be another in a line of great mentors for me. I felt it. And I knew that I had my life back on track.

✷

As time wore on, I decided to venture back out to explore the gay side of Allentown. I spent time in the bars and met a few men. Sometimes it would result in a one night stand, but I never had what I would call a true boyfriend. Between wrestling and work, I couldn't be gay in public, and I could not have a boyfriend. I don't know if I could have handled a relationship like that anyway.

But one night, as I nursed a beer at what had become my favorite bar, I was approached by a woman—strange, because this was a gay bar, and I was known there as a gay man.

"Hey, handsome," said the woman. She was small, very tan, with a short spiky haircut. She wore a white tank top and many earrings. I think I saw a tattoo on her arm.

"Hi," I said, wondering what she wanted.

"Listen," she said. "I've seen you here before, and I think I need you to be a part of my team."

I laughed. "Well, if you like chicks I don't think we're on the same team."

She smiled. "No, not that. I participate in the Gay Games."

I stopped in mid-swig. "The what?"

"It's kind of an Olympics for gays in the area," she said. "You're a big guy, physically fit, right? You could really help us out — and you could meet some other guys. It's just for fun, you know. We play tug-of-war, obstacle courses, things like that."

Immediately, I said no. "Not interested."

"Why?"

"I'm just not." I turned back to the bar.

She got closer to me. "Are you afraid?"

"Afraid? Of what?"

"Of someone seeing you?"

That's part of it, I thought. "No, I just don't want to do it."

"I think you're afraid."

"You don't know what you're talking about."

"Oh, I don't?" she said, giving me a stare. "I'm a gay woman. How do you think my life has been?"

I didn't say anything. I didn't look at her.

"Give me your number," she said.

"Why?"

"Because I'm going to call you. And I'm going to ask again."

I thought about it. Part of me wanted to go, to hang out with other gay people, to not care about what anyone thought. I wished I could.

I gave her my number, but I did not commit to anything. Still, it sounded like fun.

"Thanks," she said, giving me a sweet smile. "By the way, I'm Rachel."

"I'm Chris."

I only had to wait a day for Rachel to call me back.

"So, what have you decided?" she asked.

"I haven't decided anything."

"Chris, you know you want to go. I know you want to go. It's time to man up and commit," she said. "You know none of your straight friends are going to be in a 50-mile radius of our Gay Games. You need to do this for you."

She made a lot of sense. I needed someone to kick me in the ass.

"OK," I said. "I'll do it."

"Good," she said. "Because I really want to win the tug-of-war."

Ken, age six, and Chris, age four, holding a trophy from hockey (*top left*); Chris, age seven, at his First Communion (*top right*); Ken, age ten, and Chris, age eight, on a trip to Niagara Falls (*bottom left*); Ken, age six, and Chris, age three and a half (*bottom right*).

IMAGES COURTESY OF JACK AND BARBARA KLUCSARITS

(*clockwise, from top*) Chris with two of his nieces; the Klucsarits family (Chris, Mom, Ken, Dad) at a relative's wedding; Chris holding a 9/11 sweatshirt. His face tells all.

PHOTO BY GEORGE NAPOLITANO

ABOUT TO MAKE PERRY SATURN TAP
(PHOTO BY GEORGE NAPOLITANO)

MORTIS UNMASKED
(PHOTO BY GEORGE NAPOLITANO)

CHRIS IN THE WWE

ABOUT TO
PUNISH
BRIAN KENDRICK

PHOTO BY MIKE LANO

CHRIS KANYON BATTLES PERRY SATURN

(PHOTO BY GEORGE NAPOLITANO)

✱

I had no idea what to expect when I showed up for the Gay Games.

I was dressed in a T-shirt and shorts, and the sun sparkled on a surprisingly warm spring day. I knew I'd made the right decision when I saw the other men who'd come out to play. Many were physically fit, big guys who were attractive and outgoing. *Maybe this day will be alright,* I thought.

"Like what you see?" It was Rachel, who'd come with several girlfriends.

"I think this may have been a good idea," I admitted.

I entered almost all of the competitions, helping Rachel's team win a lot of events. I ran and swam in the relay races, navigated the obstacle course and yes, we won the tug-of-war.

Later, covered in mud from the tug, I even gave my number to one of my competitors. Tall, dark and handsome, Matthew was a local delivery man, and he caught my eye immediately. I knew I wanted to get to know him better.

When the day was over, I felt liberated. Nothing could hide my smile.

"It's like coming out to yourself, isn't it?" Rachel said.

"Yeah, it is. Thanks for convincing me to do this."

"No problem. Take care, Chris. Maybe we can do this again sometime, huh?"

"Yeah," I said. "I think we can."

✱

I first noticed the kid when Afa was having me work out with another wrestler. From the corner of my eye I could see him over at the edge of the ring, leaning over, saying nothing. He just watched.

He was a skinny kid, with a shock of black hair, dark skin and thoughtful eyes. He was too young to be in the school. I wondered what he was doing.

When I was finished, I went to the locker room to shower and get changed. After I came out, Afa was talking to the kid.

"You not old enough yet," he said. Then he put his arm around him. "Someday you can get in ring. Not now. Must be 20 year old."

"I'm 19," he said.

"One more year, ok?"

"Do I have a choice?"

"No."

"Then I'll keep watching."

"Good. You learn much while watching."

Afa looked up to notice I had come out of the locker room. "Chris, meet Billy Kidman."

I shook the kid's hand. "You a wrestling fan?" I asked.

"Not just a fan," he said. "I'm a wrestler myself."

It couldn't be. I was what people were looking for in a wrestler, not this kid. He was five-foot-nothing and 180 pounds if he was lucky. How could he do in the ring?

I immediately liked him.

"Great. Let's work out sometime," I said.

Afa frowned. "No. Must be 20. He only 19."

"He's old enough to vote, right? Old enough to fight for his country. Maybe he should be able to wrestle too," I said.

Kidman smiled. At that moment, I knew I'd made a new friend.

"I think about it," Afa said.

✴

Billy was a good-looking kid, and I loved the fact that even though he couldn't step in the ring, he was still willing to stay and watch. That showed he had the kind of love for wrestling that I had.

Afa taught us a lot about the business side of wrestling. At certain times he would take us to WWF tapings and shows anywhere from New York to Connecticut to Pennsylvania. At that time in the spring of 1995, those shows were huge productions. After coming from Smoky Mountain, where shows were taped in high school gyms, these shows were performed in front of thousands, and the shows were on television—not satellite dishes. Outside, we'd see the evidence this was a huge operation—there were production trucks and cables everywhere. And we saw all the big-time wrestlers, from Kevin Nash to Shawn Michaels, from Bret and Owen Hart to 1-2-3 Kid.

There we saw firsthand what it was like to be in a big-time locker room. We saw the lessons we'd always heard about and that I'd glimpsed at Smoky Mountain. Go around, introduce yourself, then stay quiet. Don't make eye contact and never speak unless you are spoken to. As a jobber, you are there to make them look better. Pay your dues and always listen. It was all a part of locker room etiquette.

As part of Afa's group, we were asked to help out every now and then. Sometimes the WWF would tape 40 shows, and we were asked to take beatings from the local winners. All in all, I was getting more experience in another major circuit.

And Billy Kidman was always there, watching.

✱

During my first match as a jobber in the World Wrestling Federation, I learned a little bit about how the hierarchy of wrestlers had their matches set up. First, we met Tony Garea, a thick-looking Italian who assigned all the jobbers our roles. Tony knew how good you were, and he set up the matches like this: If you were a big-name guy, but you didn't happen to be a talented wrestler, you were matched up with a jobber who wasn't that good. If you were a guy who was talented, and getting a push from the writers, you were matched up with a jobber who was talented and could make you look good.

I was lucky, because Afa told Tony I was good.

Because of that recommendation, I had a good pairing in my first match. I was to wrestle Kevin Nash, an up-and-coming giant. A former Tennessee basketball player, he was nearly seven feet tall, and would later go on to be a champion.

Before the match, Tony came up to me. He was excited.

"We really need Nash to look good tonight," he said. "We're going to put the belt on him soon. He's getting the push."

I didn't get a punch in the entire match. I let Nash beat me senseless — or at least, I made it look that way in front of a crowd of 8,000 that night. No one knew who I was, but they saw a good performance from this jobber.

Afterward, when we went into the locker room, I followed the etiquette I had learned by saying nothing. All I did was change. Afa came over to me and put a hand on my shoulder.

"Good," he said.

And when Nash entered, he made a point to tell the room what he thought. "Afa, you brought a good guy in here," he said, and he made sure all of the wrestlers in the locker room heard him. Then he looked to me. "Good job."

All I did was nod. It was a big night.

Three weeks later, Nash was a champion.

From that point on, I was matched up with good guys, and many times, I was able to wrestle 1-2-3 Kid, who was athletic and could really wrestle. It was a time where we could rub elbows—and throw elbows—with the heavyweights in wrestling, something you couldn't do in other sports. When you're playing minor league baseball, you don't get to play with the major leaguers every day. But we did.

And every night, we were paid $250 for our troubles. I'd have paid more than that to do what we were doing.

By that time, Kidman had gone from watching to wrestling, though he didn't get much experience. While he could train at Afa's school, he was having trouble because no promoter ever wanted him due to his small size.

"Sometimes I wonder if I'm ever going to get in the ring," Kidman told me one night.

"Look, man, you're 20," I said. "You've got time."

"No, man," he said. "No one's interested in small wrestlers now."

"Not yet," I said. "Be patient. There will be a time when people want to see small, athletic wrestlers."

"I don't know. Sometimes I wonder if this is for me."

I knew he needed a lift. "Hey," I said. "You know Pat Patterson? The booker for WWF?"

"Yeah, of course," he said.

"You know what they say about him?"

"What?"

"They say he's gay."

"No shit?"

"Yep. And they say he's been gay for a long time, and that he likes good-looking wrestlers."

"Shut up."

"Yeah, man. I think you could do it. Just sleep with him, man. Then you can wrestle."

"Cut it out."

"Just a suggestion."

Kidman, who lived with his parents near Afa's wrestling school, worked at a bank for his day job, but his goal was to be a professional wrestler. He wanted to use his quickness and his acrobatics to develop a new wrestling style.

At a match in New York, Kidman and I watched as "Razor" Ramon—one of four wrestlers, along with Nash, Michaels and 1-2-3 Kid, who made up what was known as the Clique—blew out his shoulder, leaving him unable to perform his finishing move. It was a tough move where Razor would pick up his opponent, put him over his shoulder, grab him by the underarms and fall forward for the pin.

But that night, the way he tore up his shoulder, we were all certain he wouldn't be able to do it—unless he could find the right wrestler.

"What the fuck?" Razor said when he saw who he was matched up with. It was a guy as big as a Samoan. With his bad shoulder, there was no way he could do his move on a guy that big.

Razor ran into the office of Pat Patterson.

"What the fuck is this?" he said to Pat. "You've matched me up with this fat fuck, and you know I've got a bad shoulder. You motherfuckers are making it so I can't do my move."

Kidman and I watched from just outside. Patterson, a heavy-set guy with a head full of white hair and a big smile, waited for Razor to cool down.

"Settle down," Patterson said. "What do you want us to do?"

"I want you to get me a small motherfucker that I can throw over my shoulder," Razor said.

"And who would that be?"

Razor looked outside the office and didn't hesitate—he pointed to Kidman. "Him," he said. "That motherfucker's good. Let me flip him."

Patterson peered from around the door and took a look at Kidman, who was wearing a white T-shirt and trunks.

"Come in here," he said to Kidman, and I followed.

Kidman looked back at me and smiled. His face said it all: He knew he was close to fighting in the WWF. But when he entered Patterson's office, the booker just shook his head. "I don't know," Patterson said.

"This motherfucker came from Afa's," Razor said. "He's good."

Patterson stepped forward. "Son," he said to Kidman, "take off your shirt."

Kidman looked back at me, and I almost burst out laughing. Maybe Patterson did want to sleep with him after all.

Kidman did as he was told. He took off his shirt, and sadly for him, his body just wasn't that impressive. He had no real muscle tone, and nothing about it was worthy of the WWF. Patterson took one look and shook his head.

"We can't put that on TV," Patterson said.

Pissed off, Razor stormed out of the office. Dejected, Kidman trudged out.

In the end, Razor went out and did his move, screaming in pain as he slung the big man over his shoulder. But I'm not sure who felt worse — Razor, or Kidman, who again watched it all from ringside.

✳

At the time, Eastern Championship Wrestling held independent matches across Pennsylvania, and it wasn't out of the ordinary for jobbers to work both the WWF and ECW. I took the initiative.

Armed with a ton of experience, including tapes of my matches in WWF and Smoky Mountain, and my training at Moolah's and Afa's, I knew I was a good candidate to earn some time in the ECW. So I did what I'd done before — I showed up and hoped for the best.

The ECW Arena was actually an old converted bingo hall on Broad Street in downtown Philadelphia surrounded by an old industrial area, which made everything look rundown and dirty. I walked in to a flurry of activity. It was a Saturday night, and a small crowd had gathered on some dingy bleachers to watch the night's taping.

I asked around, and in a break during the taping, I met two men, Paul E. Dangerously, the ECW booker, and Todd Gordon, the money backer. When I told them about my credentials, they asked if I could come back the next day. Like that, I was in. I knew they would probably call Afa to check on me, but once he gave them a good word about me, I'd be jobbing in ECW.

At that time, there were five major wrestling circuits in America: the WWF, WCW, Smoky Mountain, ECW and the USWA in Memphis. When I made my ECW debut the next day, I'd gained experience in three of the major circuits already. My resume was shaping up well.

The ECW wasn't even on the WWF's radar, so to job for both meant nothing. But if I became a player on one and started to get a push, I knew I would have to quit the other. That seemed like a good trade-off.

That Sunday, I jobbed for someone who would become another big name — Mick Foley, also known as Cactus Jack. When I met him, he was still finding his way as a pudgy wrestler who was in need of a gimmick. But again, I let him kick my ass, and I made him look good. By this time, I'd been getting a series of good mentions in the wrestling newsletters. They recognized me as a good jobber, and slowly, I was making a name for myself across the wrestling world.

I was selling the fact that these guys were hurting me. When they hit me, they killed me, or at least it looked that way. I could sell the falls, bounces and rolls. Where others would fall, I would fall and bounce, or flail my arms. I didn't just lie there; I moved. I was animated. It was all about being in constant motion.

But there were things I needed to work on. I still sent my tapes to one man: Jim Mitchell.

"Alright, let's start with the good," Jim said one day.

"Alright," I said during one of our many phone calls.

"You're progressing," he said. "You're really showing you're able to make others look good, son. I can see why people are talking about you. You show you know what you're doing."

"I smell a big but coming," I said.

"But," he said. "You've got to improve on one thing."

"What's that?"

"You have to show some personality out there," he said. "You're a robot. You need to play to the crowd, show them you can rile them up. You ain't never going to impress anyone just by getting the shit kicked out of you. Stir them up a bit."

I thought about it, and I knew he was right. I was doing everything technically correct, but I wasn't firing up the crowd or stirring the pot. I definitely needed to develop some personality.

"Good point," I told him.

"I think you're doing real good, man, real good."

"Thanks. I think I made a good move coming back to it," I said. "I love wrestling again."

"Fuckin' A, man," he said. "By the way, I met this female last night, and my God, if you could've seen her naked body, you would have just died. She was amazing, my friend."

I couldn't believe he was telling me this. "Jim, don't you remember? I don't care about good-looking women."

"Oh, that's right — you're a fag. Sorry, I forgot."

There were a lot of times Jim would forget like that. But that's just the way Jim was.

(21)

RELATIONSHIPS, PERSONALITY AND MY GIMMICK

Several times I went out with Matthew, the man I'd met at the Gay Games. He was a great-looking guy: big, muscular and dark, the way I liked them. And he was a good guy, too. We could hang out together, and we didn't need to have physical contact all the time. We didn't need to just meet up and have sex. I learned you could have more than a one-night stand.

But I had a problem. I'd never had more than a one-night stand before. I didn't know what it was like to love someone, or to be there for someone. I relied on me. And when someone else was in my life, I didn't know what do.

After Matthew had spent the night with me, I woke up nervous. What if someone came over unannounced? What if someone saw a man leaving my apartment? Allentown was a liberal place, but still—word could travel.

"Hey," I said, shaking him awake. "Hey."

He rolled over and looked at me. He smiled. "Hey."

"I think you should leave."

"What? Why?"

"I've got a lot to do," I said. "Going to be busy all day. I'm sorry. I—why don't I call you later?"

He looked at me like he knew I was afraid. He said nothing as he got up. Instead, he got dressed, checked himself in the mirror, matted down his thick, dark hair and stepped outside the door.

"I'll call you, Matt," I said.

"Alright," he said. "You do that."

I could see he was hurt. I didn't know what to say.

I didn't call him back. The truth was, I didn't know how to be a good boyfriend. I didn't know how to listen and care for someone else, because I didn't even know how to do that for myself. I couldn't be honest about how I felt, and because of that, there was no way I could be there for someone else. It just wouldn't work. I think Matthew knew it, too, because he had my number.

He never called me, either.

✷

I'd experimented a little with showing personality in the ring. Even though I was a jobber and I was getting my ass kicked on a regular basis, I could still play up to the crowd a little. In a match against 1-2-3 Kid, I started small, literally. He was a smaller wrestler, quicker, who could do a variety of aerial moves. But when I used my strength during the match, I would slam him, then play to the crowd by wiping my hands clean. Or maybe I would laugh out loud, and when I did, I got a good response from the crowd — and from my bosses. Then, of course, the Kid would go about kicking my ass.

I thought I knew what I was doing. I was wrong.

In my next taping for ECW, a seven-minute match for Monday Night *Raw*, I was paired with Bob Holly, a big bully — literally. He was a large guy, one that could match up with me in the ring, and he had a reputation for being an asshole. That night, he was playing a laughable gimmick — Sparky Plug, a race car enthusiast from Talladega. Before the match, I asked him if I could suplex him, then body slam him and throw an elbow.

He looked at me and smiled. "Sure," he said. "No problem."

After three minutes, I was supposed to take control before he regained control and pinned me. It didn't work out that way.

When it came to be my turn to take control, I picked him up and slammed him to the mat. Then I chose that time to show my newfound personality. I turned back to the crowd and started acting like I was shifting gears, or "driving the car." I kept smiling and shifting and the crowd loved it. Then I turned back to Holly.

"You motherfucker," he said under his breath, just loud enough for me to hear.

Then he went to his corner, and I knew I was dead.

He ran to me and kicked me in the stomach — hard. I didn't have to make it look real, because it was. Then he hit me with a clothesline, right in the throat. I'm not sure I'd ever been so scared in my life as I was at that moment, because I knew that Holly's finishing move was an elbow drop off the top rope.

But when he did it, he held up, letting me fake the hit, and luckily, I survived. He didn't have to do that. He could've really kicked my ass.

Afterward, as I slumped off the mat and walked back to the locker room, I had to thank him. It was another rule of etiquette. I'd done too much by making fun of him in front of the crowd.

"Is everything OK?" he said to me.

"Yeah," I said.

"Good."

And we never talked about any of that ever again. Good thing, because my throat hurt for two weeks.

✶

"So I tried to show personality, and he kicked my ass," I told Jim on the phone.

"I see," Jim said. "Well then, you must've done good."

"Yeah, well my throat doesn't feel too good," I said.

"Chris, here's the problem," Jim said. "You need a gimmick. What do you like?"

I thought about it. "I like hockey."

"OK then." I heard the sound of a can of beer being popped open. "You like hockey. What if you wrestled as a hockey player?"

"Really? You think that would work?"

"Please son, I kept that awful Mummy gimmick going for months," he said, laughing. "I'm sure you could get a hockey thing going for a while."

✶

I started working the gimmick immediately.

My beloved New York Rangers had just won the Stanley Cup, and I thought I could use that to my advantage. I actually began wrestling in tights that featured the Rangers logo and the Stanley Cup. I wanted the crowd to get to know me as a kind of wrestler hockey player. Plus, it got those in the crowd who weren't Rangers fans pretty fired up, which is always a good thing.

During that time, I was able to meet the great Jeff Jarrett, already a popular wrestler who'd paid his dues in Memphis's USWA before coming to the

WWF. Jarrett and I hit it off immediately, and he was the one who first told me about Memphis.

"It's my town, man," he said.

Jarrett came into wrestling as a skinny kid with big blond hair, but over time, he'd worked himself into a good shape, and he could rally a crowd.

"You should think about going down to Memphis," he told me one night in the locker room.

"You think so, huh?"

"Do you really think you'll get a shot here?" he asked.

"I don't know," I said. "I hoped that coming here would lead to a shot in either WWF or ECW. I'm jobbing in both, and I seem to be making a name."

"But here's the thing," Jarrett said, "ECW is gaining momentum, you're right, but the WWF is using Memphis as their training ground, man. You could go down there and really show them what you've got. Then WWF would call you up and you'd be a star."

Memphis was a full-time territory, five matches a week. As of now, I was still working my day job as a physical therapist. I had money saved in the bank, but there was no way I could support myself on wrestling alone in Pennsylvania. I needed to go someplace where I could wrestle every day — or close to it.

"You might be right," I told Jarrett. "I haven't even been able to win a match in ECW yet."

"In Memphis, you may be able to get the push," Jarrett said.

I wanted to be featured somewhere, and if Memphis was the place to be, maybe I needed to move again. *Maybe,* I thought, *I need to take the hockey gimmick down south to Beale Street.*

But the biggest decision in my life stood in the way. I knew that if I wanted to go to Memphis, I would be wrestling full-time. That meant I would have to give up my job as a therapist.

Later that night, I called Jim to tell him what I was thinking.

"If you want to do it, I say do it," he said. "Remember *Glengarry Glen Ross*. 'When you die, you'll regret the things you didn't do.'"

I started making plans. I was going to go to Memphis.

★

By Christmas of 1995, I'd given a month's notice at work. I told them I was leaving to live a dream.

I knew I didn't want to go to Memphis alone, and I thought my hockey gimmick would work better as a tag team, anyway. So I immediately thought of an acquaintance of mine, J.J. Storm. He was a smaller wrestler than me, and I thought we could work a successful big man/small man team, so I asked if he would go with me.

He said yes.

Storm looked like a young David Lee Roth, and he worked a crowd like Roth too, using his charisma to connect with the people. *We could be good*, I thought.

My boss at the hospital, and especially my boss's husband, supported my move. They knew I was a transient worker, so they thought it was a good story. And if I failed? I could always come back to my job, they said.

My parents, however, were another story. They had thought I had quit wrestling for good. But near Christmas that year, I returned home to tell them I was quitting my real job to again chase wrestling glory.

"Look, we're trying not to be unsupportive," my father said as we sat around the kitchen table. "But we've seen you go after this, then quit, then go again. We just don't know what to think."

"If you have to do it, then do it," my Mom said, shaking her head.

"I have a plan," I said. It was something I'd been thinking about for a while. "If I don't make it — meaning if I don't sign some kind of full-time contract within a year — I'll go back to being a therapist."

My Mom smiled. I think she saw there was still some hope.

"OK," Dad said. "Do it. Just be careful."

My brother, however, was a constant supporter of my cause.

"Don't worry about what they say," Ken would tell me. "This is about you. You're young, and you've got all the time in the world to be a physical therapist. You don't have that much time to be a professional wrestler.

"Take the chance," he said.

✴

By February, I had my partner, my plan and $60,000 saved in the bank. I was ready to go all-out. But I wanted to pay my dues, and I vowed that I wouldn't touch any of my money unless I absolutely had to. I wanted to survive just like everyone else.

Jarrett had given me the contact for the major booking agent in Memphis, and after speaking with him, Storm and I were ready to leave within the week.

Afa was proud to see me go, and I was excited about leaving for another new place. Everything was perfect.

Or so I thought.

With just days to go, Storm backed out.

"What are you saying?" I said into the phone.

"I just don't think I want to go," he said. "I'm sorry, Chris."

In reality, I don't think he ever wanted to leave Pennsylvania. I just wish he'd told me a little sooner. I didn't know what to do. Who could move to Memphis with me in less than a week? I took a chance.

I called the one person who I knew would move to the ends of the Earth to wrestle. I called Billy Kidman.

Turns out I was right. Billy committed on the spot.

(22)

PARTY IN MEMPHIS

I shouldn't have been surprised at Kidman's commitment. At just 20 years old, he made the decision to leave his normal life behind—including his job and family—to move hundreds of miles away to chase his dream. When I thought about it, he was the perfect one to go with me. Kidman and I had spent hours practicing in the ring, and once we trained by fighting a 45-minute match. We knew each other's moves, and he provided me with the opportunity to test out my big man/small man routine. His size might give us an edge: No one that small was getting in the ring, and maybe we could showcase how special he really was. His finishing move was something really amazing—a shooting star press, where he would do a back flip off the top rope and splash land onto an opponent. It was fun to watch, and only a few people could really do it well. He was one of them, and I had tremendous faith in him.

In the days leading up to us leaving, we watched some tapes I'd gotten from Mexico. There, on the screen, were two pint-sized wrestlers who jumped and flew around the ring. One was Eddie Guerrero, who had flowing black hair, and the other was Rey Mysterio, a short-haired, tattooed whiz, and both of them put on a show.

Kidman was enthralled. "They're amazing!" he said.

I got up and pointed to the screen. "This is the future of wrestling. These guys are going to make it in America, and when they do, you're going to get your chance."

Kidman nodded. "I can't wait."

The day before we left for Memphis, I called Randy Hales — Jarrett's contact — again, just to make sure we were all set.

"Hey, Randy — it's Chris Kanyon," I said. "I'll be coming down tomorrow with my partner, Billy Kidman, and I just wanted to make sure everything was a go."

"Yeah, there's been a change of plans," the booker said. "I'm sorry, but we don't have a spot for you anymore."

✱

"I'm sorry, I don't think I heard you right, Randy," I said.

"Look, I wish I could help you, but I don't have anything open," he replied.

"Randy, I quit my job to come down there. I gave up my apartment to come down there — just to work for you," I said. "I just convinced a kid to come down there with me. We're coming down there."

"What?"

"We're going to be there for your next show on Saturday. Me and my partner will be there. And when the next spot opens up, we're going to get it."

Randy was quiet for a second.

"OK," he said. "Come on down here."

✱

We arrived in Memphis on a cold Friday night, and, working on our meager budget, we found a $40 per night room at the Admiral Benbow Hotel in downtown Memphis. I called Randy again, to tell him we were there, and he said to show up bright and early the next day, and that maybe he'd need us.

I sat down on the bed and clicked on the bedside light. It flickered a bit and finally stayed on, but I got the feeling our bulb was about to burn out. A closer look around the room revealed why it was just $40. The sheets were yellowed with age, as were the walls. The television got one channel — and that was fuzzy. In the bathroom, a roach crawled across the cracked tile. Kidman killed it and flushed it down the toilet.

"Man, I don't know what to say," I told him.

He came over and sat down next to me. "What do you mean?"

"I feel like I've got you into something that could be a real mess here."

Kidman smiled. "So what?" he said. "Chris, I've never been anywhere before. Yesterday I was living with my parents in Pennsylvania, and now, I'm with you and we're trying to be professional wrestlers in Memphis. This is one big adventure for me, man."

I smiled back at him. "Alright, I guess that's a good way to look at it."

"Yeah," he said. "We're gonna make it, man. If not here, then we'll do it somewhere else. And so what if we can't do it tomorrow? So what if we can't do it in Memphis at all? What's the worst that could happen? If they tell us no, then we go back home."

I couldn't say anything. He was right. And I knew then he was the right person to have brought with me.

✶

Memphis wrestling began and ended with the great Jerry Lawler, known as "The King." Jerry was a star since the 1970s, when he came up in Memphis and held the southern heavyweight title. He was a big rock of a man with dark hair and a scowl, and few people were more beloved in the South than Jerry. Lawler had worked with comic Andy Kaufman and their gimmicks even landed them on the David Letterman show.

The South, like in Smoky Mountain, was the place for drama, for characters and for stories. Hopefully, our story would work.

Kidman and I had the gimmick down pat. We improved on some thinking that I'd done while partnered with J.J. Storm. Our costumes consisted of hockey sticks, street hockey gloves, ripped jeans and Jersey Devils T-shirts, which were good for us because they were cheap. We even made a three-and-a-half-foot-tall Stanley Cup out of pots and pans, which we painted silver.

We crushed paper cups and wrapped them in electrical tape, using them as hockey pucks to throw into the crowd and get the fans excited. The costume worked out well for Kidman because the more clothes we put on him, the more we covered up how skinny he was. This definitely could be our gimmick, and Memphis was the place for gimmicks.

We called ourselves Power Play.

When Kidman and I showed up for the Saturday morning show, it was early, but there was a flurry of activity all around us. Because of our experience, we were not star-struck by the other wrestlers. But when we saw Lawler, we stopped for a moment. It was like we were little kids again. He was a legend to everyone, and seeing him work took a minute to sink in. Lawler was also serving as a promoter and part-owner of the circuit, along with another gentleman named Vince McMahon Jr., the millionaire owner of the WWF.

I tracked down Randy, a spectacled man with a bushy white beard, and we introduced ourselves. We were out of costume, and Randy immediately scrutinized Kidman.

"Jesus," he said, "you didn't tell me he was so small."

"Well, he's good though," I said.

"If you say so," he retorted.

"Well, if you need us, we're going to be here for a while," I said.

"I hear ya," he said, and walked off.

I looked to Kidman. "I hope this works."

Not five minutes later, Randy came back. "Can you work today?" he asked me.

"Both of us?" I said.

"No. Just you."

"Yeah, I can."

Randy left us and went back to work. I turned around and I could tell Kidman was pissed.

"They don't want me," he said. "They want you."

"Look, this is a good thing for us," I said. "I can do this until you get your shot. You know the way you move, you're going to get a chance. Something just has to click. You're going to do it."

I went out to the car and got my gear. It wasn't unheard of to show up at an event, be a part of it and not get paid. If it was just going to be me on our first day, at least I could show the crowd our idea. But Randy told me not to bring our nearly four-foot-tall Stanley Cup replica.

Kidman wasn't happy, but he understood. He took his normal place ringside, to watch, and when he did, he saw he was really being screwed. I would be participating in a tag-team match, but not with my own partner.

I was joining another guy in a match against the PG-13 tag team, two guys I'd heard of a while back and really respected. Jamie Dundee and Wolfie D, two young kids in their early twenties who'd been wrestling in the Memphis scene for a while, worked as tattooed, skateboarding alternative kids with skinhead haircuts. Both were in decent shape, and while they weren't overly muscular, they had tone, and the crowds, especially younger wrestling fans, loved their attitude.

Before the match, none of the wrestlers wanted to talk, as Wolfie D ran around everywhere trying to pump up the crowd. That was fine because it meant the match would follow the standard tag-team match formula: The babyface comes out and looks good, beating up the heel. Then the other heel, which I played, comes out and cheats to take control of the babyface — a reversal known the "heat spot," because it's supposed to get the crowd heated up. When a match is especially exciting, it is said to have good "heat." So, in the formula, when the heel gets control of the babyface, the partner of the babyface comes in to make a comeback and save the day.

Less than 100 fans were in the studio to see the match, so I wasn't that nervous. But I did know this was my tryout, being on live television was something to think about. With a pre-taped match, you can fix mistakes, but not on live TV.

But there was something else going on in my head too. This was Memphis wrestling, the place where Hogan and Lawler became champions. The place where wrestlers took fights outside the ring, where they used props and took shots at each other from concession stands. If you were a baseball player, it would be the equivalent of playing in Wrigley Field for the first time.

The first thing I noticed was that even though the crowd was small, they were right on top of us, screaming. Gradually that faded into the background, and I focused on giving the audition my all. We went through the formula, and by the time we hit the end, Wolfie D leaned in and said, "Time to go home."

I was thrilled, because I knew I could again use the DDT to make my mark. Luckily for me, Kidman had moved to the control room, where he watched with Lawler and the others. When Wolfie D went for the DDT, I was ready. I was dropped, I landed, my hair hid my forearms and I hesitated again just for a minute, so I could balance, then I fell straight to the mat.

Later Kidman told me the place went nuts.

I stuck it, and apparently, it looked real — and great. When we left the ring, Wolfie D. and Jamie came up to me and thanked me for making them look good. I told them it was my pleasure.

Then Lawler came up to me and shook my hand. "My only advice," he said, "is that you almost make it look too good. Because you take that hit so hard, you need to stay on the mat longer. People think you're dead when you fall like that, so get up slowly. Keep selling it to the end."

I told him I would.

"They loved it," Kidman said. "That was phenomenal."

"Thanks, man," I said. "We're going to get you a chance."

Back in the day, wrestlers weren't paid when they made television appearances. It was looked at as a privilege, a chance to make your name, so no money was expected. Not much had changed since then. For these matches, you were paid $40 a night. That's it.

Randy, the squirrelly promoter, came up to us in the locker room. He was excited.

"We want you to join us on the road," he said.

I looked at Kidman. "How many spots do you have?" I said.

Randy looked at Kidman too. "We've only got one," he said. "But don't worry—we'll work him in."

Kidman's eyes got big.

"We'll do it," I said.

It was a good first day in Memphis.

✱

In one day, we'd established ourselves as good enough to be in the regular schedule in the USWA. In a normal week, we would drive 1,600 miles in the Taurus, making our $40 per night and dreaming of the big time. It was exactly what I wanted.

Our normal schedule went something like this: From 10 a.m. to noon on Saturday, we'd start in Memphis, where I'd participate in the live show; then we'd drive three hours to Nashville that same day to make a night show. When that was over, we'd drive back to Memphis that night, and Sunday was an off day. Monday night, we worked at the Mid-South Coliseum in Memphis, while on Tuesday, we'd play to crowds at the Gardens in downtown Louisville, Kentucky. Wednesday, we'd travel down the river to Evansville, Indiana, and Thursdays and Fridays were reserved for "spot shows" in places like Tupelo, or Jackson, Mississippi, but we never knew where until that week.

We were paid for four nights of work, and even when Kidman wasn't used, he would get his money because he was standing by. Still, we were only pulling down $160 a week apiece, and if we were going to survive, we needed to find a better place to stay.

Lawler came through for us in a big way. Turns out his son worked at the Memphis Best Western, which was located just beside the airport and was known for being one of the nicest places in the city. Lawler's kid hooked us up with rooms for $25 per night. So $175 of our combined $320 went to our room. We tried to use the rest for food and gas, and most of the time we would use hot plates to cook up rice and beans, while we boiled our own iced tea.

Even though I had the $60,000 in the bank, I didn't want to use it. I wanted to pay my dues, and I knew that if I lived differently than anyone else, I wouldn't be doing it the right way.

✹

I'd always heard Bill Dundee was a real prick.

Since we were wrestling against PG-13 (which included his son Jamie), Bill, who was also a bit of a legend, was always hanging around. He was only five-five, with childlike facial features and dark black hair, and a lot of people said he was such an asshole because he had "small man's disease." That is, he was jealous because he was short, so he overcompensated for that fact by acting big, trying to gain a couple extra inches with his attitude.

He was also kind of strange because he came into wrestling after performing as a tightrope walker in his native Australia. About a week after Kidman and I started, he came up to me with something to say.

"What's your gimmick?" he asked in that thick Australian accent.

I had my gear on, and I thought the answer was obvious. "I'm a hockey player," I said.

"Let me ask you this," he said, a smug look on his face. "What are hockey players known for?"

I was already irritated by his line of questioning. "I don't know — scoring goals?"

"No. Try again, mate."

I sighed. "Skating?"

"No, you dumb motherfucker."

Now I was pissed. "Now wait a minute—"

"You're doing a gimmick and you don't even know what the gimmick is," he said.

"What?"

"Fans know about hockey for one thing — the fighting," he said. "I like your outfit. If I were you, I would go out there every night and I would throw my gloves off and pound the other guy in the face. Fans would love that gimmick."

"OK, man," I said. "Thanks for the advice."

But I never took the advice. I thought Dundee was just yanking my chain, critiquing me and being an asshole. But if I had thought about it, I might have seen that he was helping me, telling me an important rule about gimmicks and the crowd. I thought I was a real wrestler, and I was too good to just go out and beat people up every night with my fists.

Maybe I should've listened to him. But other than that one instance, no one in Memphis ever tried to help me and Kidman. So why at that point, would I have listened? I didn't. But I should have.

✱

I always forgot how young Kidman was. I could always relate to younger and older guys, so it wasn't difficult to talk or live with him. But there were quirks. As Kidman continued to struggle with the fact that he wasn't being used in the tapings or the shows — and since Randy told us they would work Kidman in, they had done so only a handful of times — the kid would let his frustration out in different ways.

One way was talking to his mother, and he called her just about every day. Another way was the video game in the basement of our hotel. It was called Crazy Ball, and Kidman would play it for hours at a time, in fact, I took to calling it Kidman Ball. (For the fun of it, he started referring to me as Kanyon Ball.) But his real obsession was porn.

I'd brought along my VCR, and I used it to record matches and watch tapes of other matches. But Kidman found out it was good for something else. Because of a technological glitch, we could search the hotel channels on the VCR, and if anyone in the hotel had ordered a movie, we could search the channels, find it, and watch it too.

And sometimes, the movies were dirty. The possibility of watching free porn trumped everything else in Kidman's mind, and every time we'd come home, he would have to flip through the channels to see if there was porn. If there wasn't he would just have to check later.

"I'm going to the can," I said.

When I went into the bathroom, I'd left the television on a game show. When I came out, Kidman was flipping through the channels on the VCR, looking for porn.

"Nothing, huh?" I asked.

"Nope."

Later, while we were watching a wrestling tape, he sat up like he had an idea.

"Can I check again?" he asked.

I sighed. "I guess."

He tried again, but to no avail.

"I'm going to play video games," he said.

And so it went. Frequently, he did find porn, and it was not the kind I wanted to see. But still, I had to feign interest so Kidman didn't think there was anything wrong with me. The good thing was, with our schedule, I didn't have to make excuses about why I wasn't seeing women. I had no time; really, none of us did, so it wasn't difficult to keep my secret. Sometimes I would go down to the hotel bar and hope to meet someone, but it never happened. I never really tried.

After three months, Kidman was used only 12 times. It was a constant source of frustration, and after a mistake he made one night, Kidman quit coming on the road with me. It was a simple mistake, and looking back, it was another lesson to be learned. But at the time, it was extremely important.

In a match with Wolfie D, Kidman and I were able to use our tag-team idea, and it was working well. When we got to the end, Wolfie pile-drove me and Kidman. Taking the pile driver is difficult because it's dangerous and it has to be sold in the right way. Wolfie basically put our heads through a table, and when that's done to you, you need to hesitate for a long while before you get up and leave the ring.

Kidman didn't. After the pile driver, he waited a couple of seconds, then stood up and staggered off. It didn't look real, and he heard about it from Lawler. After that, he said he'd only come on the road if he was needed.

On a Saturday night in Nashville, he was needed. He drove up with me that night and said he was tired of not getting noticed. He said he was going to try the shooting star press.

"You think you can do it?" I asked.

"Oh yeah," he said. "I'm going to do it, and they're going to love it."

Because I'd been wearing the hockey gear during my fights, when Kidman showed up in the ring that night wearing his hockey gear, audiences knew we had an allegiance. It was a good way to let people know we were a team. Kidman was matched up against another small dude — a skinny black guy. They put on a good performance, and near the end, Kidman showed the wrestling world what he could do.

After the other guy was thrown to the mat, Kidman climbed up to the top rope, and as he did, the crowd started to get excited. Kidman faced his opponent, then leaned forward and jumped. In the air, he did a flip, and when he came down, the plan was to land on his belly, on top of his opponent.

But he didn't land it. At the last minute, the black guy moved, and Kidman landed on the mat. It didn't work. And it didn't matter. The crowd loved it, and the cheering I heard then for Kidman was louder than any cheering I'd ever heard. I felt so good for him in that moment. It was like everything he wanted to do was wrapped into that one move.

When he came out of the ring that night, I gave him a hug.

"You did it, man," I said.

He just smiled — and it was a smile as big as Tennessee.

(23)

OUT OF A JOB, ON TO THE POWER PLANT

Things were happening behind the scenes in the wrestling business that would affect us, and we had no idea. Memphis, a longtime WWF stronghold, had cut a deal with the rival WCW too, and because of that deal, the USWA would serve as a training ground for both entities. It was a good business move for the Memphis organization, but since WCW was sending eight of its up-and-coming wrestlers to our circuit, it meant the end for about eight of the current USWA wrestlers.

Wrestlers like me and Kidman.

"Look, I'm sorry, but we just can't afford it," Randy told us. "You guys are working hard. You're making a name. I'm sure you can keep doing it somewhere else."

We were just heading in to a two-week break from our schedule, and I was planning on going back to New York, while Kidman was planning to go back to Pennsylvania. When we came back, we'd have two more weeks to go, and then we would be let go. Over the break, we had something to think about.

Before we left, Wolfie D tracked me down in the locker room.

"It's a tough break," he said. "I'm sorry it had to work out this way for you. But I think you need to stick with it. Don't quit. You'll make it."

Wolfie D told me to talk to Kenny Kendell, another wrestler who'd spent some time in the WCW and had just arrived in Memphis as part of the new transition. I sought out Kendell, and we had a conversation that proved to be invaluable.

"How much do you make?" he said.

"Just $160 a week," I said.

"Jesus, my man. If I were you, I'd go down to the Power Plant school in Atlanta, then I'd go to Florida on May 1st for the five-day taping. There are four tapings a day, and you get paid $150 a match. There are no championship belts there, but they tape about three months worth of shows at once. You can make some money and get noticed."

I took the news to Kidman and presented it as an alternative.

"I don't think so, Chris," he said.

"What do you mean? We can keep the gimmick going, man. We can do it." I said.

"I don't know." Kidman remained unconvinced. "We came out here and gave it a shot. What did I say? If it didn't work out, we could just go on back. I think I need to go on back home. I'll work with Afa. We can get in that way. ECW is going to be huge."

I shook my head. "I got let go in Smoky Mountain. I tried the WWF and ECW, but I didn't get the push. I'm getting let go in USWA. I need to go and try WCW."

"Hey, man, if you got to do it, go and do it," Kidman said. "But I don't think I can go with you."

✱

After our two-week break, I came to Memphis and finished my two weeks, while Kidman stayed behind in Pennsylvania. It was a good learning experience for the kid, but I was convinced that by not going to Atlanta and Florida, Kidman had given up on wrestling. I was sure that he would never get what he needed in ECW.

My last day in Memphis, I checked out of the hotel and drove to Birmingham. From there, I went on to Atlanta, where I stopped as the sun was going down. From Interstate 20, I saw the buildings of the massive city of the New South, and I immediately thought I was going to like the place. I'd been to some cities before—Memphis, Nashville and Louisville, for instance. But I was from New York, and I could tell a big city when I saw one. Atlanta was a big-time city.

I drove around until I found a nice city park in Midtown. I left the car and bought a six-pack, took it to a bench and drank a beer as I watched the sun set. *I could like it here*, I thought.

I put in a tape and listened to some music. Peter Gabriel's "Don't Give Up" blared through my headphones. That seemed appropriate. I walked for a little while, and two blocks down the street I found a gay bar. Nice. Then I found an old Victorian home where I could rent a room for $500 a month. I found places for all of my things and I sat down on the bed, developing a plan. I would go down to Orlando, where WCW was taping, and I would prove to them that I could wrestle. Then I would use my skills to get back to Memphis, where I could then develop my gimmicks and eventually, I would make it to the big time.

Kenny Kendell had given me the name and number of the Power Plant, and of Brenda, the woman who worked there. I was supposed to ask for Jody Hamilton, who was in charge of the school.

"Hello?" a woman answered.

"Yes, is this Brenda?"

"Yes." She was curt.

"Yeah, um, hi. My name is Chris Kanyon, and I'm a wrestler, and Kenny Kendell told me to call you and ask for Jody."

"No, I'm sorry. You can't speak to Jody."

"I'm sorry? Really?"

"Yes, sir."

"Why can't I speak with him?"

"You need an appointment made by Jody to talk with Jody."

And then I heard a dial tone.

I called back. I tried to explain my situation. She hung up again.

Rather than risk another shut down from Brenda, I called all of my contacts. Luckily a few of my friends knew where the Power Plant was, and some others knew the taping was taking place at MGM Studios in Orlando — but no one knew how to contact this Jody person. Not Jim. Not Afa or Moolah. Not anyone in the USWA. It was April 30. The taping started on May 1, and I had no idea how to meet Jody.

I trudged down to the bar I'd seen before — The Prince of Wales English Pub — and sat down for a beer. The bartender, a good-looking young guy with blue eyes and a Southern drawl, brought me the beer and stayed for a minute.

"Haven't seen you around before," he said. "Tell me your story."

He probably got more than he bargained for, but I told him my story — at least the wrestling part. I left out nothing, and I told him my latest problem.

"I think my career may be done," I said.

"Well, that sounds silly," he said, wiping down the bar. "I can figure this one out for you. If I were you, I'd go on down there to Orlando. Just show up, and then you show them what you can do."

I smiled. I doubted it could be that simple. But then again, I showed up at Afa's and that worked out. Kidman and I showed up in Memphis and that worked out. Maybe I could go for the trifecta.

"Maybe you're right," I said. That bartender never knew it, but he made a world of difference to me.

The next morning, I decided to go to the taping. I drove down to MGM, bought a ticket and became a part of the crowd. I walked to the top of the rail overlooking the ring area, searching for the infamous Jody, whom Kendell described as looking like a "fat version of the comic book character The Thing."

So as I looked for a fat man in an expensive suit, WCW security man Doug Dillinger started walking over to me, a scowl on his face. I knew I didn't have much time, or Dillinger was going to ask me to sit down. When he was about 10 feet away from me, a lady with a headset came through the main entranceway. I caught her eye and motioned for her to come over.

"You need something, hon?" she said. I explained my situation, and she seemed like she wanted to help. "Hold on one second," she said. "I'll be right back."

In the corner, Dillinger seethed. I could tell he was looking forward to chewing my ass. The woman returned about a minute later from the bowels of the arena. "Jody says he can see you."

I hopped the rail and walked back with her. Behind us, Dillinger looked like someone had shot his dog. In a back room, the woman let me in a thick door. There sat the fattest man I've ever seen. He wore a black pinstriped suit and he had a wad of chew in his mouth. When he spoke, his lips did not move.

"Kendell says you're a wrestler," he said. He did not look up.

"Yes, I am."

Jody spit some of his dip into a paper cup. "You got tapes?"

Did I have tapes? Boxes of them. "Yes, I do."

"Leave me some tapes," he said. "I can't get you on the taping — it's already booked. But come back here on May 10, 2 p.m. If you're as good as Kendell says, we'll have some work for you."

I left, and I was happier than I'd been in a long while. May 10. That was my brother's birthday. Should be easy to remember. When the nice woman let me out of the arena, I discovered I was in the theme park. I looked around. No one knew I didn't have access to the park. Before I left, I decided to enjoy the rest of my day at MGM Studios — for free.

✷

"You were right," I told the bartender of the Prince of Wales. "You told me to go down there and show them what I could do, and you were right. I did it, and now I've got a tryout."

"Well there you go," the bartender said. "I had a feeling it would all work out."

Enjoying celebratory beers at the bar, I couldn't believe my luck. After coming back from Florida, I was on cloud nine. I'd gone from being really low — not knowing at all what I wanted to do, or how to do it — to having a plan. I was in a familiar place again, facing another tryout to continue my wrestling career, and it had gotten to be a comfortable feeling. I had my foot in the door, and once I did, I knew I could show my stuff. I would convince them I was valuable enough to keep.

The Power Plant had been receiving a lot of publicity in the wrestling magazines. It was very highly regarded and quickly gaining more popularity. As the days wore on, I counted down until May 10. Again, it was easy to remember because it was Ken's birthday, and I made sure to give him a call that morning. By noon, I decided to head out. In my head, I pictured the Plant as a freestanding building, in something between a residential or suburban area.

It wasn't anything like that at all. It was off the beaten path, in an industrial park, near a part of town known for its high crime rate. If I hadn't had directions, I wouldn't have been able to find the place. None of the buildings had signs, and all of them looked the same, with loading docks and few windows. To make matters worse, there was a water purification plant just down the street, which made the whole area smell like shit.

I arrived early at 1:30 p.m. and parked my car. When I got out, I held my nose and walked into the lobby of the building. Compared to my other wrestling school experiences, this was completely different. And amazing. The room was 75 feet long by 40 feet wide. In the front were offices and storage space. This was more than a training center, it was also a holding area for many of the items they used on the show. There were extra canvasses, ropes, turnbuckles and skirts featuring the logos of eight years of pay-per-view matches. The walls were lined with multicolored banners and sections of steel cages from matches past. In many ways it was a lot like Pete's, a museum of amazing wrestling artifacts. I felt like I was looking into Vince McMahon's basement.

On a shelf by itself, I spotted a silver helmet that looked like it came from a *Star Wars* storm trooper. It was covered in glitter, and I recognized it immediately. In the 1980s, there was a terrible gimmick involving a nearly 400-pound wrestler named Fred Ottman. He started in the WWF as Tugboat, but then came over to WCW, where he was called the Shockmaster. He wore the silver glittered helmet, and his voice was disguised to sound a bit like Darth Vader. The Shockmaster got a huge build-up, and it all culminated in one live television show, where he made his first appearance. It didn't go well.

Four veteran wrestlers were feuding on the show when the Shockmaster burst through a wall. His impressive entrance was ruined when he tripped over some of the fake wall, and his helmet fell off. He groped around for the glittery helmet and finally got it back on, and as he tried to regain his composure, viewers could hear a few wrestlers laughing. "I told you it was going to happen," one even said on the air. In one moment, Fred Ottman had gone from being the next big thing in wrestling to being an embarrassment, relegated to small, unpopular cards. It was a symbol of one of the greatest goofs in wrestling history, and it made me realize how everything can go away in an instant.

I walked across to an office, where a door stood cracked open. A gold plate read "Jody Hamilton." I knew Jody had wrestled with a group called the Assassins back in the 1970s, so he knew the business. And it explained why he was so big. Before you knew the guy, he used that heft as part of his intimidation over others. He did not laugh or smile freely. He was all business. I knocked on the door, making sure not to open it.

"Come on in," the raspy voice said from inside.

I walked in, and there he was, once again in a dark suit, sitting behind a desk cluttered with papers. He had huge lips, which glistened a bit from the tobacco juice coming from the wad of chew in his mouth.

"Hi, sir," I said, sliding inside the office. I stood in front of the desk and felt like, for some reason, I was a student walking into the principal's office. Jody looked up from some paperwork, and the message on his face was clear: He had no idea who I was, or what I was doing there. My confidence sunk like the *Titanic*.

"Who the hell are you?" he said.

So I explained myself again. I went through the whole story and reminded him of how I was told to go back there, at 2 p.m. May 10, the day of my brother's birthday. Jody looked down again at his paperwork. He did not move, other than to spit some tobacco juice into a small paper cup that sat on the desk. He grunted.

"What are you doing here now?" he asked. "I told you to come back on May 8, at 10 a.m."

"What?"

"Yeah," he said, still refusing to look up. "May 8 — that's what I said. 10 a.m. Why would I tell you 2 p.m.? Everyone's gone by that time. Everyone comes in around 10 a.m., not 2."

I just stood there feeling helpless. Was he joking? In wrestling, playing practical jokes, or "ribbing," is common, but was Jody ribbing me? I didn't know, but I wouldn't put it past him. It's part of the entire way of the wrestling world. By nature, wrestling people — that is, those who want to be involved in wrestling for a living — are immature. They are self-conscious, and some overcompensate for those issues by putting up a façade of overconfidence. It makes sense when you think about it. Wrestlers play-fight on television for a living, trying to convince people it is real. People tend to think wrestling makes you turn into this kind of person, but they're wrong. As wrestlers, we choose this profession because we're already that way, and the environment plays on our personalities. In wrestling, there are no statistics to measure your performance. It's all subjective, based on fan reactions. That draws a certain type of person. And while not everyone is immature 100 percent of the time, it is a common thing.

"Why would I tell you to come here in the afternoon?" he said.

I didn't know what to say.

"We always get here at 10 a.m.," he said. Finally, he looked at me. "Come back tomorrow."

I was again filled with hope. "What time?" I asked. Immediately, I regretted it.

"I just fucking told you," he said in a calm voice. "We get here at 10. Why don't you come in at 9?"

I nodded. "OK. Thanks again, sir."

The next day, I showed up at 8:45 in the morning. Of course, no one else was there. I sat in my car for about 30 minutes, watching all the others walk into the building. I finally decided to go in, where I waited until Jody showed up at 9:45. This time, when Jody saw me, he told me to get my gear on. That seemed like a good sign.

In the other wrestling schools I'd been to, there was one ring, and most of the time that one ring could barely fit in its room. As I walked into the back of the Power Plant gym, past the offices, I counted four rings. At least 30 wrestlers were stretching, taking part in exercises and milling about. Normal wrestling etiquette would have the new guy introduce himself, but I was nervous, so I didn't tell anyone who I was. Plus, they had no idea where I'd come from, or what kind of experience I had. For all they knew, I was a complete amateur. Mike Winner, one of Jody's trainers, came over to the group of guys and told us to get ready.

We started off with squats, bending down and touching our asses on the floor. We did it 500 times. I thought I was in good shape, but those exercises can make you tired in a hurry. Still, the one thing I'd become known for in the ring was my stamina, and it came in handy during those kinds of drills. When we'd finished, Jody came out. He pointed to me.

"Come here, kid," he said. "Mike, take him into the ring and work him out."

For eight minutes, Mike kept it basic with me, as we worked on simple moves like elbow lock-ups and suplexes. He was a good partner, someone who would let you show what you could do. I was nervous, but I knew I could make him look good, so I fought those butterflies and together, we danced around the ring in a simple practice match. From the side of the ring, Jody watched it all. Mike and I communicated well in the ring, and near the eight-minute mark, he pinned me. We got up and shook hands. As I left the ring, I looked over to Jody, who was walking back to his office. He closed the door.

What the hell? I thought. *What should I do now? Should I go in there?* I grabbed a Gatorade and sat down on a bench. Mike had gone to another ring to work out with the others, who were all doing their own thing. I felt lost.

Forty-five minutes later, Mike came back over to me. "Jody wants to see you now," he said.

Great. As I walked over to his office, I reeled off the number of things Jody could say to me. He could ask me to leave, which would be awful. He could ask me to stay, which would be wonderful. He could ask me to stay, but could then require me to pay $3,000, which I really did not want to do. Yes, I had the money, but in the world of wrestling, someone with my experience would not have to pay to work out at the gym.

I walked into the office, just as I'd done before, and I stood in front of the desk. Jody did not look up. "Sit down," he said, so I did. Without looking at me, he took a Post-It note from his desk. He wrote on it for a few moments before folding it once in half and passing it to me. I didn't know whether to take the note, or to wait to be told to do so. After a few seconds passed, I figured I should take it. I unfolded the note and saw six dates written down, from late May through June. A price was attached — $150 a show.

"Can you make those dates, kid?" he said, looking up for the first time.

"Definitely," I said.

"Get a booking sheet," he said.

I was getting my shot. These matches were televised. These matches were the big time.

"Thanks so much," I said, trying to contain my gratitude. "Jody, can I ask one more question?"

He nodded.

"Do you mind if I come here every day and train with the guys? I'm used to having a school where I can go try something new and stay in shape."

He raised his eyebrows, and I think I saw the beginnings of a smile. "Kid, that's the best thing you could've asked me. Of course you can."

As I drove home that day, I was the happiest I'd ever been. I'd made it through a lot of big moments in my life so far, but in my mind, this was the start of something bigger. I knew that if I could make it here, I was on the road to being a professional wrestler. I would be able to support myself, like my parents wanted. I would show all the folks back home, from my friends and family to Pete, that I'd made it. It felt like I was finally climbing the entrance ramp to my career.

I celebrated that night at my favorite bar, in the town I was growing to love.

Life was good.

11

THE FALL OF CHRIS

"To be that man, you've got to beat the man."
RIC FLAIR, WRESTLER

(24)

DIAMOND DALLAS PAGE

I would go down to the ring every day. In the few days I'd been working out there, I learned I was one of the most experienced wrestlers at the Power Plant. Because I'd learned so much, I could help teach the others, and I was a valuable asset to Jody and his crew. The bonus for me was that whenever a popular wrestler came in to work out, I would get to work with him, because I had the most experience. One of the first semi-popular wrestlers I met was a 36-year-old sponge from New Jersey named Diamond Dallas Page.

I'd seen Page on TV and could tell Page could become really popular. He was just starting to get a push at that time, and after watching some of the things he did, I could see why. Page, who had a day job running some nightclubs in Florida, began his wrestling career as a manager. Like Jim Mitchell, Page had the gift of gab. He was a good talker, but after some re-thinking, he decided he wanted to give wrestling a shot himself. Because he'd started late in life, he and I were very close to the same age, wrestling-wise. But as a former promoter, he thought about the production of the match, which gave him an edge. He introduced a huge guy as a bodyguard, and he loved to have members of his crew hold up signs like Olympic judges grading his moves. Of course, the grades were always good. He had long blond hair and a goatee, and at six-four he was a fit and imposing 230 pounds. He was still a relative rookie, but his wrestling balanced pageantry and aggression, and he had good moves. I liked it.

When I worked out in The Power Plant, I went 100 percent, even in practice. It wasn't odd to see me bouncing, or "bumping," on the mat hard. I enjoyed it, and that's the only way I knew how to do it. But someone thought I should be more careful. When I came out of the ring one afternoon, Page was waiting for me. That was odd, considering how we'd never been formally introduced.

"Chris?" he asked.

"Yeah, hi," I said, toweling off from practice.

"I noticed you in the ring there, and I just wanted to tell you I think you're really doing well," he said. To me, that was a major compliment. "I was worried though."

"Really?" I asked. "About what?"

"You know I like to be physical out there," he said. "We use speed and intensity in the ring. I try to play that up as much as I can. But you, you take it to another level."

"Thanks," I said, wondering why he was worried.

"Well, I want you to know I think you should ease up a little," he said. "A famous wrestler told me once that we all have a certain number of bumps in us. Every one you use here is one less you can use at the end of your career."

"You think I should ease up in practice?" I said.

"Yeah, just a little," he told me. "Save it for the big lights."

From that moment on, I knew Page was a friend of mine, and I also knew that I would not stop practicing hard. I always practiced like I was performing in front of six million viewers. I couldn't just change who I was. The only time I would hold back was when Page was in the room.

"Thanks, man," I said.

"Don't mention it," he told me.

✶

At the end of one day, we were finishing up practice, and I was planning on taking my car to have it worked on at a local garage. Page had come in late that day and happened to be leaving at the same time as me.

"Hey, man," he said as he saw me leaving. "You going anywhere?"

I got the sense he wanted to hang out, so my car problems could wait. "No, I'm not doing anything. You?"

"I was just going back to my place—it's an apartment complex where all the wrestlers live," he said. "I was just going to hang out, to sit by the pool. Do you want to come along?"

Hell yes, I did.

As Page drove us over to the apartment, I felt like I was getting a peek inside the life of the professional wrestler. And I felt like I was starting to belong.

"You need a gimmick," Page said. "Do you have any ideas?"

It was funny he brought it up, because I did have an idea I was thinking about. Now that Kidman and I had split, I ditched the hockey gimmick, which was probably a good idea since it wasn't connecting with the audience anyway. Instead, I had another idea. When I was growing up, I'd seen a movie called *The Wanderer*, which told the story of a man searching for his lost love and his lost innocence. I thought it would be cool to explore that a little more, and to have a character that combined that idea with a *Rebel Without a Cause* kind of character. I'd have the leather jacket, the white T-shirt with the rolled up sleeve hiding a pack of cigarettes. And I'd be wandering, searching for something. I told Page the idea.

"That's good," he said. "No one's doing anything like that right now."

We talked more about it as we sat by the pool at the complex, and as we got to know each other, we went from being acquaintances to friends. We exchanged phone numbers and he told me to call him if I needed anything. I told him I would.

From time to time I was able to wrestle some others big names, guys I'd seen on television, like Triple H, a former bodybuilder; Terry Taylor, a fan favorite from the south; and Chad Fortune, who besides wrestling had played professional football and driven monster trucks. But nothing could have prepared me for the drama surrounding my first televised match.

Now that I was making $150 per match, I could finally tell my parents that I was making some kind of money.

"No, I haven't even touched the savings account money yet," I told them on the phone one day.

"It sounds like things are going real well for you, son," Dad said.

"Not only that, but I'll be on TV Saturday night," I said.

"This Saturday?" Mom said. "Will we be able to see it?"

I told them they would. I'd been on television before, when I wrestled as a jobber in the WWF, but this was something different entirely. In this instance, I knew I would be on TV for the first time in the company that would make me a professional wrestler. That weekend, we were scheduled to go to Charlotte for a cross-promotion with a NASCAR race, where we would shoot a Saturday night live show for TBS from the streets of Charlotte, North Carolina. I made sure to tell all of my friends to watch too, but we didn't account for one thing — rain.

All of the wrestlers were waiting in a hotel as it rained outside, wondering if we would still go on. As we kept getting regular weather updates, I kept calling my parents, anxiously explaining the situation. I didn't want the big night to go wrong: I felt that they needed to see what I was doing. They needed to know I was having some success, and TV would do that. Minutes before the show, I had to call them one last time.

"No, I won't be on," I said. "We're still going to wrestle here live, because there's a big crowd in the streets, but it won't be on TV. They have some old tapes they're going to run instead."

"Why won't they put it on?" Mom asked.

"I don't think it would look very good with us all wet," I said. "Can you call my friends and tell them not to bother?"

"Sure," she said. "I'm sorry you don't get to be on, Chris."

"Me too," I said. "But don't worry, I'm doing fine and I'm sure you'll get to see me on some other time, OK? Probably next week. I've got to go, OK?"

"OK. I'll tell your father. Love you."

"Me too."

In my first match, which was not seen on television, I wrestled the Blue Bloods tag team of Bobby Eaton and Steven Regal, whose gimmick was hoity-toity British etiquette. The British-born Regal told Page I'd done well considering we had to wrestle in the rain. Page then told him it was my first match in the WCW, and later, we all went out for a party. But it wasn't just any party — it was a birthday party for WCW head man Eric Bischoff.

We walked into the bar, and there, surrounded by the faces I'd seen on TV, was Bischoff, living it up as his people paid for his drinks and the celebration. Page and Bischoff had been friends since the days when Page was a manager, and since then, the two had gotten closer as Page's popularity began to take off. Bischoff, a well-dressed man with short gray hair and a square jaw, grew up in Detroit and Pittsburgh, where he started wrestling as an amateur in high school. Bischoff earned fame by taking over the WCW at a time when it was a joke compared to Vince McMahon's WWF. Enter media mogul Ted Turner, who famously got into the wrestling business looking to compete with McMahon. With Bischoff as Turner's executive producer and vice president, the WCW began to hire away WWF wrestlers like Hogan and Randy Savage. Flush with new talent, they developed Monday *Nitro* to compete with the WWF's *Monday Night Raw*, and the two promotions went head to head for years.

Bischoff was the man who was doing it all. And there I was, right there with him. He was friendly that night, but he was also shitfaced, and I didn't want to say much because I was new. As the night wore on, and people got more drunk, Page introduced the two of us.

"This is the new guy," Page said to Bischoff, pointing to me. "He's definitely going to be something. He's someone to keep our eye on."

I took it all in. Of course, they were drunk and Page could have just been joking around. But still, for my first night of wrestling in the WCW, this wasn't too bad. Sure, the match had been a bust because we weren't on TV. But my new friend Page had just told the man in charge of the WCW that I was going to be "something."

I hoped I'd prove him right.

(25)

THE STRANGE LIFE OF A SINGLE GAY WRESTLER

The next Tuesday, we were taping in Gainesville, Georgia, and I had to wrestle Booker T, a great wrestler who'd been a champion and was known for his dreadlocks and crown combo. Before the match, Page actually went over to Booker T and told him who I was, that it was my second match, and that I could do anything, so he should be confident the match would look good. It did, and this one actually made it on TV. When it was over, Booker was so happy with the match, he hugged me and said thank you. Then he went back to Page and said I did really well.

But the big thing was my family was able to see me on television, and it lent some credibility to what I was doing, though they were still unconvinced this would lead to a career. In five months, I'd moved from Memphis to Atlanta, still trying to find a permanent contract. My parents reminded me of that fact, as well as the promise I'd made to them. In their eyes, I had seven months to sign a contract, or I would leave the business and go back to physical therapy. My brother kept telling me to stick it out and ignore what my parents were saying. I knew they were worried about me, and only wanted what was best for their son. And in a way it was a good thing I'd set up this deadline, because it really kept the pressure on. I told all of this to my brother one day, as I was getting ready for my parents to make a visit. They were coming down to Florida because their lifelong best friends who'd retired to Orlando were celebrating an anniversary. I was thinking of going down to see them.

"Yeah, you should do it," my brother said. "You know they want to see you. Mom wants to make sure you're eating enough, and they both want to see your face."

"I know," I said. "I love them so much – I just don't want it to be awkward."

"No big deal," he said. "The only way it's awkward is if you let it be. They want you to be happy, but they also want you to be safe and OK and making a lot of money. They want to see you survive. You're doing that, right?"

"Yep."

"Then it'll be fine."

Ever since my brother had gotten married to his girlfriend, he'd gotten very wise. He went through with his plans to become an accountant, and he was living the American Dream and thinking of starting a family. I liked talking to him more and more. I took his advice and made the trip down to Orlando, where my parents were meeting their friends for the party. It was a big time for me professionally, as I was making an impact in the WCW, and Page was excited about my Wanderer gimmick. I was also thinking of moving into the wrestlers' apartment complex. I had a lot to brag about, I thought.

The anniversary party was held in an apartment community room, and it was a '60s theme. When I walked in, there were tons of Sonny and Cher combos walking around. Peace signs covered the walls and a disco ball spun overhead. *Nice*, I thought. That's when I first saw the DJ. He was big and muscular, but he had a little gray working at the sides of his crew cut. He wore an earring, and when he smiled, his perfect white teeth stood out against his brown skin. He was gay. I knew it from the way he looked at me and smiled. I never thought I would find someone hitting on me at my parents' friends' wedding anniversary party.

I found my parents, and we sat down for dinner. It was good seeing them for the first time in a few months, and after telling them about my recent success, they seemed at ease. But across the room, the DJ was not taking his eyes off of me. My parents' friends also had their family sitting at our table, and I knew their son Patrick was gay. But he had come out of the closet, and everyone knew it. During a break in dinner, he got up from his seat across the table, walked over to me and whispered in my ear, "The DJ can't take his eyes off of you," he said, before walking back up to the buffet line.

I looked at the DJ, who was about 30 feet away from our table, and it was true — he was still looking at me. Our eyes met and he smiled. I watched as Patrick walked back up to the buffet line, and it occurred to me that he may now know my secret. When he came back to the table, we stared at each other. Neither of us said a word. As the evening wore on, the families mingled and visited with some of our other acquaintances. Some had moved down from the old neighborhood, while others, like my parents, came down from New York to visit. In the middle of the party I looked over at the DJ again, and he was gone. It was almost a relief, until I realized he was behind me.

"Hey," he said. He was an attractive guy. I liked his smile and he had blue eyes.

"Not here," I said. I walked outside. Soon after, he followed.

I was nervous. It was one thing to get caught being gay, but it was another thing to be caught by your parents at a party for their friends.

"Are you gay?" he asked when we got outside.

"Yeah," I said.

"Well, do you want to do anything?"

I shook my head. "Man, this is my parents' friends' gig here. I can't do anything now. No one knows I'm gay."

"Why don't I give you my number and you can call me sometime?"

I hesitated. "OK." It turned out his name was Antonio, and he lived only 45 minutes from Orlando. I put the number in my pocket.

After the party, as we began cleaning up, my Mom told me she had a few days free. Dad was going fishing with some other friends, and she had a request.

"I want to see some wrestling," she said.

"Really?"

"Yes. What can we see?"

I checked and there was a pay-per-view in Orlando the next night. We were in luck. I also knew that we didn't need tickets. I could get us in, and there were always open seats near the camera side of the ring. We could sit there. The next night, we headed out to the show. I was just impressed my Mom wanted to go.

"Well, I wanted to see for myself what you're doing," she said.

We entered through the back of the arena, where various wrestlers were running around, making sure they were ready. Not 30 feet away from us, fully geared and gleaming with oil, Hulk Hogan was stretching. He was oblivious to everything around him, but there he was, and it was the first time I'd ever been that close to him. I had never formally met him, nor had I spoken to him, and this wasn't the time.

But how could my Mom have known the unwritten rules of wrestling?

Clutching her big yellow purse and taking tiny steps toward him, she couldn't hide her excitement.

"You know," she said, in a voice a bit louder than normal, "Hulk Hogan really isn't that big."

I could've died right there.

Hogan looked up and scowled at us. He didn't know who we were, or more importantly, who I was. Mom had no idea what she'd done, so I said nothing, and we just kept walking.

Hours later, when the match was over, Mom and I drove back to the hotel. In the car, I couldn't help but tell her how I felt.

"I had a good time tonight, Mom," I said. "This was really cool."

"Me too, Chris. Me too."

She looked drowsy, and I knew it was time for her to get to bed. I took her back to her hotel, where Dad had already gone to sleep. "Thanks for coming out to watch wrestling with me," I said.

She smiled. "I love you," she said.

"I love you too."

She shook her head. "But Hulk Hogan really isn't that big at all."

✱

When my folks were on their way back to New York, I should have been on my way back to Atlanta. I wasn't. Instead, I was driving 45 minutes north of Orlando. I called Antonio to see if he was busy; he said no, so I told him I was on my way. As I drove up to meet him, I wondered again what my family would have thought if they'd known I'd gotten a date at the party—a date with a man.

When I arrived, I saw Antonio lived in a small apartment off to the back of someone's house. It was secluded, but it was almost a little too secluded. Almost a little scary. There was no way anyone could know what went on in that little apartment. I got out of the car and walked up to the door. I knocked.

"Yeah, OK, sure," Antonio answered the door, a phone to his ear. Dressed in leather pants and a red button-down shirt, he looked nice. He motioned for me to come in. It was a neat little place, with modern art and a leather sofa. There was a rug that looked like a tiger on the floor, and soft lighting throughout.

"Well, just do what you can," I heard him say. He'd walked into the bedroom, but the conversation was still clear. "Sure, we'll be here." He hung up.

"Sorry about that," he said to me, walking back into the living room. "I was just talking to some friends." He put on some soft music from an expensive-looking stereo system. "How have you been? Did your parents go back to New York?"

"Yeah," I said, sitting down on the sofa. "I'm not sure I want to talk about my parents right now, though."

"I understand," he said, sitting next to me. He wore some kind of cologne that I liked. It made him smell clean and fresh.

"This is the first time I've gone to someone else's place," I said. "I haven't had many experiences before."

"I understand," he said. "We'll take it slow."

He started kissing me, and it felt good and steamy, like a long shower. It had been a long time since I'd explored another man, and I wanted this badly. As we kissed, I started unbuttoning his shirt, slowly. We'd been making out for about 15 minutes when he led me to the bedroom. It was dark, but I could tell there were red satin sheets on his bed. We fell on to the sheets, rolling around the bed.

Then the doorbell rang.

Antonio stopped kissing me. With his shirt half-unbuttoned, he got up. "Hold on one second," he said with a smile. *What the hell?* I thought. My pants were undone, and I had to roll over to look back toward the door. My eyes adjusted to the light, but I still had to shake my head to believe what I was seeing.

Antonio came back to the room with another man and a woman. The man, who had Latino features and slicked black hair, was shirtless, wearing leather pants and boots with spurs on the heels. The woman, who had short blond hair and bright red lipstick, removed a trench coat to reveal a black bra, panties and shiny thigh-high boots. She held a long black whip in one hand and a brown paper grocery bag in the other.

Oh my God.

"Do you mind if my friends join us?" Antonio asked, smiling. "I thought they'd make things a little more fun."

"I, I don't really know," I said. "I'm not sure I'm really comfortable with all of this."

The girl weirded me out. I didn't want to have sex with a girl, even if two other guys were there. If it was just the other guy, then maybe, but these two were dressed strangely, and — this was a big factor — what the hell was in that bag? What they were going to do with me?

"How about this," I said. "How about I just watch you guys for a while."

The three looked from one to the other, then back to me. "That's fine with us," Antonio replied. Losing no time, the two men got naked, and the woman got on the bed with her boots on. I walked over to the door, where I pulled up a chair and sat down. Reaching into the bag, the woman pulled out a black muzzle and a red gag ball.

Holy shit, I thought.

Antonio got up on the bed, while the other man ordered the girl to put the gag in Antonio, who was bent over like a dog. Then she whipped him once, and even though he had the gag in his mouth, Antonio whimpered. He looked at me when he did.

Jesus Christ.

The woman took off her bra and slowly rubbed her breasts over Antonio's back. Then she grabbed the whip and tickled his ass with it before snapping it over him again. All the while Antonio looked at me. Behind him, the other man grabbed his head, flipping Antonio around and kissing his chest. The girl rubbed herself on the other man's back before whipping him.

This is fucked up, I thought. And as the three began having sex, amid moans and whimpers, I left the house. I got into my car and made the long drive back to Atlanta. Forget getting lucky, I was feeling lucky just to have gotten out of there.

✱

In Atlanta, I'd begun to realize how lucky I was. I wasn't aware of it when I arrived, but the gay scene in Atlanta was one of the most vibrant in the country. I lived in Midtown, a hub for gay activity, and I had made it a habit to frequent the bars, because when I did, I got a lot of attention. I never dated at all, because there was no point. How could I have a relationship when I was scared of outing myself?

I was in good shape, and I learned early on that when I walked into a gay bar, I could easily have my pick of any guy in the place. I was young, toned and good-looking — a hot commodity in the gay world. At 25, I saw myself as a regular Casanova. In college, I remembered how hard it was for my friends to pick up women. But with gay men, there are no games. Everyone wants the same thing, and no one's shy about it. At certain times, I'd gone into my favorite bar and spent five minutes there before I went home with someone. Guys want to hook up every night, and that's what they do.

Once I walked into a bar and the bartender was really good-looking. He came over to me without saying a word and we started making out, right there in public. Another time I was having a drink when a man walked in, saw me and motioned me to come over his way. I did, because the man was one of the most gorgeous guys I'd ever seen.

"Do you want to have sex with me?" he asked.

"Yes I do," I replied.

We left immediately and went back to his place.

In Atlanta I'd learned to be more comfortable with myself and my sexuality. I realized I wasn't taking much of a chance to go out to a gay bar and find myself a companion. And the more I did, the happier I became. I was doing what I loved for a career and being who I wanted to be in my personal life.

As long as those two worlds never collided, I knew I would be fine.

(26)

CALIFORNIA DREAMING AND MAKING MY NAME

At the Power Plant, I'd established myself quickly. Jody had a saying early on: "Kanyon is good, and we want to see our guys against someone good." When new guys came in, they would have me wrestle them, just as I wrestled Mike on my first day. I could take people through a series of moves to see just how experienced someone was. And many times, it worked.

When a six-three, 230-pound wrestler named Disco Inferno came into the Plant, everyone took notice. Disco used a dancing gimmick, dancing in the ring and while he was being introduced. We knew it was something that would polarize the audience, so the only question was whether he was good enough in the ring. I knew from the start that he was. He was loose and he made things fun. And when Jody saw Disco in the ring with me, he knew, too. Disco used finishing moves like the Village People's elbow, which was really just an elbow drop while "YMCA" played in the background. He was made for TV.

Helping work out those guys was good for me, and I felt even better that Jody had that kind of faith in me. The WCW environment was different than when I jobbed in the WWF. Even the lingo was different: In the WCW, jobbers were known as Enhancement Talent, because we made the others look good. I liked that distinction—it gave us an added importance out there, and it made it seem like they had more respect for what we did. WCW was a regional company with a national focus, so we would travel to sites all across Georgia, and we would go back to those same places time and again. That was how, even as a jobber, I began to stand out. It was rare for someone in Enhancement Talent to make a name for himself, but because I could sell the beatings so well, people began to take notice, and the newsletters (and by this time, some Internet sites) were singing my praises. I felt like it wouldn't be long before I showed everyone what I could really do. All it took was one little favor from Jody.

In July, WCW produced a wrestling match for a pay-per-view called Bash at the Beach, where wrestlers would fight in a ring set up on the beach. It was held at Huntington Beach, California, and when I heard about it, I knew I wanted to go. A friend of mine from college had moved out to that area, and I really wanted to go and visit him. I wanted to be able to wrestle on the pay-per-view too. Armed with those two reasons, I asked Jody if he would let me go — an unheard of request at that time by a member of the Enhancement Talent.

But Jody said yes. I think even then, he knew I was ready for big things. On July 16, 1995, I appeared on the pay-per-view to wrestle Johnny B. Badd, a Buffalo, New York, native who had hair like Little Richard. Johnny was smaller than me — five-ten, 230 pounds — and after all my time wrestling with Kidman, I'd learned how to make a smaller man look good in the ring. Johnny also liked to use the shooting star press, and throughout the match I knew I was doing a good job. And it would pay off in a big way. In the back of my mind, I knew Eric Bischoff was doing the television commentary for the fight, and it was the first time he'd ever been the commentator for one of my matches.

We had a short, three-minute match, but when I got out of the ring, the other guys in Enhancement Talent came over to me and told me what Bischoff had said. He'd made a point to talk me up, and in the end, Bischoff was pretty complimentary, saying, "You can expect to see a lot more from Chris Kanyon in the future." I smiled when I heard that. Johnny shook my hand and I went backstage, which really just led me outside a door to a bank of trailers on the beach. I sat down on the steps, and looked out on to the water. Out of nowhere, a figure came out of the trailer and walked my way.

It was Bobby "The Brain" Heenan, an outstanding wrestler and manager who'd worked with Vince McMahon, Jesse Ventura and Andre the Giant.

"I came all the way out of my trailer just to say you did a great job and shake your hand," Heenan said.

"Oh my God, thank you," I gushed. I didn't know what else to say.

That's when I knew I was getting bigger. As the summer wore on, the WCW's head booker, Kevin Sullivan, even wrote a storyline for me to win my first match over Disco, though Sullivan was only letting me win to get at Page. Sullivan was a five-ten wrestler from Boston, who had been a professional since 1970. He'd done a little of everything, including portraying himself as a devil-like leader of a wrestling cult. He had a voice that was high and scratchy, and he did not like the fact that Diamond Dallas Page was a close friend of Eric Bischoff's. Because of that, Page could offer input on Sullivan's storylines, and Page was virtually untouchable. Sullivan wanted to be left alone to write the storylines, but he wasn't — Page would always have more power. So that summer, Sullivan gave me a victory, because at the time I wasn't much of a big deal. But in doing so, Sullivan could take down another Page guy — Disco — who was getting a push. When he was confronted about the situation, Sullivan said he was actually helping me, another of Page's friends.

When I won, I acted the part. I hugged the ref. I thanked God. I went crazy. But little did I know, being Page's good friend was a blessing, as well as a curse.

✱

The one thing that could counteract the negativity of Kevin Sullivan was the positivity of Terry Taylor, another wrestler I'd faced at the Power Plant. Taylor helped Sullivan write the matches, and Terry also knew a lot of the writers for the national newsletters. Because of that, he was able to make sure I got my name in them. At six-one and 240 pounds, Terry was famous for a gimmick called the Red Rooster, which had him perform moves like the Chicken Wing and the Cock o' the Walk.

With the encouragement of Disco and Page, I was fleshing out the Wanderer character I'd been thinking about. But to make it look good, I needed practice, especially when it came to my interviewing skills, which I'd never really used before. One weekend I went over to Page's place, where he and I, along with Disco, did some practicing.

"You guys promise you won't laugh?" I asked.

They both promised.

Disco set up a tripod and worked the camera. I went into Page's bathroom and changed into a white T-shirt, a leather jacket and dark jeans. I slicked my hair back and pulled it into a ponytail. Then I slid some cigarettes into my T-shirt sleeve, which I rolled up. I wanted to look like the Fonz, from *Happy*

Days, and I even had a catchphrase worked out: I would point to the crowd, flip up my collar and say, "Heeeeeyyyyyy." I looked in the mirror and smiled. I looked the part, anyway. It seemed like a good idea, but I was still learning, so I also knew I could fall on my face. But there were a lot of wrestlers I'd seen in the locker room who were faltering, barely hanging on, and I knew it was hurting the business. I even told Page that if he ever saw me like that, trying to hold on, to tell me, because I didn't want to wrestle like that.

I checked the mirror again and satisfied, I stepped out into the living room where the camera was set up.

"Nice!" Page said, and Disco started clapping.

"Hell yeah!"

"Please," I said, "no autographs."

"Alright, the thing about the character," Disco said, "is to relax. Just let yourself come out through the person you're playing." Disco ought to know. He'd been playing his character for forever. From behind the camera, he said, "Whenever you're ready, man."

Page came over to me. "I'm just going to pretend I'm interviewing you after a match, OK?"

"OK." I fidgeted with my hands.

"Are we rolling?" Page said.

"We're rolling," Disco said behind the camera.

"Alright, this is Diamond Dallas Page ringside with the Wanderer, who took out the Big Show tonight after a fantastic super kick, culminating an intense 10-minute match," Page said. "Wanderer, tell us about yourself and how you were able to defeat the Big Show tonight."

Page pointed the fake microphone at me. I was tongue tied for a moment. "I, um, thanks, Page. I am the Wanderer, from the East Coast, and I, well, I wander the land, and I was — um, I was — I was able to take down that big giant of a man because he was in my way, you know?" I flipped up my collar. "I'm just wandering, looking for my baby." Then I looked at the camera and pointed. "Heeeeeeeyyyyyy!"

Disco tilted the camera away. I looked over, and dammit if he wasn't laughing. Then I looked at Page, and he was holding his hands over his face. He was laughing too. When they both saw me looking at them, they stopped hiding and laughed long and hard. And even though I was pissed they were laughing, I started laughing too, because I knew it was just that bad.

I needed work, and judging from the reactions of those two, the Wanderer was not a character that could work. In Memphis, they said play a role that's more like you. Was I like the Wanderer? I didn't really know. I definitely wasn't like this version, anyway.

"Dude, that may be the worst thing I've ever seen," Page said.

"Gimme a break," I said, laughing. "It was my first try."

"Let me have that tape," he said to Disco, who was still laughing between his teeth. Disco gave him the tape.

"I'm keeping this," Page said. "Someday, this is going to be really funny."

✱

Little did I know, but as the summer turned to fall, I heard whispers that Jody and the others wanted to develop a character for me, something I could practice with and make my own. Every now and then Page would tell me they were working through several different possibilities, but as the calendar year wore on, I only thought about one thing: I'd made a promise to my parents that I would have a contract within a year. I told the same thing to Page, and he said he would talk to Eric Bischoff.

"Set up a meeting," I said. "I want a contract."

By that time, I — as well as the other wrestlers — knew I was more than a passing talent. But as long as I was working per match they could still drop me whenever they wanted. I had no security. Finally in October, Page set up the meeting with Eric. We walked into the CNN Center in downtown Atlanta. WCW's offices were on the 14th floor, and when we got off the elevator, all I saw was nice furniture, paintings and an amazing view of the city. WCW owned the entire floor. We walked into Eric's office, where he sat in an oversized burgundy chair. It seemed to swallow him.

"Sit down," he said when Page and I walked in. He was reading a thick book and he did not look up at us.

We sat for a few moments.

"What are you making now?" he asked. Again, he did not move or look at us.

"Well, I make $150 match," I said.

Eric closed his book, slid it to the side and looked at a desk calendar. "This is the end of the year. Because of our budget constraints, I can do $450 per match for you. Come see me again at the end of the year, and I'll bump you up more."

I didn't hesitate. I didn't need to. "OK," I said, and I shook his hand. There was no negotiation. There was no haggling. I knew what I wanted, and that was a guaranteed contract. I signed up with Bischoff that day, with the understanding that I would get another raise in a little more than two months. After I signed, I told him thank you, and we walked outside to the elevators. Before I made it there, I broke down.

"Congratulations, man," Page said.

"I can't believe it," I said, as tears rolled down my face. "I've wanted this my whole life."

"Now you've got it," he said.

I couldn't wait to call my parents. When we made it to the lobby of the bustling CNN Center, I found a pay phone and made the call.

"Mom?" I said. "This is Chris. Can you put Dad on the phone too? Thanks." When they were both on at the same time, I relayed the news.

I was a professional wrestler. For real.

They were pleased I was making enough money to support myself, and they were even happier I had some kind of security now. I told them I'd be making more money soon, and that when I got a regular character on TV, I could be really big.

"We're proud of you, son," Dad said.

"Yes we are," Mom echoed.

And that meant the most of all.

✶

Until you get your first contract, you're always just an independent wrestler. You're exactly the same as any old schmo wrestling once a month at the local rec center. But when you get that first deal, you're for real. And it was definitely a different feeling. In six months I'd gone from unknown to signed, and it made all of that work and traveling worth it.

As we neared Thanksgiving, Kevin Sullivan even came up with an idea for me. He had a gimmick: Men at Work. On its face, it seemed like a gimmick that was a little generic and underdeveloped. But hey, it made me feel good they were thinking about me, so I took what I could get. Men at Work would feature me and Mark Starr, another enhancement wrestler who worked down in Florida. Starr, who also sported long, dark curly hair was an acquaintance of mine, and when we heard we'd be wrestling together, we went about arranging our costumes. We were rough construction workers, so we needed simple costumes: Blue jeans, black Magnum boots, worker hats and flannel shirts. It was perfect.

Mark was a traditional wrestler, very solid and old school. He didn't participate in any high-flying acts, but he was pretty good. When we talked about the idea, we were happy to be a step-up from the guys getting beat up every week, but we were also concerned, because it didn't seem like we had something that would really stick with fans. I had an idea —we could be construction workers who were also Chippendale-type strippers. We could go out there and play up the construction angle, then strip as part of the act.

No one liked the idea, and I wasn't even totally sure I could do it either. So we decided to make the best of it. We would be the toughest, most ornery construction workers we could be.

Knowing that I would soon be getting another raise (which would put me at about $30,000 in annual salary) I bought a Jeep. Page and I were leaving the Power Plant in the Jeep one day when we drove past a construction site. As I slowed down, we noticed the site seemed abandoned. It was late in the day, and it looked like everyone had gone home for the day. Without a word, we got out of the Jeep, grabbed a couple of pylons and some orange flags, and we even hauled away a sawhorse. I knew we could use all of it in the act.

As we drove away, neither of us spoke. We didn't have to.

(27)

SUCCESS AS MORTIS, OVERSHADOWED BY NWO

Mark and I never knew when we might get the call. We were just told to be ready. Then, just before a taping in mid-November, Terry came to us and told us to have our characters ready for next week. This was it. We'd have an entrance and graphics on TV. We'd get to use our props and I'd finally get to practice a character. And who knew? Maybe we'd get popular, and maybe we'd get a push. You never knew.

Our entrances were everything we could have hoped for: Surrounded by all the construction equipment, there was smoke and music, and we came out like two guys who had something to prove. And that was appropriate, of course, because we did have something to prove.

We looked at each other. We'd made it. We were on TV, doing what we wanted to do. *This*, I thought, *is the life.*

✶

During the Men at Work gimmick, things were definitely improving for us. We got a few wins, a couple of them over major acts, guys who were tag team champions. That was a thrill, but we still had the feeling that we could do better. The Men at Work gimmick was fine, but I wondered what I could do to get more exposure. As the new year wore on into the spring, the gimmick took a hit when Mark got injured. Injuries are always a part of wrestling, and his was a back injury that spelled the end of his participation in the group. So instead of Mark and me, we recruited Mike Wenner to be my partner. It didn't start well.

Mike, the first guy I'd wrestled when I got to the Power Plant, was nice, but always struck me as a little weird too. Still, as long as the gimmick kept going, I figured I was lucky to have anyone with me. Mike was a good wrestler, but he always dressed in a flamboyant style, very effeminate. He'd seen what Mark and I had been wearing while we wrestled, so I figured Mike would do the same.

I was wrong.

During our first match together, Mike showed up dressed in tight black jeans, which were high waters, meaning they didn't reach all the way down to his boots. And the boots—these were not the construction worker boots Mark and I had worn. These were dress boots, which did not go with the look at all. And to top it off, he tied his flannel shirt into a knot, pulled up over his bellybutton.

"What is this?" I asked, pulling him to the side before we were supposed to go on.

"This is my outfit," he said, smiling.

"We don't look like a construction crew," I said. "We look like the Village People."

Mike just laughed. "Let's have fun, huh?"

I didn't know if I could have fun when my partner looked like that. We were supposed to be big, tough construction workers. This looked bad. But during the match, I decided it could be good television, so I joined in, trying to make it as ridiculous as possible. I used my tape measure to plot out where I was going to land during a move, but then I would overshoot it. I knew at that point I was growing as a wrestler, because I was learning how to play up to the crowd, and for the most part, it worked.

Little did I know, things were going on behind the scenes, things that would take me to a new level of stardom.

✷

"I can't do this," I told Page. "Did you see Mike out there? Did you see the way he was dressed? This will *not* work."

"I hear you," Page replied.

We were backstage after the match. It was April 1996, and Men at Work had survived for six months. Still, after one match with Mike, I was ready to roll.

"What can I do?" I asked Page.

That's when Page told me of a new gimmick, sure to be one of the most fantastic in the history of wrestling—at least that was the way it was being sold through a seemingly endless array of commercial spots. It would become known as "Blood Runs Cold," the brainchild of Eric Bischoff, who desperately wanted to cash in on the popularity of martial arts–related video games and cartoons. The idea would pit four characters against each other: Ernest Miller as a karate character, Bryan Clark as the helmeted martial artist Wrath, Ray Lloyd as the icy warrior Glacier, and another character which would take the form of a snake. Wrath and the snake would fight Glacier and Miller.

"Eric needs someone to fill the role of the snake character," Page told me. "I told him he should use you. Why don't you come to one of our meetings and look at some of the ideas."

I told him I would. It excited me to think I could be a part of something so big, and Page said it could be the break that took me to the next level.

The following day, I met up with the Disco Inferno and Page, who took me to AFX Studios in downtown Atlanta. We were there to meet with Bischoff, some other wrestlers, and creative effects guru Andre Freitas, well known in the effects world for his movie work. Together, we were supposed to brainstorm more about Bischoff's idea.

The place was part mad scientist's lab and part pottery studio. Everywhere there were molds and faces and things that were being created and invented. Bischoff was taking all of this seriously, sparing no expense. He wanted Blood Runs Cold to be the next big thing, and he was employing these effects masters to help with the ideas and costumes.

In the AFX elevator, Page leaned in toward me.

"I told Eric you should be the snake character," he said. "But he didn't think you were right."

My heart sunk. Then why was I here?

"But don't worry," he said. "I talked him into it."

It rose again.

"Thanks, man," I said.

"Don't mention it. You're right for this character."

We got off the elevator and walked into a large room with dark walls and a long mahogany table. Bischoff was there, along with a few other wrestlers and a man I identified as Freitas.

Bischoff opened the meeting by telling us that for years, he'd been studying the video game industry, comparing it to what kids and teenagers were interested in. He said he'd made a connection: Martial arts. Bischoff, himself a black belt, wanted to develop a cast of characters, which could someday expand to as many as a dozen, who specialized in a dark form of martial arts, similar to the video game *Mortal Kombat*. After the characters were established, the possibility for merchandise — T-shirts, games, etc. — would be endless.

"This is going to be the biggest thing," Bischoff told us. "The marketing's going to be huge. You name it, we're going to have it. We want to invest in you."

We all knew that with Freitas involved, everything was going to look good. During the course of three hours, we listened to everyone's ideas, and most of the characters sounded like they would be very popular. But I was concerned about something. The snake character did not seem as well thought out as the others, and I wondered if we needed something different.

Since I was a kid, I'd always been interested in the *Ghost Rider* comic book. Sometimes I would go down to the corner store, and if I wasn't reading the wrestling mags, I was looking at *Ghost Rider* comics, which told a story about a motorcycle-riding skeleton. Something about that glowing skull stood out in my mind.

"Maybe we should go with a skull rather than the snake," I said.

Everyone looked at me.

"The marketing for a skull would be exceptional," Freitas said.

Bischoff smiled. He looked at me. "I like it," he said. "We don't want to be too much like *Mortal Kombat*, and one of the characters is a snake. Maybe moving away from that is a good idea."

"I always liked *Ghost Rider*, the comic, when I was a kid," I said. "That's where it came from."

Bischoff nodded. "I'm definitely open to it. It sounds like it could work."

As we left, Page gave me a pat on the back. In one sentence I simultaneously justified Page's faith in me, as well as put my own mark on the character. I'd done well. And if Bischoff was right — and I had no reason to doubt him — this was going to be an unbelievable opportunity for everyone involved.

✯

After five years working in the business, my push was going to happen. My character's name would be Mortis, a death-themed character with a skeleton mask and black cape. But Glacier would be the star of the show. We taped promos for television saying "The World Is About to Change." They showed snow and alluded to a new icy character.

It was a lot to live up to.

As part of the deal, we were pulled off of television, in part to learn and keep creating the characters. But we also needed to learn some martial arts, and learn to understand each other. For six months, we would work out together at the Power Plant. This had to be good—the WCW was spending $30,000 apiece on our characters, including our costumes. My mask and shoulder pads, for instance, were molded exactly to fit me.

While I kept feeling like I'd made it to the Show—that's what we called making it big in wrestling—I couldn't help but think about my old friends. And I wondered how I might be able to bring them along for the ride.

✣

I still talked with Jim Mitchell every now and then, telling him of the people I was meeting and the opportunities that were coming up. Jim, who was working in a furniture factory during the day, was nothing but supportive of me. We talked about how he might be worked into some of our acts, but we just never knew what we could do. Kidman, on the other hand, never called me. It was something I would always respect about him. Not once did he ever ask if I could get him a job.

Kidman was back in Pennsylvania, making a name for himself on the small circuit. I would see his name in the wrestling magazines, and slowly, Kidman was developing into a popular performer.

Mitchell, on the other hand, was not soaring as high. He was doing the same gigs on weekends and evenings, but he was not getting anywhere. But unfortunately for him, I didn't have much pull yet. Page was my only hook, but there wasn't much of a need for managers on the circuit at the time.

"Don't worry," I told Jim on the phone one night, "I know that you pick your spots up here, and sooner or later I'm going to figure out how to get you up here."

But I had to get myself settled first and make sure the platform I'd been given was as steady as I'd hoped.

✣

That summer, one of the greatest wrestling gimmicks of all time came to fruition—and it was not Blood Runs Cold. While we were training, preparing to be the next big thing in wrestling, Bischoff was also working another angle. In retrospect, it seems easy to see how big it would be. But at the time, no one had any idea.

Scott Hall and Kevin Nash, two of WWF's stars of the time, were signed by the WCW. Bischoff was finished playing second fiddle to Vince McMahon's WWF, so he convinced parent company Time Warner to pony up the money to improve the talent. Hall and Nash were signed away, along with a mystery third person, and they said that together they'd dominate the talent in the WCW. The business coup was worked into their storyline, which had them coming from WWF to take over WCW. It was a wonderful idea, one Bischoff supposedly got from a similar Japanese storyline, but no one knew just how big it would be.

The third member of the team was revealed at the Bash at the Beach, July 7, 1996. I was there, sitting with Glacier, as we watched as Hulk Hogan, one of the most famous names in the history of wrestling, came out to thunderous boos. Hogan was a heel now, going against the establishment as part of what he called the "New World Order" of wrestling.

The secret third member was no mystery to insiders, but no one knew how the crowd would react. Immediately, the fans began throwing cups and garbage — anything they could get their hands on. They hated it, which of course, meant they also loved it. I'd never seen a reaction like this. And I knew what it meant. The New World Order, not Blood Runs Cold, was the new "big" thing in wrestling.

I turned to Glacier, shocked at what I'd seen. "There goes our push," I said.

Later, Bischoff would actually take part in the scenarios with the nWo, and in one instance, he was power-bombed off the stage. It was amazing to see, and the fans loved it. Sometimes I would count how many T-shirts I saw supporting the nWo in the first few rows. I always stopped at 50. Bischoff looked like a genius. As the nWo continued to gain in popularity, the Monday show began to draw a bigger audience than the WWF, and together, they outdrew Monday Night Football — an amazing feat.

But for those of us in Blood Runs Cold, we knew we were going to always be, at best, second banana.

✱

Because of the nWo, our push was delayed. No one wanted to start anything while the biggest gimmick in the history of wrestling was at its peak. To make matters worse, Bischoff had his hands full with the nWo and no more time for us. His vision for Blood Runs cold had become nWo tunnel vision.

We were told Kevin Sullivan would write for us instead. We lost our writer and our support, but the commercials, which told everyone the world was going to end, were still running. It was still building Glacier up to mythical proportions. The delay time helped out at least one person, though — Jim Mitchell.

During the Christmas of 1996, Disco Inferno came to me with an idea. We knew my skull character was going to be called Mortis, a Latin word for death, and that I would be some kind of strange death-like human character. But the problem was a character like that normally wouldn't talk. It would be strange for a beast like this to also have the gift of gab.

"I think Mortis needs a manager," he said. "That would solve the problem of you having to talk. Your manager could say the things you needed to say."

He was right. I agreed.

"The problem is, do you happen to know anyone who could do that?" he asked. "We need to get someone, like yesterday. Do you have any friends?"

Did I? It was the role Jim Mitchell was born to play.

We sold the idea to Page, who then took it Bischoff. I got one of Mitchell's tapes and passed it along. Mortis was scheduled to have his first match in three months, and we needed someone to step in right away.

Over in South Carolina, Mitchell was still trolling the independent circuit, working at the warehouse and drinking himself silly. He was in that state when I called him late one Friday night.

"Yeah?"

"It's Kanyon," I said.

"Hey, man," I could hear him turn down a stereo. "What's shaking?"

"Remember when you called me and told me you were taking me to Smoky Mountain?"

He perked up. "Yeah?"

"Well, you took me to Smoky Mountain," I said. "I'm taking you to the Show."

He hollered on the other end. "You are fucking kidding me?"

"Nope."

"Woooo-hooo!" he screamed. "Me and you, together again — in the Show!"

I'd never heard him happier.

✶

Mitchell packed up his stuff and moved in with me in Atlanta. He was convinced he was going to be reprising his role of Darryl Van Horne, the character he'd created as a tribute to Jack Nicholson. (Even the name was stolen right from a character out of a Nicholson movie — *The Witches of Eastwick*.) Mitchell said this character would "own" Mortis and would pimp him out for wrestling matches.

Sullivan wouldn't hear any of that.

Based on Sullivan's own desire to use the devil motif, he met Mitchell and immediately told him three things:

"No devil, no Jack Nicholson, no Satan worshipping," Sullivan told him. "You play it straight."

Later, Mitchell wondered what the hell was going on.

"I'm managing a skeleton guy!" he told me. "How am I supposed to be a straight, normal guy when I'm managing a dude in a skeleton suit?"

I told him I didn't know. "Sullivan's already going to be against me because I'm friends with Page," I said. "There's no way to win with this guy."

So Jim went back to the drawing board. He would walk around the house, stewing about what this character was going to be. One thing he definitely knew, it wasn't going to be was a simple, straight guy. After a few days he settled on James Vandenberg, a collector of oddities who traveled the world. While in Thailand, Jim said, Vandenberg stumbled across my character in an underground fighting tournament. Vandenberg then convinced Mortis to come back and participate in American wrestling, Jim said.

I loved it. It was perfect.

✶

Living with Mitchell was great because I didn't have to pretend with him. He knew I was gay, and he didn't care. At night, I was still trying to go out to the gay bars and explore — something that was becoming increasingly more difficult.

In Atlanta, some of the gay bars remained open for 24 hours, but near the 3 a.m. mark, the places would clear out, then fill up again with a straight crowd wanting to continue a night of partying. It was during those gay–straight twilight hours that the scene became tense for me.

Late one night (or, if you prefer, early one morning), I was partying with some gay acquaintances at an amazing place not far from my house. It was a dance club, but one with two complete floors—one for dancing and one for privacy. The clock had just struck 3 a.m., when I noticed the place clearing out. The hetero crowd was about to come in. When the door opened on the lower level, I was terrified to see Disco and Raven walk in with some other guys from the Power Plant. They weren't regulars.

Fuck, I thought. *What are they doing here?*

I had to get around them and get out. I made my apologies to the group and went down to the lower level dance floor, people blurred into a writhing mass of bodies under the staccato strobe lights. Scents of sweat, cologne and perfume grinded against fried food and beer. As I wove through the crowd, I kept my eye on the door. I watched as the wrestlers stood by the door for a moment, taking it all in, pointing at some men making out in a corner. I circled around to a side, my back against a far wall. The group, no more than six, started to move toward the dance floor.

Toward me. I froze.

They were temporarily distracted by the men dancing and kissing in front of them, interested but clearly uncomfortable. They took another step toward me, paused, and then turned for the bar.

Away from me.

I made my way through the crowd and found the door. I hopped outside and headed for home, where I could be safe. Walking through the cold, I knew that once I was on TV, my anonymity would, for the most part, be compromised. *My days in the club could be over*, I thought.

So I changed my way of meeting people. I bought a computer.

(28)

THE ONLINE DATING SCENE

"This is it, man," Page said. "This is the way people are going to be keeping up with wrestling in the future." He pointed to his new computer.

He was talking about the Internet, which allowed people to follow matches all over the world by logging in and keeping track of what others were doing. It was like getting every wrestling magazine and newsletter in the mail at the same time. Amazing.

"What are you doing?" I asked.

"I'm chatting with some fans online," Page said. "You can meet people and talk to them. It really is incredible."

"You can meet people?" I asked. "Like, anybody?"

"Oh yeah, on AOL you can go into all kinds of chat rooms," Page explained. "And some of them are dirty." He smiled.

I smiled back. "Wow."

I went out the next day and bought a computer. I wanted it for two things: to track wrestling and to meet other gay men.

"What the hell is that for?" Mitchell asked. His eyes were bleary. It was 1 p.m.

"I want to get on the Internet," I said.

"What the hell is that?"

I explained as I hooked it up. Through AOL, I was able to set up a celebrity message board forum, where I could keep people informed of what I was doing. It was like an early version of my own web page. There, I honed my skills in dealing with the media as I chatted with fans. Still trying to keep up the façade that it was all real, I'd talk about how I hated Glacier and things like that to stay in character.

Of course as soon as I was hooked up, I started looking for gay men. I didn't have a picture, but I really didn't want a lot of people knowing who I was anyway. In any case, back then it was common for most people not to have a picture.

One day when I was on the computer, Jim came into the room and sat on the bed.

"What the hell is all this stuff?" He gestured around the room.

I looked around. There were garbage bags, filled to the top, all over the room. There were suitcases, still packed, from months ago. There were piles of newspapers, magazines and stapled pieces of paper stacked in all corners. I didn't know what he meant.

"It's just my stuff," I said.

"Your stuff?" he asked. "What's in these bags?"

"Bottle caps."

He looked at me again. "Bottle caps?"

"Yeah. So what?"

"Dude, why do you have all these? And these newspapers? And what are all these papers?"

"These are emails I've gotten from people," I said. "Fans, some guys I met online. A lot of people."

"Why do you keep all this stuff?"

"I don't really know. What if I need it someday?"

Mitchell just shook his head. "Man, I don't mean to judge here, but that's weird." He laughed. "And you know if I think it's weird—it must be really fucking weird."

I looked around the room. I didn't even think about it. I was just a pack rat; I kept everything. I shrugged it off. Jim was in no way qualified to tell me how to live a normal life.

I was finding I could have some pretty intimate conversations with guys online. But as was my habit, I would print out all of my conversations, even the ones where I would talk about intimate situations. I knew I couldn't just leave these lying around, though. I wanted to have people over to my house for wrestling parties, and I absolutely did not want my private homosexual Internet conversations lying around.

I bought a box — six inches high, fireproof and big enough for some important papers. Mitchell called it Pandora's Box. "If anyone ever finds that thing, you're screwed," he said. "It'll be opened and all hell will break loose."

I padlocked it just in case.

✳

Three weeks after I bought the computer, I was on the Internet talking to a guy named Mike. He said he was masculine — something gay men always want. Since seeing *The Karate Kid* when I was little, I always had a thing for Ralph Macchio.

When I asked what Mike looked like, he responded "a little like Ralph Macchio."

I couldn't believe it.

We moved from the Internet chat to the telephone. I was in my room, but I had the door open, and Jim — sitting in the living room — could hear everything I was saying.

"Ask him how many dicks he's sucked!" Jim yelled, laughing.

It was humiliating. But Mike admitted he'd been with a few guys before, which I thought was no big deal. We talked for three hours, and Jim kept asking for the phone. "I want to talk to him," he said. "Let me talk to him!"

Finally, I gave Jim the phone.

"Mike!" he said, as I stood watching. "Let me ask you this: Have you ever taken a dildo and jammed it up your ass?"

Oh my God. "Jim — I don't think —"

He ran into the other room. "Mike — have you ever sucked off a guy and then spit it back into his mouth?"

"Jim!"

"Mike, do you get along with your parents, and what do they think of you being a faggot?"

I grabbed the phone back from Jim, went into my room and closed the door. After a few more hours I came out. "What the hell were you thinking?" I asked Jim.

Mitchell smiled and stood up. "Hey, man, I was just trying to help you out."

"Well, what did you think? He said he looked like Ralph Macchio. I really like him."

"He sounds nice," Jim said, sitting back down.

"But?"

"Well, he says he looks like Ralph Macchio?"

"Yeah."

"Sounds like he looks a little more like Ralph Kramden."

"Why do you say that?"

"Just saying, man. Just saying."

✶

I really wanted to see Mike, but he acted weird when I asked him to come over. I didn't know why, but I finally convinced him to drive over the following day. I didn't want Jim there, so he left for the dirty bookstore down the street. Jim always liked to spend time at the dirty bookstore.

He grabbed his coat and as he walked out the door, he popped his head back in. "Remember — Ralph Kramden," he said, smiling. Then he closed the door.

From my window I could watch Jim walk down the street. I could also see the cars coming from the opposite way, and I was watching for Mike's. I watched for an old red Mustang, and when it turned down our street, my heart started beating faster. When it pulled into our parking lot and the engine stopped, I thought I might burst.

Then the door opened. And out came the spitting image of Ralph Kramden, straight out of *The Honeymooners*.

I couldn't believe it. But it was true.

I thought back to what Mike had told me during our conversations: He was masculine, well-built and looked like Ralph Macchio. Outside, a man was walking up to my home, and he was short, overweight and bald. He was not well-built and he looked nothing like the Karate Kid. He looked like the Dirty Old Man.

Shit. What had I gotten myself into?

This man was obviously a liar. And in his hand he carried a single rose. *Oh my God*, I thought. I wanted someone masculine, not someone who brings me flowers. Jesus.

Mike came up and knocked on the door. I made my way down and took a deep breath. I opened it.

"Hi, Chris," Mike said. He smiled. His teeth were yellow.

"Hi, Mike," I said.

He gave me the flower. What the hell was I supposed to do? I took it and as he came in, I sat it on the counter.

"Well, come in, sit down if you want," I said.

He did, and I sat on the opposite side of the couch. "Do you want a drink?"

"Sure," he said.

I got him a small cocktail and sat back down. We did not speak.

"So," I said. "How about those Braves?"

"Hmm?" he said. "Oh yeah, the Braves. Good team. Good team."

"Yeah." I twiddled my thumbs. He coughed into his hand.

Everything about Mike repulsed me. His gut hung out from his untucked shirt. He wore a loose-fitting khaki jacket over that, along with sweatpants. Sweatpants!

"Look, um, Mike," I said. "I really enjoyed our conversation last night, but uh, this isn't going to work."

"What?" he seemed genuinely confused.

"This is not going to work. I'd just like to be friends."

"Oh, well, ok," he said. "That's nice."

He knew why. He knew he'd misrepresented himself to me. I was angry, but I was trying to hide it and be polite. I sat on the couch and watched him finish his drink. Slowly, he got around to the last drop, and when he did, I think he realized it was time to go.

"So, uh, I guess I'll call you," he said, getting up.

"Great," I said.

Minutes later, he was out the door, and I watched the Mustang drive away with as much as anticipation as I'd had waiting for it to arrive.

I called down to the dirty bookstore, where Jim was talking up the old woman who worked at the counter. "Come on back," I said.

"What happened?" he said.

"Just come on back."

When he walked in the door, he saw the story on my long face.

"Macchio?" he asked hopefully.

I shook my head no. "Kramden," I said. "Completely Kramden."

"Dude," he said, "you gotta know that in life, most people tend to lie."

I knew that better than anyone.

Right off the bat, I learned people misrepresented themselves on the Internet. In another instance, I met a man who said he was 27 and muscular, and he lived a block away. I was tired that day, but some companionship sounded good, so I walked to his house.

The man who answered the door was 50 years old and out of shape.

"What the fuck?" I said.

He smiled. "Well, you're here now anyway, we might as well do it." He opened the door.

"Dude, you are fucking lucky I don't beat the fuck out of you," I said. I walked away and vowed never to do it again.

I came up with some rules. I never wanted these people to know where my house was. I knew that if they found out who I was, and that they discovered I didn't want people to know about my sexuality, then they could blackmail me. I wasn't being paranoid; I was being realistic about what it would take for me to keep my secret.

So I always went to their place. It occurred to me then that being a closeted gay man is all about a kind of justified paranoia. When I was young, I knew I had to hide it. There was never any thought of telling my parents. I never revisited that decision. Maybe I should have, but I didn't. Instead, it became ingrained into my head to keep the secret. And the longer I kept it, the more paranoid I got that I would be outed. I should've learned from the experience with Jim — he didn't care about me being gay, and the friendship was actually better now that he knew. Again, I didn't realize that.

Aside from one great experience when I met a man at a restaurant, my socializing was relegated to the secrecy of the Internet. I, like most gay men, wanted to meet Mr. Masculine, but everyone was just too feminine for me.

When talking with gays, I would say I was a contractor. While they thought I meant I built decks, I really meant I was an independent contractor-wrestler. Some would want a picture, so I would send a picture of my body with my head cropped out. I explained I was closeted, and that it was dangerous for me to reveal my identity.

Then it got to where that wasn't accepted anymore. People needed a head and body shot. Luckily for me, a guy sent me a picture once that looked a little like me, so I ended up using that when I had to.

While surfing online one evening I came across a man who actually posted his picture. While he still looked like he might be too feminine, I decided to risk it. After chatting, we agreed I should come over to his house, which wasn't very far away. I pulled up to his door, and when he opened it, I knew I'd at least found someone who was good-looking.

Then everything went wrong.

The man's name was Randy. He was petite, with a toned body but he still looked a little feminine in the face. And with the way he stood—weight perched on one leg, arm flexed out, hand dipping downward—he looked like a stereotypical effeminate gay man.

But far worse, he recognized me.

"Oh my God! You're Kanyon!" Randy said, putting his hands on his cheeks like Macaulay Culkin in Home Alone.

Oh Jesus.

He screamed.

Oh fuck.

The scream turned into more of a shriek. I was sure the neighbors could hear.

Randy yelled for his roommate, who came running down a flight of stairs. This man was so gay he made Richard Simmons look like a drill sergeant.

"Johnny!" my once-promising companion yelled. "Look who it is!"

Johnny's shirt—which was cut off at the abs—was tie-dyed and sported a huge peace symbol. When he saw me, he stopped cold.

"Hello, Mr. Kanyon," he said, extending a limp hand.

What a fucking nightmare.

Randy, started hyperventilating. "Oh my God," he kept saying, over and over.

I walked into their apartment, which was immaculately clean, and I tried to get Randy to calm down. "Look, man, this is no big deal," I kept saying. "Just chill."

We sat down on a leather sofa, and once Randy had gotten his wits about him, he reached under their glass coffee table. "You have to sign my album," he said, giving me a dark blue picture book.

I opened it up and I couldn't help but laugh. The book was filled with pictures of wrestlers, or at least wrestler's crotches. Randy flipped through and stopped.

"That's you," he said.

Yes, it was. I looked at a picture that was supposed to be me getting pinned, with another wrestler laying on my chest. Instead, the picture was nothing but my crotch. He gave me a pen and I signed.

"You know I can't stay," I told him, and he looked like a wounded puppy. "No one can know about me, right?"

"Oh yeah, of course," Randy said. Behind him, Johnny nodded.

"If I read online tomorrow that you met me and I'm gay, I'm going to have to come back here and beat the fuck out of you," I said.

Their eyes were wide.

I hated saying it, but I had to. It wasn't me, but I had to become someone I wasn't to cover up the secret.

So I left. He was way too feminine for me anyway. I'd have to try to find love online elsewhere.

On the drive home, I thought about why I disliked feminine gays so much. Part of me disliked them because they cast a bad stereotype on gay men, but the more I thought about it, the more I realized I was being hypocritical. They were being honest with themselves, while I wasn't. I was afraid of people disliking me, but there I was, disliking them.

(29)

NEGOTIATIONS

As the marketing and training for Blood Runs Cold wore on, I knew the other guys were making more money than me. For Bryan Clark, who played Wrath, it made sense. He was a veteran of *WrestleMania* and I didn't mind him making a high salary. I'd heard he was making about $275,000 a year. *No big deal*, I thought. But for Glacier — a guy who'd never before been on TV — to come in and make $210,000 a year, that seemed a little much, compared to the $30,000 I was making. I'd been to multiple wrestling leagues now, and I'd been in the WCW for more than a year. The worst of all was probably Ernest Miller who was Eric Bischoff's kid's karate instructor. Ernest "the Cat" Miller had never done anything in wrestling, yet he was making $250,000 annually. I thought that was absurd.

Of course, I didn't have an agent. The only ones who did were the Hulk Hogans of the world, those who were established. It didn't make sense to have one because you didn't have much bargaining power. If I threatened to back out, Eric could just find someone else to do the job. But Eric was a fan of martial arts, so Ernest could get his money, and Ernest had some experience in martial arts tournaments.

In March 1997, I told Page I wanted a meeting with Bischoff. Practices with the Blood Runs Cold gang were strained, in part because I could not believe the other wrestlers were making more money than me. My anger focused all on one person: Ernest Miller.

"You've got to lock up tight, like this," I said, during one of our first practices in the ring. I showed him the proper way to do it. He didn't care. He almost didn't even pay attention.

"Locking up," he said, smiling. "You know, in karate, we don't have to lock up. We just kick ass."

At that point I was 26 years old and the business of wrestling was an absolute obsession. *If you're in the business, you need to respect it and love it*, I thought. Ernest didn't do that — he didn't take it seriously and he didn't respect those of us who did.

We worked every day at the Power Plant — and we trained him from scratch, taking eight months to do it. We got up every morning, got down to the Power Plant and were in the ring from 10 a.m. to 2 p.m., then we'd go to karate class until 5. From there, we'd head back to the gym for cardio and leave around 8 or 9.

Ernest making more money was a travesty, being that he was so disrespectful. On top of that, he was overweight. And while we took our training very seriously, he had the biggest job: He had to learn how to wrestle, then incorporate it into martial arts, then try to figure out how to make a character.

Miller strolled in and out whenever he wanted, and what hurt the most was he wasn't good. Actually, he was one of the worst wrestlers I'd ever seen.

Mitchell said it best: "When you punch him in the face, he does the Swarm of Bees," he said.

That meant Miller would wave his arms around and try to swat bees from his face. It didn't matter what move you put on him. You could kick him in the stomach and he would do it.

"Dude," I would say, "you may want to try something different. A different reaction could be good."

"I'm a world champion in karate, and you guys aren't world champions in wrestling," he said.

Right there he showed how clueless he was.

"We don't need to learn karate from you," I said. "You need to learn wrestling from us, because that's the name of the game."

Several times we got heated and had to be held back. But it was guys like Miller that made me wonder if we could pull it all off. And to think he was getting paid so much, while we were showing him how to do everything. Something about it just wasn't right.

Brian and Ray always felt bad for me. Brian never let me pay for anything, and he went out of his way because he thought it was unfair. We knew we weren't going to get the nWo-like push, but we were working so hard together, we knew we'd have something, and with Eric there for us, we were really optimistic.

Later, a large group of us went to a KISS concert in Atlanta. I sat with Glacier, and as we walked around, talking to people before the show, he turned toward the stage.

"Look at all of this, man," he said. "A year from now, we won't be able to do this without being bombarded with autograph requests."

I hoped that was true. I'd been gaining a little more steam within the company, even though I hadn't been on TV, I did create a finishing move for Page for a pay-per-view. In the process he taught me a big lesson:

"The people will believe what you tell them—if you keep telling them it," Page said. So he did. For weeks, he kept telling crowds he was going to perform the Most Dangerous Finish on the Planet at the pay-per-view. Now we just had to come up with something.

I had the idea of Page using his diamond-cutter move on four guys in a row. Then he would pin all of them in reverse order. But by that time, the first opponent would have come out of it, so they would wrestle again, and Page would land the diamond-cutter again for the final pin.

It worked beautifully.

But all that time off of television had me scared. It was well known that Bischoff could fire those who were "out of sight, out of mind." He fired Stone Cold Steve Austin, who had been hurt, and I was a big fan of him. I told Page to tell Bischoff not to fire him.

"This place is crazy," Austin said. "If you don't show your face, people forget about you, or they fire you."

Two weeks later, he was fired.

✱

Eric wanted to see a different kind of fighting style, but I also knew people didn't want to see karate; they wanted to see wrestling. So we created a new style. Obviously, we wanted to incorporate a lot of martial-arts style kicking, extensions and arm movements. We came up with an idea where I would be thrown into the ropes, and Ray would follow me there, rolling then jumping to elbow me in the chest as I came off the ropes. Another move involved Ray outside the ring, leaning against the ring posts as someone held a chair above his head. I used a super kick to send the chair into his head.

I was a fan of ultimate fighting, so I was imitating Ken Shamrock, who had a stance with his hands out in front of him, palms forward. It was something that just looked different.

We also knew our entrances would be unique. We spent $250,000 for a snow system for Glacier. The whole arena would be dark, filled with powerful martial arts music.

We were doing everything Eric wanted, and doing it well, so I was confident going into our meeting. I didn't have a set figure in mind. I knew what the other guys were making, but I didn't know how high I should go. I was thinking $85,000 — a little more than double, but not triple what I was making.

I made the trip up to the nice office again, and I was nervous through the initial exchange of niceties. Then Bischoff casually dropped the question I'd been dreading.

"How's Ernest coming along?" he asked.

I had to think before I responded. "He needs patience," I said. "He does what he does real well."

"Well, you make him look good. I heard you don't get along real well."

Shit. "Well, I get along with a lot of people, but not with everyone. I just think we have different perspectives on wrestling."

"I know what you mean," he said. I felt better. He'd heard about Miller's bad attitude. "So, you're here for what?"

I swallowed hard. "Well, I've been working here for over a year, and I think I'm doing well." I told him my life story about how I love wrestling, which I'd written down on a sheet of paper. I got all the way up to college, describing how I found wrestling schools, how I was making $70,000 a year but quit to make $40 a night wrestling. I told him how my parents were angry.

"But, Eric, I was happier making $40 a night than $70,000 per year," I said.

"Chris, put the paper down," Eric said. "Stop reading the paper. Tell me what's in your heart."

I stopped. I thought back to a conversation I'd had with Page.

"To tell you the truth, Eric, DDP told me that you thought I was sitting on my ass, and that sitting on your ass and making $30,000 a year isn't bad," I said. "If you think I have been sitting on my ass, you're out of your fucking mind. I want this gimmick to work. I need this gimmick to work. And to hear that really hurts."

There was silence in the large room. I think both of us were shocked I was that honest.

"Let me explain," Eric said. "When I came here from Minnesota, I had a wife and kids, and I had to collect cans and cash them in to put food on my table. We had to struggle to make ends meet. When I hear $30,000 a year, it means a lot more to me. When I say you were doing nothing, it doesn't mean you were doing nothing, it just means you're not collecting cans. That's hard work."

He drummed his fingers on the desk. I sat back, feeling very small. I was grateful he opened up to me, but at the same time, how could I ask for more money after hearing that?

"How much were you thinking?" he asked me.

Fuck. How could I ask for $85,000 now? I started thinking. Two times 30 was 60, and I could back off that — $55,000.

"How about $55,000 per year?" I asked.

"I can't do that," he said.

What? I thought. "Why?"

"I was thinking 100."

I thought he meant $100 a week. It took me a minute. Did he mean one hundred *thousand* dollars a year?

"Do you mean $100,000 a year?" I asked.

"Yes."

I didn't hesitate. "I'll take it," I said, shaking his hand. "Thank you so much."

I went down to the lobby and again called my parents. This time, there were three people crying on the phone.

(30)

DEATH ON THE AUTOBAHN?

While nWo dominated North America, Blood Runs Cold was shipped over to Europe to promote the new characters. In Germany, they'd been seeing the promos introducing Ray. They knew that supposedly, the world was about to change. The Christmas tour was going to give Ray and I a chance to work together a little bit. The names on tour included: Alex Wright, Big Van Vader, Lex Luger, Buff Bagwell, Eddie Guerrero, Harlem Heat, Disco and Paul Orndorff.

After arriving in Germany — with all of my gear — we stopped at our hotel, where I heard there was an enclosed pool on the roof. I went up to check it out, and the first thing I saw was three young women, walking around topless, their perfect bronze bodies there for everyone to see. I was not in Atlanta anymore.

I looked over and sitting down, sipping a drink, was Paul Orndorff, the legendary Florida wrestler who played football and was known as "Mr. Wonderful." Orndorff had come up through the Memphis territory with Lawler, and he was always a favorite of mine growing up. Unfortunately, he had a nerve injury that caused his arms to atrophy a little. He must have been close to 50 by that time.

I left to go back downstairs. I met up with Disco, and as it turns out, we were also matched up with Orndorff on the trip. The three of us met in the lobby before going out to dinner.

"Chris, did you go up to the roof?" Orndorff asked me.

"As a matter of fact I did," I said. "I saw you up there."

"Oh my God, those women," he said, like a dirty old man. He closed his eyes. "I started to imagine me saying, 'You come over and gimme blowjob?' and one saying yes. After, I'd just say, 'Thank you for blowjob.'"

Disco and I couldn't handle it. We laughed like we were in third grade.

"What?" Orndorff asked. "I just want her to gimme a blowjob."

✶

Ray and I had our match down.

When it came time to perform in front of the German crowd, we did, and it went fine. That's the best word for it — fine. The intro was great — Ray had the ice and the snow. I came out with the spotlights and smoke. It was very entertaining.

"Something's missing," Orndorff told us.

We'd taped it, and later we tried to figure out what was amiss. I was almost 27, and only five years into the business — I didn't have the experience to see what was needed. But it was obvious when I performed that there was no intensity in the match when I got on Glacier. I wasn't vicious enough.

"You need more energy," said Orndorff, who had experience as an aggressive heel. "You need to be more vicious."

"Thanks, Paul, I'll work on it," I said.

But I kind of rolled it off because being vicious was what he did.

In reality, he was right. I didn't know it then. We still got a good reaction from the crowd, and at the time, I thought that was good enough.

I was wrong.

✶

We never should have let Orndorff drive on the Autobahn.

The WCW paid a young guy to drive us around, and when Orndorff told him to take us to the Autobahn (where there are no speed limits), the young kid knew he could not let Orndorff take the wheel.

Disco and I knew Orndorff was legitimately crazy, we just didn't know how crazy he was.

"Please let me drive, kid," Orndorff begged.

The kid — no more than 20 — just kept smiling and shaking his head no. I don't think he spoke English. The windy road was also covered in fresh snow.

"I can't believe this shit," Orndorff said, as we laughed from the backseat of our BMW. Orndorff loved to smoke, and in Germany they had a kind of snuff, a flavored tobacco you actually snort up your nose.

He showed the kid the snuff. "How about I give you some if you let me drive?" he asked.

The kid looked at the snuff, then the wheel. He nodded his head yes. Disco and I were shaking ours no.

The kid pulled over, and they switched places. Orndorff gave him some snuff and then the terror began.

The old wrestler grabbed the wheel and turned into a child riding his first tricycle. The speedometer topped out at 120 mph, and we were fairly certain we were going to die.

"Yeahhhhh!" Orndorff screamed.

The situation only got worse when he jammed too much snuff into his nostril and screamed again — this time in pain as it burned his nose.

"Take the wheel kid!" I screamed from the back.

"Kid, if you don't, we die!" Disco shouted.

Whether he knew English or not didn't matter. The kid saw Orndorff pull his hands from the wheel to his burning face. The driver reached over and grabbed the wheel. He contorted his body so that his leg could reach the brake. He jammed his foot on Orndorff's.

The world spun as the car made doughnuts on the most famous freeway in the world. When we came to a stop, we were all alive. Orndorff's face still hurt a bit, though.

Disco looked to me. "How do you say 'Thank you' in German?"

✻

Orndorff might have been crazy, but he had a good reason — concussions.

Essentially bruises on the brain, concussions are a part of all contact sports, including wrestling. As in football, the head is constantly jostled in wrestling, and falling to the mat, or taking a misplaced chair shot sometimes resulted in a concussion.

I remember my first: it happened at Pete's during a practice. My head slammed to the mat and I saw a bright flash. Opening my eyes, it was difficult to get up. I suffered an intense bout of déjà vu, and for a moment, I wondered what had happened. Later, I went home suffering from nausea.

I would suffer 10 more concussions during various times in my career. It was just part of the job. But that didn't mean it wasn't serious. Concussions can result in severe brain damage, memory loss and worse. I knew Orndorff had a problem when we were talking to him one night at a German bar.

Orndorff had wrestled for a long while, and Disco and I were well versed in the history of the sport. During the course of the conversation, it seemed we knew Orndorff's career better than he did.

We knew that Orndorff made his WWF debut as a heel, trained by Piper, in the early 1980s. It was then Orndorff took the name "Mr. Wonderful."

"No, I came in as a good guy, then wrestled Hulk in *WrestleMania*," Orndorff insisted.

I looked to Disco. We had only been at the bar a few minutes. Orndorff wasn't drunk.

"Are you sure about that?" I asked him. "You were involved in a pretty big storyline with Piper when you came in."

"No," he said again. "I wrestled Hogan when I came in."

Wrong. Disco and I knew that the night Orndorff made his debut, Hogan beat the Sheik for the title. Again, I looked to Disco, who shrugged. Orndorff was involved in one of the biggest storylines in wrestling history, debuting with Piper as a heel, but he didn't remember it.

We were convinced Orndorff's concussions had clouded his memory. How else would you forget?

✱

Nights out in Germany with those guys were always eye-opening. It was strange seeing them, the same people I'd grown up watching, in social environments. I learned about them as people, and sometimes it wasn't pretty. One night we were out with Big Van Vader, a 400-pound behemoth from Colorado. He was talking to Orndorff and they were both using racial slurs. I grew up in a very racially diverse environment, and I wasn't comfortable with those kinds of words. It felt awkward *not* to say anything, but I didn't want to be called out.

I remembered a time in the mid-1980s when Orndorff was going against Mr. T, and Orndorff acted like a monkey and called him a porch monkey. I remembered watching that and thinking how brutal the match looked for Mr. T.

This explained why a lot of the things they did looked so real.

I had to leave. I couldn't stand it anymore. I made an excuse and went back to my room.

*

I'd always thought Vader was dumb. Once I watched as he broke a guy's back in North Carolina. Another time, he told Hogan he was going to do the shooting star press — and at 400 pounds, he almost killed himself. Then there was the night he messed with Paul Orndorff. It was the worst backstage fight I would ever see. Before a Bash on the Beach, Orndorff came backstage to let us know it was time to get ready. For some reason, Van Vader ignored him. Vader was always a bully, and because he was so big, he got his way — most of the time.

But even with atrophied arms, Orndorff was an amazing wrestler.

"Vader, you got an interview," Orndorff said. "You got to get ready early."

Vader, sitting across from me in a chair in our office, didn't move.

Ten minutes later, Orndorff came back. Vader was still sitting in his chair. "Hey," he said, pointing at Vader, "get ready. You've got an interview."

It was time for me to leave to get ready, so I did. And when I came back, I saw something that took me completely off guard — Vader was on the floor, and Orndorff was kicking him in the face.

I followed the fight as it spilled over into a dressing room. People were screaming and when Vader came out, his entire face was swollen shut. He could barely see out of his eyes. The walls were splattered with blood.

In the other corner stood Orndorff, who didn't even look like he'd been in a fight. He breathed heavily, staring at Vader.

Vader came back at him, because he apparently hadn't learned his lesson. So Orndorff beat the shit out of him again — with one arm. He was too quick, his moves too precise, and with Vader already blinded, the fight was even easier than when it began. Technically, as a fighter, Orndorff was amazing, and Vader learned it that night. He never had problems with Vader again.

(31)

THE RETURN OF KIDMAN, THE DEBUT OF BLOOD RUNS COLD

Germany was an interesting time, but I was ready to get back to America, so we could work on our gimmick and make it better for the U.S. debut.

By the spring of 1997, my career was flourishing. I was back at the Power Plant working out. Every few months, the Plant would give tryouts for guys who wanted to be in the Show. They would test people by making them do squats—1,000 of them, with breaks after every 200. Then there were sit-ups and running. It was all a test of heart, and I understood. You want your wrestlers to have heart.

Sgt. Buddy Lee Parker, who had a state trooper gimmick that he used, ran the tests. He was very tough and very physical, and he pushed the kids to get the most out of them.

I always wondered if some of my friends could come up for those tryouts.

It'd been a year since I had last talked with Kidman, and I thought about how he was doing. I'd read in one of the newsletters that WCW was thinking of signing Rey Mysterio, a little guy—just five-six and 160 pounds—who would fly around the ring, and he really impressed Kidman. They weren't talking of bringing in any other guys, but a sliver of door had opened.

Mysterio had to have someone to fight, someone of comparative size and skill. Someone like Kidman.

I immediately talked to DDP. "If they bring in Mysterio, we're going to need someone to fight him."

He agreed. "Do you know anybody?"

I told him about a kid I knew in Pennsylvania. A talented guy named Billy Kidman.

Page talked to Bischoff, who told us to bring him in. He wanted us to try him out.

I got to make the call.

We'd only talked once or twice after we'd left Memphis. But for 18 months, I kept tabs on him. I knew he was successful up there — he'd won some tournaments, and he'd been making a name for himself, even though it was just a small, independent league. He'd even won the Super 8 — a gathering of the best cruiserweights in the country.

Kidman and I both tended to isolate ourselves sometimes, but when we finally reconnected, it was as if we never stopped.

When I called him up, I could tell he was happy to hear from me.

"I see you're doing well," I said. "I've got some good news for you."

"Yeah?"

"Yeah. They're thinking of bringing in Mysterio. But they need someone to fight him."

"Really?" I could hear the excitement in his voice.

"I think if you can make it down here for a tryout, you'd do well," I said. "They're excited about you."

"I'll see you tomorrow," he said.

And the next day, Kidman came to Atlanta.

I knew that was the kind of response I would get. I'd gone to bat for him, because I knew he would want it. And of course, he did.

✱

I picked up the excited Kidman at the airport the next day and took him over to the Power Plant. There were only a few people there, but we just got in the ring and did our thing. We knew each other's moves, and could read each other just like Flair and Steamboat. It didn't take long for people to notice. I introduced everyone to Kidman, and then — when enough people were around, I told them to watch his finishing move — the shooting star press.

He landed it. The whole gym went nuts.

Page got on the phone.

"Yeah, Eric?" he said. "We found our man."

Right off the bat, Kidman signed a deal for $700 a week.

✷

The Blood Runs Cold gimmick made its debut that year, with Glacier coming out first, over Christmas. The plan all along was to build up Glacier, to make him into a super good guy. Then, on the other side, build me up as a super bad guy. It was unique watching part of your own angle starting, knowing I was going to debut later in the year.

Glacier's entrance was phenomenal, with laser lights, snow falling from the ceiling, and music coordinated to a series of kicks and punches. Nothing could have lived up to the hype of changing the world, but that was cool. Glacier went on to win a few matches. It was important for him to start off with a winning streak, so the fans got into it. Then we could introduce me as his enemy, and the rivalry would begin.

But I could already tell there were some chinks in the armor. There was almost too much karate at times, and I could tell the fans didn't love it as much as we thought they would. Glacier's signature kick, the Cryonic Kick, wasn't going over so well, and with each week, he was getting fewer cheers. Part of it was because the kicks were so good, the opponents he was pitted against were shying away from the contact.

It didn't look good at all.

In the original plan, we were supposed to shoot promos for me too. Mitchell and I were supposed to be on a boat, heading back to face Glacier. There would be smoke, and bats and skulls all over the boat. Dozens of guys would be rowing the boat as I peered into the distance, waiting for my chance to take Glacier down.

None of that ever happened. And after three months of fighting, Glacier did not beat a top-level wrestler. They told us we would be on pay-per-view, then they told us we wouldn't.

The only build-up we did was Mortis and Mitchell doing an interview. There, we got to explain how Mitchell's character found Mortis at the underground wrestling tournament in Thailand. But we didn't get to do enough to set up the rivalry.

I was able to get in one great line, though.

When the announcer asked us what we thought of taking on Glacier, I answered, in my raspy voice, "What is a Glacier? It's a slow moving block of ice."

It was all a lot of fun. But still, you just got the feeling that with nWo still going strong, we were being left behind.

✶

Mortis debuted that spring in Charleston, South Carolina.

We were nervous. After all the training, the creating of the costumes, and the expectations, this was it. I was frustrated because we were promised a build-up, but I felt we'd gotten nothing. I had a gut feeling Glacier was going to win the match, but I thought I should win to make up for the three-month push he'd gotten.

After looking at the footage from Germany, we realized Paul was right. I needed to sell the character more, so we worked on it. We were all concerned about what the crowd reaction would be like.

As soon as we got to the building, they called us into the office and told us what they wanted.

"Glacier wins," Kevin said.

I bit my tongue. Glacier hadn't been getting the best crowd reaction, and because I was under a mask, I knew few people would know me. Still, that's what they wanted. It was time to put on the show.

Before the entrance, Jim and I waited behind the curtain. I looked over to him.

"Welcome to the Show, buddy," I said, offering a hand.

"Welcome to the fucking Show, my man," he said, shaking it.

✶

The entrance was everything we wanted it to be. The lights were lowered for each of us, and when Glacier came in, the snow and music rained down. Classic. For me, they played an eerie organ music, which added to the overall creepiness of the scene.

When we entered the ring, we were ready. We showed our innovative stuff—I would throw him into the ropes, then roll with him, and kick him as we bounced off. We used the chair, and kicked it into each other. The crowd loved that move. But because Glacier hadn't defeated a big-name wrestler yet, they had no idea how to take him.

At ringside, Jim, in a black suit, green tie and ponytail, was screaming. He was talking about where I was from, filling in more of our history.

"Remember Taipei!" he yelled. "Take him out like you did in Taipei!"

When Glacier used the Cryonic Kick to pin me at the end of our nine-minute match, the crowd roared, and my spirits soared despite having to take the loss.

As soon as the match was over, Wrath made his debut appearance to save me. Then Jim hit Glacier with what we called our "skeleton stick" — basically, a black walking stick with a skeleton on the tip. I started beating the hell out of Glacier, so in this case, everyone won. Glacier got the victory, but I got some of my heat back by beating him up at the end.

It was a good start.

We still believed the gimmick could be big. While the nWo had the angle, we had the tools. We were innovative and new, and we all thought we were tapping into that Martial Arts craze. This could make us all big, big stars.

Unfortunately, we were wrong.

(32)

HEELS, SULLIVAN AND THE BUCKET

A week before my rematch with Glacier, I hurt my heel.

On the bottom of our wrestling boots there is a dense foam, thicker than a wrestling mat, which provides some cushion when you land. I was always taught that when you land, you spread your body as much as you can, from your ass to your back to your legs, and you bend your legs so your feet can take the impact.

But for the Mortis character, I didn't wear any wrestling boots. I used amateur wrestling shoes, which have no padding, just a little rubber on the bottom. But I still took falls the same way, and my feet were suffering the consequences.

Everyone at the Power Plant knew that when I practiced, I went 110 percent. Sometimes, like Page told me when he first watched me, going that hard in practice wasn't a good thing. During one practice leading up to the Glacier rematch, I hit my left heel hard and instantly, I knew it was really bad. I could barely walk.

"What am I going to do?" I asked Page. "I've got to go on in two days."

I'd only been featured on one other pay-per-view in my career. This was a big deal, and I didn't want to look bad. I visited a massage therapist and that didn't work. I got a hydrocortisone shot, and the pain still wouldn't go away. Finally, Page gave me one last option.

"Have you thought about acupuncture?" he asked.

"Like, someone sticking a bunch of needles in me?"

"Yeah."

I thought about it. "Man, I'll try anything."

"I know a place," he said.

As we drove down to Atlanta's Little Five Points area, I thought about the predicament. I'd never even considered anything like acupuncture as a real solution to help injuries, but at this stage of my career — and at this stage of the gimmick — I needed to be OK. If acupuncture could help, I needed to give it a try. Everything in wrestling starts with the feet. You could never fake your way through a match with hurting feet.

Atlanta's Little Five Points neighborhood was like stepping into another world, one filled with incense, beads, pictures of dragons and funky music. It was Bohemian and strange — and it appealed to me because it was different and it didn't care.

Page pulled the car into a parking spot on the side of the street. He got out and led the way.

"Here it is," he said, pointing to a shop that looked like something from Chinatown — discreet, with no name or sign, just a placard in a dark window that read "Open."

Inside, the room was dark, its walls covered in paintings of dragons and other mystical scenes. I could smell incense burning in another room and it almost made me dizzy. From a back room, a small Asian man appeared, dressed in a black robe. He looked like Mr. Miyagi from *The Karate Kid* movies.

"Hello," Page said as he bowed. "My friend needs help with pain in his foot."

Miyagi said something I could not understand.

"In his foot," Page said, and he pointed to my heel.

I had to balance on my good heel, so as not to put weight on the other. And when Miyagi saw me in obvious pain, he understood. He said something to Page and clapped his hands. Then he looked to me.

"Come," he said.

I followed him to the back room, which was behind a dark curtain. There, a young Asian girl, who I assumed was Miyagi's daughter, stood in front of a bed. Behind her, there was a long tray filled with dozens of needles. The needles were also hooked up to electrodes.

"Welcome to the world of electrical acupuncture," Page said.

"I hope this works." I took off the jacket I was wearing and laid down on the bed. For the next 30 minutes, thin needles, almost like tiny hairs, were used to cover my entire heel, foot and upper ankle. Small wires ran from those needles back to a machine, and I could feel bursts of energy running through my foot. Strangely, as I felt the energy, I also began to lose the feeling of pain.

When the young girl began taking the needles out, I could still feel the warmth of the energy, and when she was finished, I didn't feel any pain.

"Amazing," I said to Page. "The pain is gone. I don't feel any pain at all."

"They know what they're doing," Page replied.

I got off the bed and put my full weight on the heel. Nothing.

"Oh my God," I said. I jumped up and down, landing on my previously throbbing heel. "I can't believe this. These people work miracles."

Then Miyagi came back into the room. He handed me a slip of paper. "Forty dollars," he said, smiling.

For forty dollars I was healed. I would've paid four times that amount. I handed over the money and walked out of the shop.

"Well," Page said. "What do you think?"

"I'm a believer," I said. "I can go wrestle right now."

✱

The next day I was to take part in a live event, the last show we'd film before the important pay-per-view. My ankle and heel felt wonderful, and I was confident the pain wouldn't return, but I had another issue.

I was sick. As in, I had a bad case of diarrhea.

All day that Saturday I spent hours on the john, wondering why I had to get sick. Why, after I'd just fixed my foot problem, did I have to come down with some shitty stomach bug? What rotten luck.

All my friends knew I was sick, and word got around to the producers and writers that I wasn't feeling good. I was really hoping that would convince them not to use me in that night's show. But I should've known better.

I should've known Kevin Sullivan would screw me.

When I came into the arena that night, I hoped for the least amount of work to do. I was in no shape. Instead, Sullivan had me doing the most work possible. He had me coming out from underneath the ring to attack Wrath. I could have cried.

Under the ring?

He knew that in order to pull off the illusion of having a wrestler come out from under the ring, the wrestler would actually have to be there, waiting, under the ring, for about three hours. The wrestler would have to be dressed in full costume and under the ring before the studio audience arrived, then the wrestler would have to wait throughout the entire show until it was time to burst onto the scene, land his moves, and rush backstage.

Three hours underneath that fucking ring. But I had to do it. Kevin told me to, and I did not want to show weakness, so I did it.

There's an old trick wrestlers use when they had to wait under the ring for surprise moments like this. They took a bucket with them. They took toilet paper. They took a book or something to keep them occupied, and a small TV to watch the proceedings. If you had to go, you went in the bucket.

I'll have to do that too, I thought.

So I did. I waited down there for three hours, and when the time came, I put on my Mortis suit, went out and did my job. The match went off without a hitch and I looked great on TV. But I did not feel great.

I used the bucket three times.

And when I was finished wrestling, I had to hit the toilet again.

But I did it. And I never said anything about it to anyone. I couldn't complain, because then Kevin would know he'd gotten to me. I didn't want that to happen.

But to this day, I've always wondered one thing. I wonder who had to clean up that God-awful mess I left behind?

✱

That Sunday, we wrestled on the pay-per-view. I'd gotten over the stomach ailment and I was good to go.

But I was still frustrated. I lost to Glacier again, and Ernest made his debut. He had an uphill battle never having wrestled before. The fans didn't know who he was, and I don't think he was comfortable. He was somewhat charismatic, but wrestling never was his realm.

He was very consistent on the style of his kicks, and when he fought me, we could make it look like he took my head off. Most guys would just throw up their hands to block a kick, but I didn't have to. I made it actually look like he was kicking me in the face. It became known as "taking the kick," and the crowd went nuts for him when he fought me.

But it was tougher when he faced others. We knew all of this was working up to one big tag-team match the following month. But in reality, I think we all knew this was it — this was going to be the end of the feud. No other characters would be added, like we'd discussed. We were not going to be licensing any merchandise or getting built up anymore, as we'd discussed. We were officially eclipsed by the nWo, and because of that — and Sullivan's reluctance to give us any help — we were fading in the eyes and minds of the fans. They didn't know who to cheer for or care about. It was falling fast.

We put a lot of time and effort into our moves and making them as good as we could. As much as we'd been fighting with Sullivan, we still felt like we'd come a long way, and that even made it more gratifying. The fans weren't 100 percent behind it, but they also weren't totally bored with it, either. They thought it was interesting, and that was OK.

We had one shot to make it into something bigger — the Bash at the Beach tag-team match the next month. It was like the World Series for Blood Runs Cold. We knew that if we did well there, we may have something special.

✱

A month of training later, in July, we were ready. It was the shot we'd waited for. We were going to be featured as a tag team, fighting each other in the opening match, and everyone would be watching.

When we got to the arena that night, we were told Wrath and Mortis would defeat Glacier for the first time. It was up to us to decide how to do it. We had all of our moves down, and we thought we had what it took to make it look amazing.

Halfway through the match, we all knew we were doing spectacular. We wanted to keep trying out new things, and we also wanted to get Mitchell involved.

One of the best moments came when Wrath picked up Ray for a power-bomb, pulling him onto his shoulders. I grabbed Ray's neck and rested it on my shoulder. With Ray's legs around Wrath's head, and his shoulders on my shoulders, Wrath dropped to a knee, while I dropped to my ass. We called it the Power-Bomb Neck-Breaker, and the crowd loved it. We also used a leg-drop to the back of the head, which looked good, and we worked in a reverse Boston crab, which Bobby Bald Eagle taught me.

With each kick and move we made, the crowd responded with cheers. It was the best thing we'd ever heard. As we neared the 10-minute mark, it was time to finish.

We had something special planned.

My foot was close to the ring apron, so Jim came out with a large chain and looped it over my foot. I stood up and put a spinning kick on Glacier, a move we called the Super Kick. Having the chain on my foot when I kicked was a little extra something, and the crowd loved it.

The only problem? I hit Ray in the chest. I was supposed to kick him in the jaw.

No matter. Ray hit the mat after the Super Kick and I covered him — one, two, three for the pin. We'd won the feud. The crowd roared.

Afterward, I was a little upset I didn't land the kick right into his jaw, but it was hard not to love what we'd just accomplished. We wrestled the perfect match — or at least as close to it as we could've come.

"Hell yeah, man!" Ray said, high-fiving me.

The five of us hugged and let the moment sink in. We did exactly what we wanted to do.

"Hey, guys," a man was tapping me on the shoulder. I looked over. It was one of the production guys. "Kevin wants to see you in the booking room."

"Oh fuck," I said. "Here we go."

"Same old shit," Mitchell said, imitating Sullivan. "'You've done too much.' 'You need to hold back.'"

"Yep," Glacier said.

Still amped with adrenaline, we headed for the booking room. There, Terry and Kevin stared at us as we walked in. When we all made it into the small room, both Sullivan and Terry stood up and clapped for us.

We couldn't believe it.

"That was one hell of a match guys," Sullivan said. "That's what an opening match is supposed to look like."

I got goose bumps. It felt like redemption to us.

"Thanks," Ray said.

"Yeah, it would've been perfect if you could have just caught him in the chin with that last kick, Chris," Terry said.

That itself was like a kick in the chin. Of course, they would use that one instance to get us back. But the match was so good, I couldn't let that bother me. It was just about 10 minutes of perfect wrestling.

Behind the curtain, me, Jim and Wrath wondered aloud if we'd done enough to keep the gimmick going.

"I have to think they're going to keep us all together," Jim said.

"It was too good," Wrath added. "It was too good not to let us keep going."

I agreed. "We're better together than apart. I think they'll keep us together."

They didn't. Even after wrestling a near-perfect match, one that resonated in the minds of fans, we hadn't done enough. And looking back, I realize we never could have done enough. The plans had been changing from day one, and after the Bash at the Beach, Blood Runs Cold was officially over.

(33)

FRUSTRATIONS

The Mortis character would go on to have a successful eight-month run. By October, I'd be moving on to other things. But up until that fall, Wrath and I (still as Mortis) were repackaged as a tag team, and we went on to feud with another team called the Faces of Fear, two guys I'd known because they also had an affiliation with Afa.

The Faces of Fear were two huge boys from Samoa, related to the entire Samoan clan. One was named Barbarian, the other Meng. They knew about my training under Afa, and we had bonded over that when we first met at the Power Plant more than a year ago. They were good guys, and talented, and we liked each other from the start.

That's why it was so strange when, during our first match with them, the two Samoans started giving me and Wrath a real beating. Within the first minute of the match, things turned brutal. There was no acting: real punches were thrown and real blood poured from our faces. They were physically dominating us — both were six-two and they weighed a combined 600 pounds. And Meng was one of the toughest guys in the business. There were legendary stories of him getting into fights with 10 men in a bar — and they always ended with how Meng beat them all. He was the last man I would want to get in a real fight with.

And that day in the ring, we were in a real fight.

"Fuck," I said, after I took the first punch from Meng. I looked over to Mitchell at ringside, and his eyes were big. He mouthed the words "Oh shit."

At that point, Wrath and I were faced with a decision. Sometimes in wrestling, for whatever reason, guys will start trying to hurt you. I'd learned it from Pete in New York. He said to always be ready, and this was one of those times. But how to react? Do you take the beating, or do you fight back? We had to respect these guys because they had been in the business longer than us. But we also didn't want to get our assess kicked. There's a certain amount of pride on the line, because you absolutely do not want to look like a pussy. The decisions you make in situations like the one Wrath and I faced set the tone for the rest of a wrestler's career.

The question remained: What to do?

You can't fight back in full force for two reasons. First, your job is to make the fight look real and follow the script. That leads into the second reason: No matter how hard you fight, you will not win. But we decided we needed to give something back. We had to, for our pride, for our reputations and for some reprieve for our bloodied faces. On instinct, Wrath and I both decided to fight back.

I was the smallest one out there, so I was able to give back a little. I hit Meng in the face, enough to shock him, but not enough to really hurt him. He shook it off, and the strange thing was, his expression never changed. It was as if he expected it. When Wrath came back into the match, he did the same, and as the match went on, the beatings on us lessened a bit. They were becoming less violent as we gave back. They allowed us to.

We could see that they didn't want to take the real fighting any further. In wrestling, if someone hits you hard, and you hit back, it's called a receipt. When Wrath and I got our receipts, the beatings stopped, and we finished the match as scripted, with us winning.

We went behind the curtain, and we felt like we'd been in a war. The ridiculous irony of the situation is that wrestling protocol calls for you to go over, hug your opponent and say thank you. So we did.

My face was bloody, and when I went over to Meng, he shook my hand and leaned into my ear. "Business is business — you know what I mean, brother?" Meng said.

I just looked at him. "Yeah, I guess," I said.

He looked me in the eye, adding in that thick island accent, "You know what I mean — the bosses."

That's when I knew Sullivan told them to do it. If Meng and Barbarian even hesitated or questioned Sullivan when he asked them to do that, they would have been on the shit list. They had to.

Bischoff had set up the feud, and Bischoff had requested we win this match. Because Sullivan didn't agree with the feud, he told Meng and Barbarian to rough us up.

The feud ended up being pretty successful, lasting a month and leading up to a decent pay-per-view match. Later, Sullivan tried to sneak in a victory for them, but it was foiled when Bischoff asked me before the match if we were going to win.

"No," I said, pointing to Faces of Fear. "Sullivan said they're going to win."

"I don't think so," Bischoff said. And he changed it. I'm sure that just made Sullivan even angrier.

During this time I came with another big move — a suplex of Barbarian off the second rope, while I was on Wrath's shoulders. That turned out to be something people remembered, and it helped my reputation as a guy who could come up with innovative moves.

Sullivan just kept getting more pissed that we were getting popular. The next night on *Nitro* we wrestled Scott Hall and Kevin Nash for the tag team championship. The crowd got behind us, but we lost. Still, we didn't mind. We were becoming a top-level team, and it seemed like we were on the road to becoming household names.

✶

On the road, it was just like the good old days: Mitchell was there with me, along with Kidman. We were all in the Show, and we were all doing well.

Then things started to turn. For a while, it seemed as if Wrath and I were getting a push. But Bischoff's involvement had made Sullivan so angry, that when Bischoff was focusing on something else, Sullivan would bury us. We won against no-name teams, and interview time for Jim dwindled. I started to get stressed out.

And I started taking my frustrations out on the people around me.

During a taping session in Florida that fall, things boiled over. The three of us — Jim, Kidman and I — returned from a late dinner. We walked into our hotel and I was already irritated by their stupid conversations.

"No, you will never be that popular because people will not root for a shrimp like you," Mitchell told Kidman.

"What do you do?" Kidman fired back. "All you do is stand around and talk! You're not even necessary out there. You're lucky to even be here."

I could tell they were joking, but it was a sensitive area for both. Add in their low tolerance for alcohol, and the situation was about to escalate.

"Really?" Mitchell said. "Well, let's see you take me on right now, big guy."

And Mitchell pushed him. Hard. Kidman almost lost his balance, regained it and — as we entered the hotel lobby — charged at Jim. I caught him before he could do anything.

"Hey," I said to Jim. "Kidman is my friend. If you've got a problem with him you have a problem with me."

Jim stopped. "I got no problem," he said. "No problem at all."

But we all had problems.

Our hotel was more like an apartment for Jim and me. I slept in a bedroom and Jim had the TV area, with a bed that folded out from the wall. To get to my room, you had to pass through that TV area, which was never a pleasant sight.

In the music business, the ladies that follow you around are called groupies. In wrestling, they're called ring rats. The ring rats follow you around from town to town, and all they want is an in. They either want to fuck a wrestler, say they fucked a wrestler, or marry a wrestler. Some want to break into the business. And sometimes, it even works.

Not long after the incident between Jim and Kidman, I came home from dinner and a taping ready for sleep. I unlocked the door, stepped into the TV area and threw my keys on a side table.

There, on the pullout bed, I saw Mitchell's white ass up in the air as he grinded on a local ring rat. Her moans of what I could only imagine to be fake joy filled the room, as did Jim's grunting. It was a disgusting scene, and the only thing I could do was grab my keys, turn around and leave. I stayed with Kidman that night.

The next morning, I returned, and found Mitchell asleep, face down on the bed.

"Get the fuck up," I said.

He rolled over and opened an eye. "Wha—?"

"Get up."

He opened the other. "Hey, man. Didn't hear you come in last ni—"

I slapped him across the face.

Immediately, he covered up his face with his hands and rolled over. He was naked under the sheet. "What the fuck, man?" he said.

I walked to the other side of the bed and hit him with my fist. Even though he blocked his face with his hands, I knew it hurt him. "Owwww! Fuck! What the fuck's your problem?"

"You," I said. "Have some fucking courtesy not to fuck one of those rats when I'm here, OK?"

With that, I walked out.

Later, when we were back home in Atlanta, Mitchell apologized for the timing of his tryst. He also said he wanted to pay me back some money he'd borrowed. A few months prior to the Florida tapings, Mitchell decided it would be best to get his own apartment in Atlanta. I thought he was probably right.

"Look," he said to me on the phone. "I've saved $100 and I want to give it to you. I know I owe you some money, and I want to pay it back as prompt as I can."

"You don't have to do that," I said.

"I want to. It means a lot to me. Come on, I'll pick you up, we'll go eat and I'll take you back to my place."

"OK."

Something told me this could be a bad idea, but I let him pick me up in his car — an old, beat-up Cadillac. We got some food and I went over to his apartment anyway. It was my first time there — most of the time, he was still coming over to my place. From the outside, the apartment looked fine. It was simple and neat, red brick with white trim. Tasteful.

On the inside, I couldn't believe it.

"Hey," he said, opening the door. "Welcome."

I looked around. There were hundreds of crushed beer cans on the floor, covering up an old blue sofa and a tattered easy chair. Pizza boxes were littered about. The place smelled like a dirty bar — all old beer and stale food.

"I know I have the money somewhere. Gimme a minute," he said. He rifled through old newspapers and magazines, throwing trash from one side of the room to the next. I did not want to know what the bedroom or bathrooms looked like.

"Dude, it doesn't matter," I said.

"Yes, it does."

I kept getting more irritated, and part of me could not figure out why. I knew I should be laughing, but instead, I was getting so angry. Hulk-angry. I tried to control it as best I could.

After 20 minutes of looking, the search was called off.

"I'm sorry, man. I don't know what I did with it," he said. "When I find it, I'll get it to you."

"OK."

On the way back to my apartment, he could not stop talking about the money. "I mean, I just saw it, you know? Strange."

"Just pull up front when we get to my place, OK?" I said.

"OK."

As we pulled in to my building, he turned away from the front, and pulled into the back of the building. I lost it.

"What did I just say?" I screamed. "I asked you to pull into the front and you pulled around back! Fuck!"

"Hey, sorry, man I—"

I got out of the car, slammed the door and went to the rear of the beat-up Caddy. I kicked at the taillight once, then twice, then again, until I completely smashed out the glass.

"Kanyon, what the fuck are you doing?!"

His words echoed in my ear as I went into the building, went upstairs and slammed the door to my own apartment. I needed some time alone.

✶

Jim and I avoided one another for a while, until it was impossible to do so. The next week we roomed together in Columbia, South Carolina, our old stomping grounds. It felt good to be back in the area after being away, but Jim and I still did not socialize.

One night Wrath and I had been out to dinner, and when we got home, Jim was there, waiting for us. He hadn't made it home the previous night, and I wondered where he'd been. He was smiling.

"Where were you, anyway?" I said.

"I hooked up with a Rat," he said. His eyes were dancing.

"OK, so what?" Wrath said.

"So this time, I got video," he said, and he pulled out a tape.

Wrath started laughing. "No way."

"Oh yeah."

"Well, let's see it," Wrath said.

I could care less to see it. In fact, it just reminded me of walking in on him in our apartment. But still, they put in the tape.

And we started watching a bare-assed Mitchell as he had sex with a filthy-looking woman. It went on for a few minutes.

"Now watch this," he said.

We watched as Mitchell, holding the camera, pans over to a plastic bag. He opens the bag, and produces the Mortis mask — the very same one I wear in the ring! I couldn't believe it.

"Oh my God," Wrath said. I don't know if he was stunned or repulsed or both.

In the video, Mitchell puts the mask on the Rat and starts fucking again.

Wrath was speechless. Mitchell was laughing. I felt the fury start to boil again. At the time, I felt protective of Mortis — it was my character. On the video, she started doing some of my moves while he fucked her.

It got worse.

He reached into the bag again and took out the Mortis stick — the one with the skull on the end — and he put the skull end inside of her.

That was it. I thought of Kidman. And the whores. And the car. And the money.

"You motherfucker!" I grabbed Jim and pushed him as hard as I could on to the bed.

"Now guys, calm down," Wrath said.

That's when things turned into some crazy Quentin Tarantino movie.

From his pants pocket, Jim drew a gun and pointed it straight at me. I couldn't think. I only reacted. I grabbed his neck and fell on him and onto the bed.

"Guys, what the fuck are you doing! Shit!" Wrath said. I could tell he was freaking out.

"Let the gun go," I told Jim.

"Let my fucking neck go," he said to me.

The exchange went on several more times before I became fed up.

"Fuck it," I said. I put my full weight on his wrist — either it was going to break, or he was going to let go. He let go. In the background, the moans of the homemade porno could still be heard.

I grabbed the gun and held it in my hand. I'd never held a gun before.

"You pulled a fucking gun on me," I said. Jim writhed in pain on the bed as he held his wrist.

"Well," he said, "you beat my car up. You beat me up. I had to protect myself, don't you think? How was I to know what you were going to do next?"

Wrath pointed at me. "*You* calm down. Jim, come with me." He pulled Jim from the bed and led him out of the room. I was alone.

I walked over to the TV and turned it off. Then I looked at the gun for the first time. It seemed old, like something from a Western movie. It was cocked back, so I clicked it back into place. Then I pulled a small lever and removed the cartridge. I'd watched enough TV to know how to do that. But I also knew there may be one bullet still left in the chamber. I pointed the gun at the door. *No, I thought. What if there is one more bullet left in there and it goes through the door?*

I pointed the gun down, toward the bed, and pulled the trigger back.

My eyes were blinded by a flash, and my ears hummed from the loud cracking sound the gun made.

I looked at the bed, where a small hole was still smoking. The hole went through the blankets, through the mattress, through the box springs and into the floor, where a small divot was made.

I was in shock. I didn't really think there was another bullet in the gun. The room smelled like gunpowder, and as I walked to the door, I wondered if anyone was outside. I opened it and peeked my head out. Two cleaning ladies, wearing long skirts and hairnets, looked back at me with questioning eyes.

I knew that if I had pulled the trigger at the door, I could've possibly killed them — or someone else.

Shaking, I made my way to the bathroom. I had to wash my hands. I had to do something to make myself stop shaking. I sat the gun on the sink and started washing, scrubbing furiously.

Then the door, which I had left propped open, flung wide.

Jim ran inside, looked to me in the bathroom, saw the gun on the sink, and smelled the gunpowder in the room.

"No, Chris!" he screamed. "No! Don't kill yourself!"

I stopped scrubbing. I looked at him. He looked at me.

And all I could do was laugh. Me? Kill myself? It was the funniest thing I'd ever heard.

"I thought you were going to do something awful," he said, sitting on the commode.

I laughed. "No, man. Don't worry about me."

We were better, then. Our troubles seemed to be past us. We were both a little crazy — I knew that. I thought something may be abnormal about my reactions to his behavior, but I didn't see it as a major problem. I definitely didn't see it as indicative of something serious.

Later, I would look back and realize something in me was just not right.

(34)

INJECTING THE NEEDLE

When I started wrestling, two of my goals were to win the World Heavyweight Championship, and to do it cleanly. By that I meant I wanted to do it without using steroids. I knew I was a role model, and I wanted to always be able to tell kids they could make it in the business without using drugs.

"Look at me," I would say to them, "you can do it. You can make it without the steroids. I did it. I'm proof."

It was harder than I ever imagined. By 1997, things would happen to force me into a new way of thinking. I found out that one of my goals would be impossible if I didn't break the other.

*

By 1997, I thought my shot was over, and I didn't know what to do. Other wrestlers would have loved to be in my position, to participate in my routine in the WCW. We had the live show we aired every Monday, as well as another show we taped on Thursday. In between, there were shows we taped on Saturdays and Sundays too. But every now and then, we would go down to Orlando for multiple tapings, knocking out tons of other shows over the course of a week or two.

But I couldn't help to feel that my star was fading. We'd spent months developing the Mortis character only to be outshined by Hogan and the nWo.

A year earlier, we'd sat in our meetings with Bischoff, who told us we would be the next big thing in wrestling.

Then we got no push. And to top it off, our characters, who were created in large part because of their ability to be marketed, were getting no attention. There were no T-shirts or figures. There was nothing.

Mortis was fading fast. I knew the end was coming. There wasn't anything I could do. As much as I pleaded with WCW officials, there was no way to make my character more popular. And Sullivan was clueless, still falling back on the "it's Bischoff's baby" excuse.

It all came to a head one day in Florida that spring.

"It's just so fuckin' frustrating," I said to Page. We were in the locker room after one of the marathon tapings. There, Raven, Page and I sat alone, and I wanted to talk about my problems.

"Why can't I get the push?" I asked. "It seemed like things were working out, and now we're fading."

Page looked over to Raven before replying. "I spoke to Kevin Nash the other day," he said. "And I asked him why you weren't getting a push."

Nash and Hogan had become almost like the head of the organization, and it was ironic, because their entire ploy was that they were taking over WCW. No one knew how real it was.

"Nash said you needed to work out more," Page said. "Nash said it was obvious that because you don't have a bodybuilder's body, you don't love wrestling as much as the others."

I couldn't believe what I was hearing. Page had been telling me for months I needed to work out more, but I would tell him I was doing all I could. I was working out at the gym six times a week, lifting and doing cardio. I was tanning, trying to make myself look good. I was eating right. I didn't know what else to do.

"You know no one loves this as much as me," I told them.

They looked at each other.

"I'm just telling you what he said, what the perception is," Page said.

"I don't know how to get bigger," I said. And after the words had come out of my mouth, I knew there was one other option—the thing I said I wouldn't do. I knew what this was about. They were letting me know that I had a choice to make.

This was about steroids.

"Do you want to stay where you are?" Page asked. "Or do you want to be a star?"

In the past few months I'd gone from thinking I was going to be a huge name in wrestling to barely being a mid-card act. I never had the bodybuilder's build, and there were few things that were going to make me have that kind of body. By that time in the WCW, wrestlers were using steroids, and I knew it. Everyone knew it. Lex Luger, who came up from Florida, was a heavy abuser of human growth hormone, instead of steroids, but it was still abusing drugs.

No one from the front offices in the WCW or WWF ever told me to take steroids. Then again, I saw the people who were getting the push — Nash, Hogan, Luger — they were all huge guys. I've heard that Hogan admitted to taking steroids, but I couldn't tell you whether or not these guys did or did not. I just know that whether they came by their size by natural means or not, they're huge, and when they got their push, it was easy to see who the management favored.

I got the message, whether it was ever said or not. Big was good. Actually, big was better.

It hurt to have my heart questioned. I'd loved wrestling since I was six years old. That hurt more than anything. They could say I didn't have the look or the charisma, but they couldn't say I didn't have the heart. And that gave me a new perspective on using steroids: I wouldn't be taking them to get big, I would be taking them to show that I had heart.

"We're not telling you to do anything," Page said. "This is your choice."

✺

It was sad knowing that Mortis was soon going to be taken away from me. Aside from using the character as a breakout in the WCW, it made my personal life easier. Being gay, it was hard for me to go out and be social because I was afraid people would recognize from me from the shows. But the mask gave me confidence. I could hide behind it and later, I could go out and know that no one knew I was Mortis.

On TV, I was hiding behind that skeleton and a black cape. In real life, I only had my face, and that was something to be afraid of. I was scared to let go of my alter ego, but I was even more afraid to let go of my other fake identity — that of a heterosexual man. I was playing a lot of roles in life, and it occurred to me that it was funny how I depended on one character — Mortis — to help me in the other secret life I was leading outside the ring.

Sometimes in wrestling, you get lost in your character and you forget what reality is. In my job, I was Mortis, a symbol of death. In my personal life, I was Chris, a guy who loved wrestling and who was pretending to be a heterosexual man because I was too afraid to come out of the closet.

What was my reality? Sometimes, it was difficult even for me to play all the roles. And in my wresting world, Mortis was coming to an end, and my entire career as a wrestler could too, if the people in charge were questioning my heart. If that were to happen, what would I do?

What would my reality be?

✱

For a few days, I thought about my conversation with Page and Raven. If my goals were to win the heavyweight title but to do it clean, it looked like I'd have to sacrifice one. What if I had to take steroids to win the belt? What if I chose not to take steroids and I could never win? My ego was telling me to take the drugs and keep my career moving, but my gut was telling me it was wrong. I never confronted Nash about the conversation he and Page had had, but I was glad Nash's opinions had made it back to me.

I read a lot of research on steroids and saw that they could do a lot of harm to the body, especially to the liver and the reproductive organs. But most of what I saw was inconclusive, and I didn't know what to make of the studies.

I went back to Page for advice.

"I can't tell you one way or the other," he said. "Steroids can do a lot of bad things to you."

He told me the drugs could affect your mood and your temper — two things I really did not need to be messing with. But still, the effects were uncertain.

"What if this is my chance?" I asked. "What if I never get to this point again and I regret it?"

Page just shook his head.

"Do what you have to do," he said.

✱

I told Page I wanted to try it, and he gave me the name of another wrestler who could get me the drugs. I spent a few hundred dollars for a three-month cycle of various steroids. When I bought them, I was given instructions on how to use them, but I had to write a lot of it down because it was so confusing.

I ended up taking the bag of items back to our hotel, and I laid out all the vials and needles on the bed. I still had the sense that there was time to turn back. If I didn't take the drugs, I could still say later on that I had a professional wrestling career without taking steroids.

I took my clothes off and went over to the mirror. I looked myself up and down, paying special attention to my abs. I flexed, and when I did, I thought I looked pretty good. *But not good enough for the WCW guys*, I thought.

I picked up the vial and the needle. It was a wonder that I could inject something inside of me and it would make me bigger. I filled up one of the vials, went back to the mirror and remembered what my supplier had told me: inject in different places — one shoulder, then the other, one buttock, then the other, one thigh, then the other.

I decided on the left shoulder first. *Is this what you want to do?* I asked myself.

Don Henley's "New York Minute" was running through my mind. In it, he says, "What the head makes cloudy, the heart makes clear." I wish I'd listened to that song and followed my heart. Instead, my ego devoured it.

I pulled back the plunger and jammed it into my shoulder. Then I did the same to the other shoulder. I could never again say I wrestled without taking steroids.

✻

After that first time, the shield was broken. Now that I'd compromised one goal, I'd do anything to make the other happen. I figured that I had used steroids once, I might as well do it again, and they was so readily available. You always think there may be something else that can get you more ripped, so you try it all.

Human growth hormone, or HGH, was also popular. Luger's gym in Marietta, Georgia, became the place to get it. I don't even know if that stuff was illegal at the time, because it was totally unknown. But it was easy to get if you had the money.

From what I understood, a doctor's prescription made it legal, so Luger had a doctor there who could give you what you needed. But I was told it was like $3,000 for a three-month cycle. Scott Steiner, who went to Michigan on a wrestling scholarship, did it. Buff Bagwell, a friend of Scott's did it too.

I didn't mess with the HGH, but I could never say I was totally clean.

I became lazy, and in a way I think I tried to self-destruct. I was so disgusted with myself for using, I tended not to be as dedicated in the gym, and I didn't eat well. And that's not the way it works. You have to work out hard to keep your tone. I screwed up in other ways too: I tended not to stack the drugs right, and I never cycled them correctly. Because of that, I never really saw the results, and I cast aside my values for nothing. Still, I kept trying steroids because I thought they could help me, and they didn't *appear* to be hurting me.

But when you take the most complicated organ in the body—the brain, the one we understand the least—and you douse it with chemicals, you affect the way you think. You mess up the chemicals that the body produces.

By that time, I was already what I would later learn to call Manic Depressive, and here I was, pumping this stuff into my bloodstream. God only knows what I did to myself. I'm certain those chemicals did something. Do I know that they caused me to later try and kill myself? No. But do I know that they didn't? Do I know they had absolutely no effect? No.

And that's the scariest thing of all.

(35)

FROM MORTIS TO KANYON

That fall, Page came to me with news.

"Eric thinks it's time for you to take off the mask," he said.

That was it. They thought the Mortis character had run its course.

"I haven't wrestled without the mask in a long time, man," I told Page.

"I know," Page said. "But they want to use you in different ways."

In my mind, we hadn't gotten a chance to fully explore the Mortis character. Mortis had never even feuded with a quality, big-name babyface. And I still thought the merchandising opportunities were untapped.

"I want to talk to Eric," I said.

Later, at a show in Oklahoma City, I spoke with him backstage.

"You don't want to do anything with more with Mortis?" I asked.

Eric didn't hesitate. "I think we've done as much as we can with him."

"I think we can market him," I said.

He sighed. "I just don't think skull merchandise will sell," he said.

It became a ludicrous remark. Six months later, Stone Cold Steve Austin would prove that a skull on a T-shirt sold — his shirt became one of the greatest selling wrestling shirts of all time.

Mitchell was scared when he heard the news that night, just before the Oklahoma City show.

"What do you think I could do?" he said.

I was honest with him. "I don't know."

"I'll come up with some ideas," he said. "Maybe I could do something with the Odditorium—like, my thoughts on the wrestling world, or something."

"Good idea," I told him. Right then, I knew he'd probably make it out OK.

✱

Raven was the first person who said he wanted to do something with me if I took off the mask. We came up with a sketch, and it worked out pretty well for me.

In the February of 1998, fans watched as the sketch opened with Raven, sitting by a boiler in the inner workings of the arena. I, still dressed as Mortis, told Raven I wanted to join his Flock—a group of wrestlers (including Kidman) who fought with Raven.

"If you want to join the flock," Raven said, "then you'll have to defeat Diamond Dallas Page for the U.S. heavyweight title."

I turned and walked to the ring, as Mitchell, in character, followed me.

"No, Mortis!" he kept screaming. "Don't do it!"

But I went ahead and wrestled DDP for the title, and the crowd backed me like never before. It felt amazing as I went through the match, because the crowd was cheering for me, as the underdog, to win. And they fully believed Mortis could defeat Page, one of the most visible and popular of all the characters. It felt like they believed in the character and we could have taken him farther.

But it was not to be. Page defeated me with a diamond-cutter, and I was dejected. The rest of the Flock came to the mat and carried me back to Raven.

"What now?" I said to him.

Then Raven kicked me in the gut and gave me another diamond-cutter on the ramp. I was finished. And Mortis was ready to disappear. Jim Mitchell dragged me away and it would be the last anyone saw of Mortis.

For two months no one saw or heard of me. In the storyline, I'd been let go from my contract. But that spring, various people from the crowd began running up and attacking Raven during his shows. A police officer attacked him, as did a vendor. Each time, it was secretly me attacking him, and it was all part of the way I was to reveal myself as Kanyon.

It was somewhat of a scary time for me, since "Out of sight, out of mind" was still one of the essential maxims of the wrestling business. But my storyline was so good I was never forgotten. In fact, I was supposed to continue attacking Raven while disguised as a lot of different characters, but instead, we only did it a few times, partly because Dusty Rhodes took over most of the writing around that time. Dusty, a legend who'd come up from Texas and was known as the working-class hero "American Dream," decided we should get on with the story. I never really thought Dusty saw much potential in me.

It was written I would make my first appearance without the mask in a match against Saturn, who like Kidman, was a member of the Flock. It was a pay-per-view match, and by this time, people knew I'd be coming up with new moves, so the crowd was ready to react. Unfortunately, they reacted with confusion.

We were in Oakland, and it was a great match with Saturn, but the storyline got jumbled as Saturn turned against Raven, so it became Saturn and me against Raven. We were good guys fighting Raven, but Saturn and I were also fighting each other. The crowd didn't know who to root for.

As each member of the Flock came out, I hit each of them with a different move. Then Kidman came out.

"You ready?" I asked.

He just smiled.

We showed the crowd a move we'd practiced back at Afa's — the second-rope pile driver. Kidman stood on top of the ropes, and I stood on the second rope, put his head between my legs and fell to the mat.

His head hit the mat, and I heard the best reaction I'd ever gotten.

Then Saturn came in to celebrate with me, and it all turned.

He pinned me, and the crowd just died, realizing Saturn was also against me. Again, they had no idea who to root for. They liked us, but they wanted to root for both of us.

A week later, Bischoff — who was not there for the show — called us in to his office.

"Your fight was the best part of the show," he told me and Saturn. "But when you guys started to fight each other, you lost me."

We knew it too. Saturn had a lot of ideas, and we worked well together. But Raven is very particular, so it was very difficult to put the three-way match together. At one point during the match, all three of us were on the mat. I had to roll over and ask Saturn, "What's next?"

"Hold on," he said. "Raven, what's next?"

"I don't know," Raven said.

"Raven doesn't know," Saturn told me.

We made up a few moves before figuring out what we were supposed to do.

Things were going better for Jim Mitchell, who had figured out a way to keep his character going. He proposed the idea of doing segments on his own that placed him in front of a makeshift "office" filled with bubbling cauldrons and other weirdness. There, he would give his views on the state of wrestling, kind of like a commentator, but still playing off his weird character. He was able to pull it off, and it worked well for him.

✷

During the feud with Raven and Saturn, I had a big moment—one that got me noticed more than any other.

Holding my opponent, I pushed his chest up and behind me, and fell on my back. We called it the Fireman's Carry Flapjack. When we fell, we were a straight tower, one person landing on his back, the other on his stomach.

I tried it on Raven and the crowd loved it.

When I looked up, the camera was right in my face. I knew it was always a good time for people to see my face and hear me talk. I was excited, so I screamed the first thing that came to mind.

"Who better than Kanyon?" I said. Then I looked away. Then I looked back. "Nobody."

When I got backstage, Page was waiting for me.

"That was a great line," he said. "Where did you come up with that?"

"Just came to me," I said, smiling.

"Well keep doing it."

Saturn agreed. So I kept at it.

The next week, I grabbed the mic. I wasn't told I could—I just did it. Hey, once you get something started, it's hard to stop.

"The last couple weeks, I been asking you, 'Who's better than Kanyon?' And you been saying 'Everybody,'" I said. "You keep getting the answer wrong. Who's better?"

"Everybody!" the crowd yelled.

"No, no, no," I said. "Nobody!" The catchphrase had caught on, and it looked like Kanyon might too.

✱

There was a time when I thought Randy Savage was going to kill me.

On a trip to St. Louis, Raven and I roomed together, and we said we wanted to catch a later flight back to the site of the next show, Monroe, Louisiana.

We woke up the next day to a blizzard in St. Louis. Racing to the airport at 8 a.m., we tried to get on six flights, but all were either canceled or we'd missed them.

In wrestling, there is an unwritten law: Do not miss a show. If you're hurt or sick, you drag yourself there. One urban legend involved Hulk Hogan, who used to book double shots on the weekends, meaning he had to get to four different shows. As the legend goes, he got stuck on the runway at LaGuardia. His show was in New Jersey, which isn't far — he could have driven there. So, as the story goes, Hogan pulled the emergency exit handle, slid down the inflatable staircase and took a cab to the next show.

But we weren't a cab ride away, and I was scared, mad, aggravated and tired.

"There is a way to get there," Raven said. "We could charter a plane."

For $2,000 we took a six-seater to Monroe, and barely made it.

When we got to the arena, I heard Savage was there with someone from the news, along with a kid he was training named Diaz, who I would have to fight.

Before the match, a cameraman came over as I was putting on my boots.

"What do you think of wrestling Diaz?" the cameraman asked me.

I wanted to give him a good sound bite. I thought for a second. "From what I understand, Randy Savage has been training this guy for a few months," I said. "Randy Savage is a has-been, and this guy is a never-will-be. I've been wrestling for a long time, and like I always say, no one is better than Kanyon."

I was pleased with it. I thought I sounded pretty good. Only later did I find out the camera crew was from *Good Morning America*, which was producing a story on Randy at the time. Oh well, I didn't think much of it.

A few days later, I was in the gym when Page rushed up to me.

"Dude, you better be careful, Randy Savage wants to kill you," he said. I assumed he was joking. I had no idea why, so I blew it off.

A couple of days later, Page approached me again. "Did you call and apologize to Randy?"

"No. Why?" I asked.

"He wants to kill you."

"What is this about?"

"I guess you said something about him on *Good Morning America*?"

"Are you fucking serious?" I said.

Some wrestlers get lost inside the identity of their characters. Savage *is* that character.

Never has there been a better example than leading up to his legendary match against Steamboat in *WrestleMania III*. People say he wanted to practice the match weeks in advance with Steamboat—that's the way Savage thinks. He takes everything to the extreme.

As an homage to him, I wrote out my apology. I didn't want to come across as too kiss-ass, or too harsh. I had to be very particular. But I also didn't want to sound like I was reading it.

So I called up Luther Biggs, who I'd met at the Power Plant, and read it to him. Although he wasn't a member of WCW, he had done a lot of work with us. Luther was a heavyset guy who loved Elvis and got lots of laughs by doing exaggerated karate moves or working his curves with sultry dancing. He came up with the perfect name for himself—Big Sexy. He used it for the first time during one of our tapings down in Florida, and after that, Kevin Nash (who came into town when the nWo started) stole the name. Nash still calls himself that today.

"And so, I am sorry if I offended you," I said over the phone. "I did not mean any harm. I only meant to set the stage for a good match."

On the other end of the phone, I could hear Luther laughing.

"No, it's OK—it sounds good," he said.

I swallowed hard and called Savage, and of course I got his answering machine. I left three minutes worth of apology, explaining that Raven and I had to charter the plane, and I was tired. I told the whole story.

A few minutes later, I got a call back. Savage has the deepest, most raspy, fake-sounding—but real—voice any wrestling fan had ever heard.

"You motherfucker—I'm going to kill you," he said. "I don't give a fuck about the plane. I don't give a fuck about the apology." Then there was a two-second pause. "You're dead." And he hung up.

I could not believe it. What should I do? Who should I call?

My phone rang again. It was Luther, laughing. "Did you like my Savage impression?"

"You fucker!" I screamed.

It was Luther doing a great Savage impression.

So, was I off the hook? Did Savage get my message? Was I still a wanted man?

*

By September of 1998, my storyline had straightened out a bit. The Flock turned on Raven, so I matched up with him against them. It was clear that pairing me against Raven wasn't working, so this was something new. I thought back to the advice I was always given: Keep the storyline going. Do what you have to do to keep your name out there. It seemed like the next logical step, and Raven was a veteran guy who could continue a storyline.

The next question was obvious: Where could we take it next?

Who knew? But the possibilities were endless. I was feeling good as a wrestler. I was making a name for myself without a mask, and because of my failure to figure out how exactly to manage my drugs, I quit using steroids. I just couldn't see the effects. I figured I needed to go back to my old ways: I needed to be clean. And if I couldn't make it clean, I wouldn't make it.

I had bigger obstacles ahead than the size of my muscles, though — namely Eric Bischoff and the bright lights of Hollywood.

(36)

TO HOLLYWOOD AND TORONTO — AND BACK

Since I'd first wrestled at the armory just a few blocks from my parents' house in Queens, I'd wanted them to see me doing what I love. I still felt guilty about lying to them all those years ago, and I wish they'd been there.

In 1999, at the Nassau Coliseum in Long Island, I was able to make that wish come true. I was scheduled to fight a match with Page and Bam Bam Bigelow. My parents didn't love to go out to these kinds of events. They didn't love the smoke and the pyrotechnics. But they did love me.

I was able to get them some decent seats — not front row seats, because the company wouldn't allow it, but decent seats nonetheless.

It was a thrill performing in front of my parents, as well as other family members who were in the audience. But that day was special for what happened after the show.

Back at my childhood home in Queens, Dad pulled me aside.

"Look at this," he said. He reached into a closet. "I found this at the toy store down the street."

It was an action figure — of me! I'd heard about it, but I hadn't told my parents about it yet. The likeness really did resemble my face.

Dad smiled. "This is when I knew my son was famous," he said. "I don't have to go to some show to figure that out."

That was when my fame became surreal to my father. Neither of us ever expected I would have my own action figure. Later, I would also be featured in two video games. That made Dad happy too.

I always thought that when someone became a star overnight, it must be overwhelming to deal with the celebrity. For me, it was much more of a gradual rise, so I feel like I was able to handle it better than most. I started off performing in small matches, then I became the wrestler who was beaten up every week. Eventually I became a small player on television, and after a lot of work I was able to have a more major role.

After that, I got my own action figure.

And my Dad loved every minute of it.

✱

I'd been wrestling as myself for a few months when I got called into Bischoff's office. I was told it was urgent.

"NBC is doing a Jesse Ventura movie in Toronto," Bischoff told me.

That made sense. Ventura, one of the most popular wrestlers of his time, was bold, brash and a former Navy SEAL. But in 1998, Ventura went on to a surprise win in the Minnesota governor's race, where he would serve for four years. All the major television networks then decided they would produce the definitive movie about Ventura's life.

"NBC called me up and said they needed someone to consult," Bischoff told me. "So I said you would do it."

I was flabbergasted. "Really?" I said. I was just getting my big solo break in the company, and I did not need to be off television at this point. "Why me?"

Bischoff smiled. "You've earned it," he said. "You have a reputation for working with wrestlers and developing new moves. You can do it. That's why."

In a way, it felt nice that Eric had that confidence in me. But it also felt strange to be walking away from the ring at such an important time in my career. Still, I had my marching orders from the boss.

"Thank you, Eric," I said. "How long should this take?"

"Well, first I need you to fly to California," he said. "So . . . maybe a few weeks."

"California! For what?"

"You're going to go to L.A., and you'll watch the actor they've hired to play Jesse," Eric said. "Then, if you approve of him, you'll all go back to Toronto and begin filming."

Inside the massive office, Bischoff's telephone rang.

"Excuse me," he said. "I've got to take this."

That was that. I was going to help with a television movie. I was scheduled to leave in a few days.

That night, I was unable to sleep. All night, I paced, back and forth — either literally, or in my mind. I was miserable.

The next day, I saw Disco, and mentioned how I couldn't get to sleep.

"Have you had the problem before?" he asked.

I thought about it. "Sometimes," I said. "Sometimes I just get so wound up I can't slow down."

"I've got a cure for you," he said. "Go to the health and nutrition store. Pick up this stuff called Renutrient. It comes in a half-gallon bottle, but you just take a little. Take a capful of it, and mix it with some orange juice. You'll sleep for at least five hours — maybe eight — and you will feel a million times better."

I did what he suggested. Thinking I may need it on the trip, I bought four bottles of the stuff and began taking it that night.

It worked. I awoke the next day after almost eight hours of sleep feeling more refreshed than I had in months. It was like a miracle cure. Feeling good, I was ready for the trip.

Not long after I arrived in California, I got a call on my cell phone.

"Hey, buddy, this is Eric."

"Hi, Eric."

"I have another task for you."

Oh boy.

"HBO has a show called *Arli$$*," Bischoff said. "It's about a sports agent and they're doing an episode on wrestling. I need you to meet with them and listen to what they have to say."

"Uh . . . OK."

He gave me a name and an address, which I wrote down.

"Just wait for a call from them."

"Sure, OK."

"Thanks."

I hung up the phone, and I was already feeling a little panicked. I had to meet with one wrestler about the Jesse movie, but then I had to meet with these other people about the TV show. OK. I figured I could do all of this.

Then my phone rang again.

"Hi, buddy, it's Eric again."

Oh God.

"Hi."

"Yeah, I need you to take care of one more thing for me while you're out there," he said.

"What's that?" I was to the point of freaking out.

"I want you to meet with some Warner Bros. executives, OK? They're thinking about doing a wrestling movie, and I just want you to talk with them, feel them out."

"Um, well, OK."

"Great. Thanks."

And he hung up.

I stood there, in the middle of the Los Angeles airport, feeling helpless. What should I do first? How did I know? My brain wasn't able to handle all of this at once. Maybe some people could, but I couldn't. I took a deep breath and walked to the baggage claim.

On the way, the phone rang again. If it was Eric, I thought I might kill him.

It wasn't. It was a representative from the Jesse movie, who gave me a time and place to watch the actor try out his wrestling moves. I knew the school and the trainer, who was famous for producing guys like Sting and the Ultimate Warrior.

The actor who was trying hard to land the role of Jesse was named Nils Stewart. Many in the movie business didn't understand that Stewart didn't have to be a great wrestler — Jesse himself wasn't a great wrestler. As long as Stewart could get by, in my opinion, he had the job.

When I arrived at the school, a few people were in the rings, practicing. One was left open for us. I brought my gear along because I wanted to show Stewart a few things to gauge his ability.

I was immediately introduced to a few people associated with the movie, as well as Stewart, who looked a lot like Ventura, with his bald head and black mustache. Stewart was also a stuntman who had a nice build and could pass for a wrestler.

"I want to get in the ring with you," I said.

Immediately, I could feel Stewart thought he should not have to get in the ring with me. He didn't even know who I was.

Fair enough.

"I'm a professional wrestler," I said, introducing myself to him. "You really should get in the ring so I can see what you can do."

Shortly thereafter, I realized we wouldn't be doing much. But we could get by.

Besides, I'd heard we were going to start filming in a couple of days, so we really didn't have that much choice. The goal was to get our version of the movie out quicker than ABC and CBS. Stewart would do fine.

As we got out of the ring and I passed my recommendation along to the movie representatives, I got another phone call. I was late for my meeting with the people from *Arliss*.

"I'm sorry," I told them on the phone. "I was actually out here working on a movie."

We rescheduled for the following day. I was already a Hollywood big shot. But I didn't feel like it at all. I felt unorganized, slightly afraid, nervous and unprepared. I wanted to go home.

I checked into my hotel — a nice place near the beach and water — and I took a capful of Renutrient before going to bed. I needed to pass out.

The next day I felt refreshed and a little better. I had the address for the set of *Arliss*, and when I arrived, my wrestler/actor was waiting for me. However, there was no script, no one to tell me what the show was about and I had no idea what I was supposed to do.

"I think you're supposed to teach me some moves," my wrestler/actor said.

"OK," I said.

For two hours, I worked with him, and we developed a few simple moves for him to use in what I learned would be a small part of the show. After the session, I felt good about what we'd done.

Then the phone rang. It was Eric.

"Why aren't you at Warner Bros.?" he asked.

"I am," I said. "I just got done showing this kid how to do his moves for *Arliss*."

"No!" Bischoff screamed. "*Arliss* is HBO! Not Warner Bros.!"

My head was swimming. I had to then reschedule with Warner Bros. for the next day. I still had no idea why I was meeting with them. I also didn't know when I was supposed to leave for Toronto. Plus, I was still on Eastern time and my head felt foggy.

I went back to the hotel, took a shot of Renutrient and fell down on the bed.

And the cell phone rang.

"Shit!" I said.

"Hello?"

"Chris Kanyon?" the voice on the other end was female.

"Yes," I said, tired and impatient.

"Yes, I am with the NBC movie group, and I was wondering if you'd arrived in Toronto yet?"

"What? No! When am I supposed to be there?"

"Today, sir."

I was about to explode.

"I can't be there tomorrow," I said. I was losing steam. The drug was taking over. "I can be there the next day."

"I will pass the word along, sir."

It was the last thing I heard before I slipped into unconsciousness.

✱

The next day at Warner Bros., I realized we were there to brainstorm ideas about a new movie, one that would be released in 2000 as *Ready to Rumble*, a wrestling comedy about two fans who want to restore credibility to their fallen hero. At first though, there was only a rough idea — and one request.

"We really want John Goodman to star as the lead role," one suit told me.

I didn't know if John Goodman fit as a down-on-his-luck former wrestler, but I guessed it could work. But I still didn't know what to say.

"Yes, definitely," I said. "I think we in the company would be thrilled to work with you on this."

I shook hands with a lot of people, and — feeling more out of place than ever — made my getaway. I was hyper, and I felt like I was ready to jump out of my skin.

Later, I learned Oliver Platt was chosen to play the lead character in that movie. I had no say in the matter. Apparently, I wasn't as important as everyone thought.

I certainly didn't feel important. With Hollywood behind me, I was ready to get on to Toronto, and ultimately, get this thing finished.

Before I got on the plane to Canada, I took another shot of Renutrient. I slept like a baby.

✱

The next day, I was in Toronto, staying in a beautiful hotel and reading the script to *The Jesse Ventura Story*. I decided I liked it, and as I read, I noticed that where a match was supposed to take place, there were no details. It just said, "wrestling match."

I took that to mean my job was to fill in the gaps. That morning I began to sketch out matches and think of moves. I had two problems. First, Jesse wasn't a great wrestler, so we couldn't do anything that was too difficult. But more important, should the movie reflect the wrestling moves of that era, or should we really be creative and just feature some great wrestling, including moves of today?

I decided I would use some of my more modern techniques for the wrestling scenes because if they were reflecting me, I wanted them to be good, and fun to watch — not boring old-school wrestling.

An assistant with the film crew met me at my hotel and took me away to the movie set. When I arrived, I immediately felt guilty.

It seemed like everyone was waiting for me.

Dozens of people wanted my time. We had to discuss props or wrestlers or stunts or the story. I felt like I was an integral part of this process. And everyone wanted to see me *at that very minute*.

Again, I was confused, and I wondered if I was going to explode. I felt as if the entire project was on my shoulders. I'd never dreamed of working on a movie before, and I had a billion questions. What was my role and responsibilities to WCW? Do I get to use our guys? Do we fly them up and do they get extra pay? I didn't know who to ask.

In an hour I knew I was in over my head.

But I always seemed to lean on the right people. I gave my old friend and columnist Dave Meltzer a call. Because of his writing and contacts, he hooked me up with the names of many of the local independent wrestlers and promoters. WCW sent us some belts we could use, and I went about talking to the guys in the independent scene about securing a ring for our use.

Things were going really well.

Then I lost my cell phone. And all hell broke loose.

✱

That night, I felt good about what we'd done. Things were progressing and I was doing my job. I went back to the hotel, took my shot of Renutrient and passed out into a deep sleep.

The next day, Stewart and I met to discuss some of the more specific moves that would be used in the film. Stewart, who wanted to do a good job of portraying Jesse, was open to anything, and that made me happy. We even discussed using a version of the second rope pile driver. I started taking him to some of the independent shows in the area, and he — as well as our director — started to get a feel for the environment.

Somewhere along the way I decided to go for the biggest name in wrestling. I wanted to get Hulk Hogan for the movie.

After a lot of calls, I ended up getting a contact for Hogan's agent. Good. But I wondered if it was stupid to even try calling. Would Hogan want to do this?

I called.

When his agent answered, I explained who I was and what I wanted.

"Why would Hulk want to do this?" he said.

Shit. I'd wondered the same thing. Good question.

"Well," I said, "this would be good exposure for Hulk. After being in the movie, he could go on Jay Leno. It would be good exposure."

The agent started laughing. Not a good sign.

"Kid, Hulk can go on Leno any time he wants," he said. Then he hung up.

Well, I struck out there. What else could I do?

I tried to call Bischoff to see who I could use for the movie. I kept getting voicemails. Slowly, I began to feel that helplessness again, like I was losing it. I'd been working forever, and by the time I looked up at the clock, it was time to go. I realized I was the last person on the set.

When I walked out to get my car, it had been towed.

Oh my God, I thought. I was on the verge of a panic attack.

"Hey, man! Kanyon!"

I looked over to see a kid, no more than 20, who drove up to the curb outside our parking lot. He pulled up in a sports car, with what looked to be a ring rat sitting shotgun.

"Yeah?" I said.

"Come on, man! Hop in!" His girl, a blonde with boobs falling out of her halter top, just smiled at me.

To some, that would be exactly what the doctor ordered. To me, it was awful timing.

"You need a ride?" he said.

"Yeah," I said. I did need a ride.

"Come on," he said.

I got in the back. Immediately, the ring rat slipped back there too. She put her arm around me and shoved her boobs in my face.

"Hey, man," the kid said, driving away. "I'm Brian. I'm a disc jockey at a local radio station. I know you guys are here working on the wrestling movie, and I want to be a promoter. That's Jill, by the way."

Jill was massaging my thigh.

"So anyway, I want to get in the movie, if possible."

I rolled my eyes. "I'll do what I can," I said.

As we rolled up to the hotel, I wanted to be anywhere else.

"Hey, baby," Jill said, "I want to be in the movie too."

"OK."

"Hey, man — you want to go to a club?" Brian asked. "You want to get a couple lap dances?"

Jill purred in my ear.

"No thanks," I said, getting out of the seat. "Not really my scene."

"Hey man — no problem," Brian said. "Get some sleep."

"Bye, baby," Jill added.

The two sped away, and I was left in front of the hotel. What the fuck was going on, anyway? I had to find my car, I had to talk to Bischoff, and I had to stop meeting locals who wanted me to get them in the movie. I made my way up to my room, which was more than spacious enough for me, and I took a shower. I just felt dirty.

I got out of the shower and prepared my shot of Renutrient. As I swallowed it, I thought maybe I should try Bischoff once more. I grabbed for my cell phone, which was normally located in my jacket pocket.

It was gone.

Jill. Jill the Skank took my cell phone. Shit.

What could I do? My mind started to wander as I realized I was in no state to look for it. Dammit.

The world faded to black.

✳

When I woke up the next day my mind was fuzzy. When it all came back I was already in a bad mood. My car was gone. My phone was gone. I had too much to do. Damn.

I walked down to the lobby of the hotel when I was stopped by a man at the front desk.

"Mister Kanyon?" he asked.

"Yeah?"

"You have a visitor."

"A visitor? Who?"

"Ike Shaw."

"Who the hell is Ike Shaw?"

"That's me."

I turned to see a man in a suit and a long trench coat. He looked almost like an old mobster, with a thin mustache and a black fedora. He was flanked by three young, tough-looking twentysomethings.

"Do I know you?"

"No, sir," he said, extending a hand. "I run my own wrestling school here."

Oh no. *Here we go again*, I thought.

"I heard you needed wrestlers, and I am willing to lend you some of my talent."

"Well, yes, we do . . . but I would need to evaluate the talent, and —"

"You can do it wherever and whenever you want," Shaw said. Behind him, his talent — a black man, a white man and an Asian man — never spoke.

"Well, I really need to get my car first," I said. "It was towed last night."

"I know where they tow them," he said. "Let's go."

I couldn't argue. I felt like I was caught in some local con. On the way, Shaw told me about his school, which sounded like a nice place away from the hustle and bustle of the city. Still, something about all of this seemed set up.

We arrived at a local garage, and Shaw went inside an office to speak to the owner. Minutes later, he came back — with my keys. I could've hugged him.

"Do you need anything else?" he asked.

"No, you've done quite enough, thanks so much," I said.

"Are you sure?"

I laughed. "Well, if you can find the skank who stole my phone last night, that would be great," I said.

Shaw pulled a box from his pocket. "Here," he said, handing it to me.

It was a new cell phone.

I stared at it blankly. "How — I can't accept this," I said.

"Please, keep it," he said. "I have many."

"Thanks so much, really," I said.

"Are you hungry?"

Just then, I realized I was famished. "Yeah."

"Let's get a meal."

I drove the crew over to a local pancake joint, and after we sat down, Shaw excused himself to the bathroom. It was just me and the kids.

"Hey, guys," I said, "is Shaw a good guy? Is he being straight with me?"

"Mr. Shaw is like a father to us," the black kid said. He did it without smiling.

"It's true," the Asian kid said. "He took me in when I was a kid and had nothing. Now I am becoming a wrestler."

I nodded. Pete had done much of the same with kids in New York.

The kids told me Shaw had converted his house into a dojo, and that they all lived there while practicing. When Shaw returned, we were eating, and he did the same.

"Do you have to work tomorrow?" he asked.

"I don't think so," I said.

"Why don't you come out to the dojo? You can watch the talent," he said.

I agreed. It sounded like a good time.

That Sunday, I did travel to Shaw's dojo. It was exactly what I needed.

I got away from the Hollywood stuff, and got back to real wrestling. Shaw's kids were good—they had talent, and they worked hard. Plus, their chemistry was something special. You could tell they came from tough places, but they knew Shaw had given them a chance. They wanted to run with that chance.

And because of that, I wanted to help them as much as I could. I knew I could get them into the movie, and if that helped, then that would be great.

Over the course of the afternoon at the dojo, I told stories, I coached and I became calm. There was no stress; there was only fun. And I feel like I provided a service to Shaw and his kids.

As the evening set in, I finally left, and as I shook Shaw's hand, I told him I would help them as much as I could.

"Because I appreciate how you helped me," I said.

"Take care," Shaw said. "And keep in touch."

The whole day calmed me back down.

But it wouldn't last.

I needed a few more guys for the movie, and coincidentally, WCW was coming up to Toronto's SkyDome for a show that following Monday.

We decided to film the show, as well as Stewart wrestling Bill Goldberg. I had no idea how that was going to go. We used about 30 wrestlers in the movie, a lot of whom were from the local area.

I asked Luther Biggs, who lived nearby in Detroit, if he wanted to be in the movie, and he said yes. But there was one condition, I said.

"No Savage impressions."

He agreed.

After Hogan's agent reacted that way, I knew this project wasn't for big money guys, but the exposure could be good for others. Raven, for instance, wanted to participate. The local guys, including a lot of Shaw's wrestlers, did really well.

I felt like I was getting the job done. But I wasn't sleeping that well anymore. I was sleeping for four hours, and sometimes I would fall asleep driving home. I started to become crazy and somewhat depressed.

I did not know then I was bipolar. It was manifesting itself as anger, not sadness. I would get rebellious with some of my crew, and I was also high as a kite — creative, but out of control. It led to paranoia. I was getting into some odd arguments with folks on the movie. In one scene where Jesse gets trained to wrestle, I was very upset with the outfit they chose for the trainer. It looked nerdy, and I got pissed.

I don't know why that bothered me so much.

It all led up to one evening when I lost it. I was slammed with panic attacks and paranoia. I locked the doors, and I thought people were coming to get me. I wanted to leave, and I didn't know who to call.

I thought the movie was going to cost me my career.

I called up Luther, who was coming in the next day.

"I can't handle it," I told him. "I'm losing it. I don't know what's wrong with me. Can you help me?"

That night, Luther came in early and met me in my room. When he knocked at the door, I was in a full state of nuts.

"What's going on, man?"

"I don't know," I said. "I-I-I, um, what are you doing? What am I doing? I don't know what's going on."

It all came out in a word salad. I was talking a million miles an hour, my mind racing, coming up with sentences, my mouth not keeping up. I thought I was saying everything right. In my head, everything was there, but I could see in his face it wasn't working.

That's when he slapped me. "Calm down," he said. "You're delirious."

I sat down on the bed and tried to collect the millions of thoughts swirling in my head.

Luther walked around my room, and on my dresser, he saw the bottle of Renutrient.

"What the hell is this?" he demanded, shoving it in my face.

I tried to get the words out. "It's my sleeping pills."

"Do you know what this is?" he asked. "This shit you're taking is fucking you up. That is a form of GHB. The date rape drug. You need to get rid of it."

Date rape drug? What? "I can't. I need it."

"No, you need to get rid of it. No doubt it helps cause the paranoia and everything else you're feeling."

"You sure?"

"Yep. And you need to sleep."

"I can't. I'm too fucking stoked."

"OK. Have you had a meal?"

"I don't think I've eaten since I've gotten here." I was out of my head.

We went downstairs, ate, and planned out what I had to do.

Luther got me back down to ground zero. I flushed my drugs down the drain. I didn't know it, but Renutrient was illegal in Canada. Later, it would be illegal in the U.S. too.

✱

To make the Ventura movie's wrestling scenes more realistic, we planned to film the WCW SkyDome matches. But our producers wanted to stop the match if there was a flub. I had to put my foot down.

"How would you like it if we stopped your movie in the middle and showed you directing?" I told our director, David Jackson.

"But people know it's fake, don't they?" he asked.

"Yeah, but we don't want to beat people over the head with it," I told him.

With tricks and editing, they were able to film it with Bill Goldberg wrestling Stewart.

Everything went well except for one thing. Sullivan was in the stands, across the arena from us in the middle section, and something was going on. He looked like he passed out, but he also looked like he was dead. A group of guys were trying to walk him down the steps to the arena floor. I ran down there as they pulled him backstage.

Shaw was there with some of his students.

"Did you see Sullivan's herky-jerky chicken-walk down the steps?" Shaw asked. "What caused it?"

"I think he has diabetes or something," I said.

Shaw just looked at me. "Diabetes, huh?"

"Yeah." I could tell he didn't believe me.

I knew what it was. Sullivan, like most of the other wrestlers, were abusing the GHB. It was the drug of choice for a lot of guys, and I didn't understand why. It made me happy I'd dumped the shit, and that instance was embarrassing to say the least.

Like all things, the show came together. Toward the end, producers told me the date they were going to air the movie, and there were two major problems: They were going head-to-head with a Cleopatra miniseries, which I think everyone realized was a mistake. But even worse, it would be aired up against a WWF Sunday pay-per-view.

"You're losing half your audience right there," I said. It didn't matter to them.

On wrap day, the director gave me a Jesse Ventura watch and a $5,000 bonus. NBC was the first to air their Jesse movie, but it drew only between a 1.8 to 2.2 rating—not good.

And it seems the few people who watched it didn't like it. The reviews were bad. The *Daily Variety* said it was terrible, but the reviewer did note, "The only thing of value in the entire movie is the eye-catching and exciting wrestling scenes put together by Chris Kanyon and David Jackson." That felt real good.

In the end, I could look back and say, "Wow, what an interesting experience that was." Too bad I was a drug addict during the whole thing.

But that just makes it more Hollywood.

When I came back, I found that morale in the WCW was down. Because of the domination of the nWo, many of the other wrestlers felt like they could never become anything. But I saw once more I'd fallen into a high-profile spot. With Raven as a tag partner, we took on Kidman and Mysterio in St. Louis and won. As a result of that, we went on to face the tandem of Chris Benoit and Dean Malenko, a fierce match-up that spawned a feud.

Benoit and Malenko were two guys who'd come into the company just after me. I'd been a fan of Chris's for a while. He was friendly, low-key and serious, but he was a good wrestler. His love for wrestling showed in his intensity both in and out of the ring. You could see it even when he was working out.

After a show that year, Jim, Wrath and I were looking for a motel, but we were told by someone at a front desk that the entire town was full.

Benoit and Malenko pulled up in a cab and saw us. They opened the door.

"It's already full," I said.

"We got some places, and there are more vacancies across town," Malenko said. "Come on in."

Sure enough, they got us into their motel, and lucky for us, there was a diner attached — one that served booze. I'd never talked with them before, but they were easy to like. Dean, like his friend Eddie Guerrero, was outspoken. He had an arsenal of one-liners and a knack for dry humor.

Early on, Jim Mitchell got up to go to the bathroom. Out of nowhere, Benoit opened up.

"Let's play one on Jim Mitchell," he said. So Benoit told the waiter to give us all shots — water for us and vodka for Jim — and to keep them coming.

Then Benoit put on a great performance.

"Oh, it burns," he kept saying, punching the table with each shot. He would overact how bad they were, and all the while, Mitchell was getting tanked.

I never thought Benoit had a sense of humor. He wasn't doing it to amuse us, he was amusing himself, but I was still laughing hysterically.

We had to leave, and Jim was shitfaced, vomiting all over the parking lot.

"Why aren't you guys . . . why aren't you . . . you're not drunk!" he kept saying.

We laughed our asses off. Benoit didn't let everyone in, but when he did you saw how genuine he was. Later, in a future blurring of reality, Sullivan wrote a feud about his wife, Nancy, leaving him for Benoit.

It actually ended up happening, and the line of fantasy and reality was blurred even more. In 2007 something short-circuited in Benoit's head. He would kill Nancy and their seven-year-old son, Daniel.

I don't think it's a coincidence that a lot of wrestlers have some short circuits.

✶

"Hello, Kanyon?"

"Yes?"

"This is Shannon Moore. I'm a cruiserweight-size wrestler from here in Atlanta, and I know you don't know me, but I'm friends with some of your friends — Matt and Jeff Hardy."

"OK, hi," I said. I had no idea why this kid was calling me.

"I just wanted to know if you had any advice for me breaking into the company?"

Hmm. I told the kid to come to the Power Plant and show his stuff.

I got another phone call that day, this one from Eric Bischoff. Apparently I had become his personal errand boy.

"Do you know who Peter Engel is?" he asked.

As a matter of fact I did. I always had an attraction to Zack and A.C. Slater from *Saved by the Bell*, which Engel produced.

"I talked with Engel, and we want to produce a show," Bischoff said. "I proposed a concept for a Saturday afternoon type show, split in half. The first half would be like *Saved by the Bell*, but a more reality-based high school with dramatic roles."

"OK," I said.

"But some of the boys in the high school have put together an independent wrestling circuit," he continued. "In the second hour, the matches would be the kids wrestling each other. It would air on Saturday mornings."

I thought that was an interesting idea.

"We need wrestlers who are good, but who look 18," Bischoff said. "I need cruiserweights like Kidman — 10 of them. I like what you did when you found Kidman, and I like the guys you found for the Jesse movie. Find me some more."

It was 1999, and Bischoff had given me the power to hire 10 cruiserweights for the television show. The first call I made was to Shannon Moore.

Shannon knew four more guys who looked like they were in a boy band. There was half of my quota right there. I spread the word, made some calls and looked at some tapes. I found some local guys in Atlanta too and recorded their moves on a little 8 mm camera. When Bischoff asked me how things were going, I would always hook up the camera and show him who I'd picked.

"Great," he said. "You've got $400,000. Divvy it up the way you want."

I decided to just give them each $40,000.

✶

During this time, I decided to buy a house — a 4,200-square-foot, six-bedroom house with a swimming pool and a small deck. And right off the bat, I let a lot of the guys stay at my place. Shannon Moore and another kid named Shane Helms both stayed with me. We made a nice enclosed tiki bar, with a hot tub and three TVs. We made our own beach volleyball court and called it Klub Kanyon. For every WWF pay-per-view, we'd have 150 people over to watch. It was a great place, and my family loved it. They also had their own bedroom and we had a nice dining room.

It was just the family home my parents hoped I'd have — though certainly my boarding house of wrestlers wasn't the family they'd had in mind.

✶

As the year wore on, the tag team took a hit when Raven got hurt. On television it looked like Page and Bam Bam Bigelow attacked Raven and me, forcing us to the hospital.

But Raven was actually hurt. After a wild series of events, Page, Bam Bam Bigelow and I were matched up as tag partners to form the Jersey Triad, and at the 1999 Great American Bash in Baltimore, we defeated Benoit and Saturn for the WCW Tag Team title. Finally, I was a champion. I had a belt. It was like no other feeling I can describe. All I can say is it was another dream that came true. Things were going so well, they even made a rule that allowed either of the two of us to defend the title. I was right up there with Bigelow, who was a former headliner at *WrestleMania*, and Page, who was a former U.S. heavyweight title holder.

Finally, I could be in main event title matches.

That is, until my phone rang. It was Bischoff.

"You've got to go out to L.A.," he said. "They're making a movie called *Ready to Rumble*, and I need you there to supervise."

Oh no. Not again. No. I was honest.

"I don't want to, Eric."

There was silence on the other end of the line.

"I wasn't asking you, I was telling you," he said.

I sighed. Thankfully, we worked it out so that I could still work the Monday *Nitro* shows. So I went off to L.A. and worked Tuesday through Saturday, but was off Sunday and Monday, so I could participate in the shows. It was a rough schedule.

I knew that I needed someone to go with me to keep me sane.

Shane Helms and I had hit if off ever since he moved in with me. Young and good-looking, with a square jaw and long hair like mine, I suppose I was always attracted to him. But I also knew Shane was straight. He had a girlfriend back home in North Carolina and even though I told him we could be out there a few months, he was quick to commit. I went out to L.A. first to learn about what had to be done, and then I said I would send for Shane.

As I left for L.A. I felt a lot better about this project. I knew I'd done this before, and this time, it was a Warner Bros. movie and I wouldn't be in charge of much. This movie was big, with David Arquette, Oliver Platt, Rose McGowan and Scott Caan. The director also did *Varsity Blues,* and that movie did real well.

I just knew it wasn't going to be bullshit.

✷

For the most part, I was right.

The whole scene was much more laid-back. The executive producers were very hands-on, very friendly, though the day-to-day guy was a bit of a ball buster. All of the crew — from hair to sets to costumes — were nothing but professional. This was when I was introduced to the Internet Movie Database. Pretty much everybody had a great resumé.

My first day out there, I went to the set of *The Flintstones in Viva Rock Vegas* to meet with my stunt coordinator. I was told this was the biggest deal of all, because I was going to be working with him every day. Thank God he was one of the nicest guys on the planet. His name was Joel Kramer, and I could not believe the movies he'd done — *True Lies* and *Terminator II*, among others.

Holy shit, I thought, *I'm working with one of the best stunt guys ever.*

They put me up in a nice apartment and I knew I was going to have fun. Working with Kramer, I met with the stunt performer and we worked out our wrestling scenes, but we had to keep reminding ourselves this was comedy. It had to be visually appealing and funny.

David Arquette wanted to do some of the wrestling himself, so we trained him, too. We used tons of wrestlers, so I acted as a liaison between the film and WCW.

On the second day I was there, I got a call from the star.

"I heard they got a ring? Do you mind if we go down there and try it out?"

It was like he was a movie star version of me. When we went down to our ring, Arquette was happy just to be on the ropes. He was smiling and you could tell that he loved it. He was an absolute fan.

After a few hours of showing him the basics, we walked out of the gym together.

"Hey, man," he said, "do you have any plans?"

"Me?" I said. "Dude, I'm in Hollywood, and I don't know anybody. I have no plans."

"Why don't you come to a party with me and my wife tonight?" he asked. "We just wrapped this movie I've been working on — *Scream 3*."

"You want me to come to the *Scream 3* wrap party?"

He nodded.

"OK."

"Look — come over to mine and Courteney's place, and you can follow us, OK?"

After one day of work in Hollywood, I was already getting invited to my first big party.

On my way over to the Arquettes' house, I thought about David. He was funny, but also nutty at the same time. Other than wrestling, I wasn't sure what we had in common or what we could talk about.

Then I met his wife, Courteney Cox Arquette, and she was so wonderful. Courteney got her break when she was featured in the music video for Bruce Springsteen's "Dancing in the Dark," then landed a recurring role on the show *Family Ties*. Of course, she later went on to superstardom on *Friends*, but she is the most normal, friendly person.

Some people, especially famous people, are intimidating. Not her. Courteney draws you in and makes you feel comfortable. She and David make a very genuine couple. Even years later, I would still receive Christmas cards from them.

So what did I think of my first real big Hollywood party?

It was lame as fuck.

It was just held at some producer's house (which was not even very big) and I didn't even recognize very many folks.

Not too long after we got there, I felt awkward.

"I'm just going to walk around, see what's going on," I told Courteney.

I came across a lineup, which I thought was a line to go to the bathroom. Wrong. People were waiting to do drugs. I watched a couple of people stagger out. I knew it wasn't my scene.

Eventually, I told the Arquettes I was tired and needed to go.

I thought it may be time to call Shane.

✶

With Shane in L.A., we had fun, and it was very low-stress for me, especially compared to my last movie experience.

Then Randy Savage went crazy again.

Out of nowhere, Savage called us. But of course, I thought it was Luther again, so I didn't take it seriously.

When I realized it was the real Savage, I was filled with fear.

"I understand you got a ring set up out there," he said.

"Yeah."

"Is there any way I can get into it?"

"When?"

"Tomorrow."

He explained he had a match with former basketball star Dennis Rodman in Sturgis and — of course — he wanted to practice.

What could I do? I said yes.

"And Randy?" I said.

"Yeah, brother?"

"Are we cool with that whole *Good Morning America* thing?"

"Oh yeah, brother. I got your message. We're cool."

I was treading carefully now.

"Why were you so mad?" I asked.

"I was right in the middle of my Slim Jim deal — a $1 million deal, brother," he said. "They were trying to faze me out. They thought I was washed up. Then, one of the Slim Jim guys watched *Good Morning America*, and saw you — someone in my own company calling me a has-been."

Oh God.

"Man, I'm so sorry," I said. "I can see how that would look bad."

"Yeah," he said. "So I was ready to kill you, brother."

He laughed.

"But I ended up getting the deal anyway. Otherwise, you would have gotten a million-dollar ass beating."

✴

Shane was feeling a little down about being apart from girlfriend of eight years. His favorite wrestler of all time was Savage, so I thought meeting him would be a good pick-me-up.

We got to the ring and, of course, Randy was there and he already had the entire thing planned out. He knew Rodman was a bit nuts, so when Rodman showed up and was completely clueless, it surprised no one. Later on, I would also train Jay Leno, who in my opinion took the whole thing way too seriously. But at least he was easier to work with than Rodman.

In fact, not only was Rodman clueless, he was also disrespectful, sweaty and unwashed. It's common courtesy to show up clean, but he didn't get it. He'd been partying for two days straight, and he smelled like it.

While in the NBA, Rodman was known for his antics — his colored hair, his technical fouls for childish outbursts and his lackadaisical practice habits. But he was also known as the best rebounder in the league, a guy who came into the NBA as a small-college nobody and turned into a champion many, many times over.

Unfortunately, he couldn't be coached. We tried to work with him, tried to incorporate his ideas, but they wouldn't work — and he wouldn't listen. Savage knew exactly what needed to be done, so they walked through it.

And Shane got to watch his favorite wrestler in all his crazy glory.

It went that way for five hours.

In one part of the match, Rodman had to hit Randy over the head with a chair. We tried to show him how to do it properly — spreading the hit flat so a large portion of the body could absorb the hit — but I knew it wouldn't matter. Still, Savage wanted Rodman to do it. We gave the chair to Rodman and he tried to do it in slow motion.

It looked pretty good.

"Let's do it at full speed," Savage said.

Shane and I could not believe it.

Rodman hit Randy like he was hitting a grand slam. He put the chair behind his back, and with those long arms, swung as hard as he could.

The smack was unlike anything I've ever heard before in my life. It had to be horribly painful, but Savage came up quick.

"Exactly, brother!" he exclaimed, high-fiving Rodman.

He acted like it didn't hurt him at all. He wouldn't show pain — not in front of another athlete from a different sport.

He did not. He would not.

✴

While there were so many similarities between actors and wrestlers — we perform, they perform — they took days to tape a minute of footage, while we made a show every night live.

It started wearing on me because we were doing so much. On Monday I spent all day at *Nitro*, then I would fly back to L.A. for the movie's work week.

In the summer of 1999, I was getting burned-out. I'd had enough. I was a tag team champion, but I actually wanted someone to take it away from me because I was getting worn down and didn't want to come back to defend it. I loved wrestling and stunt directing, but they were working against each other.

After one grueling day in Sturgis, I finally got to my hotel room at 3 a.m., the phone rang. It was Savage.

"Can you come over and help me go through this match one more time?" he asked.

I couldn't believe it. It was the voice I did not want to hear.

I walked in to Savage's room, and Rodman was there on the bed. When he saw me, he just rolled his eyes. I couldn't think of how many times they must have done this. For three more hours, we practiced. Each time we rehearsed the fight choreography, we would beg to be finished, but Savage wanted to make sure we had every last detail down. Finally, he let us go.

After all the practice, Rodman and Savage's Road Wild match went well, but at my own match that night, the belts were taken away from us. While I should have been disappointed, I was relieved I didn't have to do Monday *Nitro* shows anymore. And it helped me. Then I could focus on the movie.

✱

Warner Bros. did not skimp on taking care of me. One of my hotels was like an apartment, close to a gym. I never realized a gym could be a place to hook up with a guy until I was staying in L.A., working on the movie.

One day I was working out when I noticed a guy checking me out. I'd been on TV for a while though, so it wasn't out of the ordinary for some people to come up and ask for autographs. He was Hispanic, and pretty good-looking, and he stayed close to me, no matter what machine I was on. I felt bad for him that he was too shy to come up to me and ask for an autograph. I wanted to make it easier for him.

"You know what, dude, do you want an autograph?" I asked.

He looked at me like I was nuts, so I just walked away. But he kept looking. I went to the locker room to get my bag, and then it occurred to me — he might be gay.

He followed me in, and stood there with me. I went out to the lobby of the hotel, and I watched as he followed, still staring at me. He intentionally dropped a piece of paper, looked down at it, looked at me and walked away.

I walked over and it only said, "Miguel," with his phone number. So I called. It was obvious that he was gay and he wanted me, so I told him to meet me in my room in 20 minutes.

When I got up to my room I got a phone call from Page, wanting to know if I wanted to go to the movies. I didn't have enough time, so I told him I was going to get room service and stay in.

Unfortunately, the whole note-dropping, picking up and coming up to the room was four times longer than the foreplay. Minutes later, Miguel was finished, and he was putting his clothes back on.

I called Page back. "Yeah, man — it turns out I can make the movie after all," I said.

✶

The movie I saw with Page was *Beyond the Mat*, the story of professional wrestlers and how the sport is real, and it really revitalized me. Of all the times I thought I was burned-out, that movie made me realize how lucky I was to be in wrestling. They try to explain what wrestling is: it's comedy, it's drama, and so much more, but in the end all they can say is "It's just wrestling."

There's just nothing like it. And the people in this unique business? There's nothing like them either.

✶

There was one wrestler who always hit on me. Somehow, he knew I was gay. The closest I ever came to fooling around with another wrestler was while I was working on *Ready to Rumble*.

While we were staying in the same hotel in L.A., he called me into his room and invited me down to the hot tub. I already thought the guy might be gay, but this made it seem all the more likely.

I went down and got in. Unfortunately, the hot tub was beneath all the windows at the hotel. I figured nothing was going to happen. The other wrestler showed up with his ice bucket and some beers, and to erase any doubt, he also brought a gay porn magazine.

He got in the hot tub and asked if I wanted a beer.

"Do you like the magazines?" he asked.

"They're all right," I said.

Then his foot felt my leg. A lot of things were going through my head. Just being in the hot tub was probably too much for me, let alone looking at this mag.

"I need to go back to my room," I said.

"Do you want to come back to mine?" he said.

I thought about it. No other wrestler had ever hit on me before, but I couldn't risk getting found out.

"I'm sorry, but no," I said. "No thanks."

There had been rumors about me, and a lot of it came because of my recruiting of the cruiserweights. All of a sudden, they saw me recruiting good-looking 18-year-olds, then they saw them living in my house. It added up.

At that stage, *Nitro* was on fire. When we went to the hotel bars after the show, all the fans would go there with us, keeping up the tradition that all the wrestlers and fans watch the west coast show together. Of course, there were girls there, and most of the guys brought girls up to their rooms. When I didn't, people started noticing.

I got Chinese food with Terry Taylor once, and he asked me flat-out. "Are you gay?"

"No," I said. "Why?"

"Well, you got those cruiserweights living in your house and stuff."

Even Raven had his suspicions.

"Come on, Kanyon, I know you're gay, just tell me," he said.

"No," I countered. "I'm not."

And when Page asked, I knew the rumor must have spread everywhere.

"A lot of people think you're gay," he told me.

"Yeah, I know," I said. I didn't confirm it or deny it.

The rumors had spread to the Internet, too, and that really bothered me. I didn't want friends and family reading that.

So I did what I had to do.

Sometimes after a match I would have to pick up a ring rat and take her to my room. I'd force myself to have sex with her, even though it made me sick to do so. I hoped they'd tell everyone else what we had done.

I didn't want to go that far, but I had to. The only way to save my rep was to try to ruin it.

✱

On the movie set, they celebrate everyone's last day. They made a pretty big deal when it was my wrap day, presenting me with one of the world title belts that was used as a prop.

At the wrap party, I was drinking, which was not good for me. For some reason, I was angry, and I took that anger out on Shane. At the time, he was schmoozing with other people rather than talking to me. And it pissed me off.

I decided to confront him. Bad idea.

"I hired you!" I screamed. "You don't appreciate what I did for you! What the fuck is your problem?"

But even as I yelled at him, part of me said, *What the fuck am I doing?*

Shane, who had no idea what had gotten into me, protested. "Why are you doing this?" he asked.

I had no answer. I walked out of my own wrap party and passed out.

The next day, I felt horrible. I was apologetic, but Shane was more confused than hurt. I think he knew I was a bit unhinged.

I think I knew it too.

(37)

THE WWF AND THE EFFECT OF 9/11

I was happy to return to the ring full time, and it looked like time away hadn't hurt my career. We even discussed an angle that would use my Hollywood experience as a gimmick: I'd act like because I'd been off working on movies, I was better than everyone else.

I was able to bring my Hollywood flair to the squared circle in more basic ways, though. At our pay-per-view Slamboree in 2000, I had a move that would have made the stunt guys proud, jumping from the top of the three-tiered cage, landing on the ramp and rolling to protect my body from the impact. I tried to save Page from a power-bomb but instead got thrown off the top of the cage. I even started a feud with Page, which I thought could have really gotten me a long way, but everything was about to change.

Just after making the second movie, it was time to negotiate another contract. I was in a pretty good position: I'd found some fame, I'd worked on the movies and I risked a lot to pull off that spectacular PPV fall. But Eric Bischoff was not leading the negotiations anymore. Instead, it was a pair of suits: Diana Myers, a lawyer who was jealous of the wrestlers because we made more money than she did, and Brad Siegel, president of general-entertainment networks at TBS.

I decided to go to Eric anyway.

"What would you do if you were me?"

"If I were still in that job, I would give you at least $400,000 — probably $460,000 over three years," he said.

It was good to know before my meeting with Diana and Brad. Those two were the first in a line of what I would come to dislike as "non-wrestling" people — people who had no experience in the wrestling business, but got to make decisions about the wrestling business.

When I arrived to meet with them, it started off well enough.

"What would you like?" Siegel asked.

"Anywhere between 4, 5 and $600,000 — in that range," I said.

The two looked at each other. "I'm not going to tell you what we were thinking because it would insult you," Myers said.

"You saying that insults me," I replied.

Siegel explained the contracts were no longer guaranteed deals. They held up a chart, explaining how many shows I would perform and my progression over the years.

They offered me a figure based on how many days I could work. If I worked more than 275 days a year, I could earn $700,000. But they had eliminated house shows and decreased the number of days worked. The average days worked would probably be 70 days a year, which would equate to *less* money than I currently made.

And if I was injured? I could get nothing. I told them to go fuck themselves.

I knew for the first time the company was doomed.

✷

In what would become the first in a line of injuries, I broke my wrist in a match against Ernest Miller. Before the fight Terry Taylor had a message for me.

"We want it especially real tonight," he said.

That made no difference to me because everything I did looked extremely real. But the story of the match was that Miller would get the crap beat out of him, but he would keep coming back at me like he was out of some horror movie, so I had to sell it more than ever.

In that match, Miller and I agreed we would throw a different kind of wrestling punch. We knew that if we hit with our knuckles — like a real punch — then we could hurt each other and our knuckles. We didn't want that. Instead, at the last moment, we would bend our wrists, hitting with the heel of our hand. It looked real, and it minimized the chances of us getting hurt.

Or so I thought.

Doing that over and over, our metacarpals were connecting to our foreheads, bone on bone. I hit Miller one time too many and ended up breaking my wrist. I even needed a cast, and I had to be off television. It couldn't have come at a worse time.

✷

Every year, we'd do one Panama City show for Spring Break. Even with my cast, I was still invited to the show, so I was looking forward to a few days of rest. But with all the rumors flying, I was feeling anything but restful.

Our ratings were slipping. Even though Vince's numbers were better than ours, we were still drawing well. But our sponsors were threatening to pull out on us. It became obvious that we'd stuck with the nWo angle a little too l ng without adjusting. One strong angle couldn't carry the whole promotion..

We heard that Time Warner wanted to sell us. With the exception of Ted Turner, we knew most of the Time Warner people were against wrestling. A lot of people looked at us as the red-headed stepchild from the start, even though it was wrestling that kept cable television on the map.

Another problem was when our *Nitro* show was extended from two hours to three. You never want to oversaturate your market, and it looked like we had. I spoke with Eric, who said the "higher ups" forced him to do it. Did they want us to fail? Who knows.

We all started to wonder what it would be like to work in the WWF. Morale had dropped when we started to get beat in the ratings. We felt like it was impossible to compete. We wanted out.

Bischoff saw the handwriting on the wall. He was trying as hard as he could to collect investors to buy the corporation. Supposedly he had raised more than $200 million, and Time Warner was considering the deal. But industry insiders were already referring to the Panama City show as the "season finale." Some of us thought it could be the finale of the entire promotion.

As I went to the airport that day, I felt like I was in a better position than most. I was pretty sure Bischoff was going to gain control, and Bischoff was a friend of mine. I could recuperate for three months, get paid and get ready for another big push. If things went well, life would be good for me. And I was excited that I might get to help with a new product.

I did have one major concern: my contract was about to come up. The WCW had a week to tell me they wouldn't want me to come back, then according to the contract, I had a month left. Making $240,000 annually, I was hoping for once that I would fall through the cracks. I figured that with everything else going on, they'd forget about my contract. And if they didn't notify me of any change within the week, my contract rolled over for another three months.

I got to the airport and parked. As I walked in, I saw Ernest Miller waiting on the curb to check in. When he saw me, he shook his head.

"What?" I said.

"Bischoff's deal fell through," he said.

"What? How?"

"I think AOL/Time Warner is pulling us off television."

Oh my God, I thought. We were going to be without a network. And a wrestling company without a network was, well, absolutely nothing. We wouldn't be able to make a dollar. But it made no sense. In the ratings, we were beating every movie, every Bulls game and every Braves game. The only reason they'd want to drop us? They just didn't want to be in the wrestling business anymore.

Still, I felt like maybe in the next three months, something could be figured out. Maybe Eric could work something out. And maybe I could help. *Sure*, I thought, *things could still work out*.

Then my cell rang.

"Kanyon?" It was Johnny Ace, a representative from WCW.

"Yeah?" I said. Even then, I knew.

"This is your 30 days' notice, man," he said. "I'm sorry."

I'd been with the company for six years and now all I had left was 30 days.

"Do you still want to be on the last show, man?" he asked.

I couldn't speak. "Yes," I finally managed. "Of course."

Throughout the two-hour flight, I thought back to the time I'd thought of jumping to the WWF, but wasn't allowed to.

Just a year before, morale at WCW was sinking, and I didn't want to go down with it.

Bill Busch, who had replaced Bischoff and was negotiating contracts as the executive vice president for the WCW, said that anyone who wanted to could leave the company. Benoit and Guerrero and others made the jump. I talked to WWF promoter Jim Ross, and he offered me $400,000 to leave. Legally, we weren't even supposed to be talking, but I liked what he had to say.

"Unlike other guys who have jumped over, you would immediately be featured in our storylines," Ross told me. "Some who have come over here aren't talented. You're polished. You can do it."

On Valentine's Day 2000, I asked Bush for my release. As I waited outside his office, I heard him ask a coworker who I was. He didn't even know the names of his talent. It made me sick: just another example of the company hiring non-wrestling people to run their company. In fact, Busch was an accountant with no wrestling knowledge at all. I was already pissed over some Internet comments I'd read from Hulk Hogan that day. I had a history with Hogan, as Kidman and I had helped him train celebrities like Jay Leno and Karl Malone in the past.

"Kidman couldn't draw flies at a flea market," Hogan had said on the Internet.

I didn't for the life of me know why Hogan would say such a thing. Was he trying to set up an angle? I didn't think so — he'd never done that with Kidman before.

As I walked into Bush's lavishly decorated office that day, I only knew one thing: I wanted out.

I got to the point. "I want my release."

"Why?" Busch asked, acting genuinely shocked.

"We're on the *Titanic*, and I want to get off."

"What?"

I decided to humor myself. "Did you hear what Hogan said this week about Billy Kidman?"

"No." He looked confused.

I exploded. "You don't know anything about your industry! You promised that anyone who wanted to leave could leave! I want to leave!"

"No. I can't have people leave," he said.

"Then you shouldn't have said that! Let me go make my money!"

"We'll get in touch with you during the week."

My impatience boiled over. "Billy-Boy, you've made a lot of promises and haven't followed through. You promise I will hear from someone this week?"

"I promise," he said, looking smug.

I got up, livid. "I predict I won't get a call this week," I said. "Do you know that this Monday, WWF isn't even on?"

"No," he said.

"They're not," I told him, pointing at his face. "They're showing the Westminster dog show. And you know what? That's going to beat us in the ratings too, because people like you don't know what you're doing."

I walked out of the office and slammed the door.

That Monday, the dogs destroyed us in the ratings.

✱

I left the meeting with Busch and I called Ross.

"I'm driving to Connecticut the minute I get my release," I told him.

Ten minutes later, Jim Mitchell called me. "Heard you asked for your release," he said.

It was obvious Busch had started spreading the word.

Next, wrestling writer Dave Meltzer called, so I decided to use it to my advantage.

"No, I didn't ask for my release," I told him. "Busch offered me $500,000 to stay, and I said, 'Hell no. I don't want that from you.'"

It was in the *New York Daily News* the next day.

While I fielded other phone calls, I was headed somewhere else. I had to settle something with Hogan.

✱

Hulk was taking off tape when I found him in the locker room.

"Hey," I said.

He looked up. "Hey."

I didn't waste time. "I heard what you said about Kidman," I began. "He loves this company. I thought you liked him. Why would you say that?" I walked over to him, but I didn't sit down. I wanted to loom over him. "You're our leader," I said. "We look up to you. When you start talking bad about others, it hurts us."

"Whoa," he said, holding up his hand. "Don't get me wrong. Between you and me, I'm setting up an angle. I want to wrestle Kidman."

I was floored. I never thought he would want to wrestle Kidman. "Really?"

"Yeah, all those things you said are true. I've got a lot of respect for him. I think it'll be a good angle."

"Wow, that changes everything," I said. I sat down.

"So," Hogan said, unwrapping more tape, "you've got a spot up there, huh?" He winked. We both knew he meant the WWF.

"Yeah," I said.

"Do me a favor," he said. "When you get up there, tell Vince to save me a spot at the big table."

He slapped me on the shoulder.

"I'll do it," I said.

Hogan told the truth. A few months later, he and Kidman had a feud. It worked.

✸

Weeks passed and I never got that phone call from Busch.

Every few days I would call, and sometimes his secretary would tell me he was out. Sometimes she would tell me nothing at all, she would just take a message. Eventually, Busch used her to tell me that I would not be receiving a release from my contract. And for three months I wasn't used on television once. It looked like I was being punished.

I missed the first train out of the WCW. While I could have had a head start on the others, making a new name for myself under Vince McMahon, I had to wait until the WCW completely folded.

Over a year later, as the plane sent me to my Spring Break destination, I hoped I could be one of the first people to negotiate with the WWF. It could be a completely new start.

✸

We touched down in Panama City and I felt better about things. As I got off the plane, my first call was to Jim Ross, who had a good ol' boy persona and let friends call him by his nickname, J.R. He really played up the J.R. Ewing gimmick from *Dallas*, even while suffering from a form of palsy that caused facial paralysis, and I liked him.

"If you guys are still interested, I want to come work for you," I told him. "Thirteen months ago, you offered me that chance, and I couldn't do it. Now I can. And I want to."

He told me they would be in touch. Things were looking up.

In fact, as I checked into our hotel, I felt better and better about life — until later that day, when I saw Disco.

"Did you hear?" he said.

"Yeah. Eric couldn't do it. We're losing the stations."

"No," he said. "There's more news.

"What?"

"Vince McMahon is going to buy us."

I couldn't believe it. Disco told me he'd heard Vince was buying up 24 contracts, and the ones he didn't buy would be paid by Time Warner. I was not one of the 24. I was being released.

I went from a manic high to losing it over the next three or four days. I mixed pain pills and alcohol. I staggered out on to the beach where I met a horde of college kids, celebrating their vacations. One of them had a video camera and as they recognized me, they wanted me to body slam them.

I did it. I was drunk and out of my mind. I didn't know where I was. Over and over I body slammed the kids. It was a sight to see.

I think you can still find it on YouTube.

✻

The night of the show in Panama City, I had cleared my head. I wanted to feel good for the last show. I did — until I saw Diana Myers.

"We're all sorry about the situation," she told me.

"Whose decision was it?" I asked. "Does Vince know about my contract?"

"It's confusing."

"I know," I said. "Who decided I had to go? Eric? Vince? I need to know."

"Please don't hate me." She looked down at the ground.

"Too fucking late," I said and walked away. She was the epitome of why we went out of business.

During the last WCW show, a bunch of us got together and cried. It was the end of an era. And none of us really knew what we were going to do next.

✻

Ross later came to Georgia and had one-on-one meetings with a lot of people. I got a meeting too — and I told them I wanted to be in. Ross said he would sign me. He wasn't supposed to, but he did.

At WWF, contracts were structured differently, guaranteeing your salary, no matter how much you worked. Plus, you got a bonus for participation in bigger matches. In one cage match, I could make $13,000 — a lot more than what I was making in WCW. And even if I got injured, they couldn't fire me. It was called a "no-cut" deal. There was one stipulation: If the injury forced me out of action for three months, they could cut your pay.

✷

So after all the battles between the WCW and the WWF, it looked like Vince McMahon had finally won the war.

People said the demise of WCW stemmed from their love of the old guys, like Hogan and the nWo. With the focus on them, young wrestlers were ignored, or given mid- and lower-level card matches that didn't encourage fans to connect with the rookies.

I could relate.

In a storyline that was eerily familiar, I became part of what was known as "The Alliance," a group of more than 30 wrestlers, including Page, Raven and Kidman, who were "invading" McMahon's WWF. I debuted in July 2001, and my performance there caused Stephanie McMahon, our part-owner, to tell Booker T to give me the WCW United States Championship. He did, and I held my first national title.

While I had been able to forge a great relationship with Bischoff, we never saw Vince very much. But when we did, he was as intimidating as any human could be — and that's just the way he liked it. He was like a kid in some ways, a schoolyard bully. He enjoyed being mean, and he'd place people in uncomfortable situations because he thought it was funny. During booking meetings, Vince would always make fun of Ross, and the side of his face that was paralyzed. As if that wasn't enough, he even made Ross once kiss his bare ass on live television.

To the outside world, Vince seems like an odd guy. That's because he is. And like many other wrestlers, you never can tell where reality ends and the fantasy begins. Is Vince the same person outside the ring as he is inside? I don't think anyone knows. But one thing is true: Business comes first.

However, when he can mix the business with the humiliation, he really has a good time. He likes to wait until the performers come to their hometowns before he really unloads the humiliation.

I saw this not long after I joined WWF. Kidman and the woman who would later become his wife (fitness model Torrie Wilson) joined up, and she told Vince she would do anything on camera. And she meant anything — bra and panty girl wrestling, making out, whatever. But there was one thing Torrie didn't want to do: She did not want to dance.

"I feel like I'm a terrible dancer," Torrie told me one day backstage. "I'm just not comfortable with it."

So Vince agreed not to have her dance in any skits. That is, until our tour made a stop in Boise, Idaho — Torrie's hometown.

The day before the show, Torrie was crying backstage.

"What's wrong?" I asked.

She looked up at me and wiped her eyes. "My family and friends are all going to be here for the show," she said. "And I'm supposed to do a dance contest tonight with Ernest Miller."

"But Vince said you didn't have to dance!"

"I know," she said. "I'm so nervous. I'm scared."

"He's just doing this because you don't want to," I said. "You can't let him win."

"What should I do?"

We talked it out and decided that Torrie would not dance. She would strip. "Dance all sexy," I said. "People will love it. You'll be a star."

The crowd ended up loving her act. I could tell she was nervous at first, but then she let it all hang out. I walked over behind the stage curtain and there I saw Vince, a wide grin on his face. He just laughed as he watched Torrie squirm. From then on, I did not want to work for him. In that private moment, when no one was watching, he showed me his true colors.

It was only a matter of time before I felt that cruelty firsthand.

✷

After being in the WWF for a while, I started to get a little push, thanks to another wrestler with ties to the management. It was Chris Jericho, a veteran wrestler with long blond hair, who went to Vince and let him know that I was the real deal. "This is the guy we need to go with," he told Vince.

A few days later I wrestled Jericho, and it's the only time Vince ever approached me to talk about anything. When he talks to you, he's in total control. But he'll pause in the middle of sentences. It's very weird, and it made me uneasy.

"We really like you," he said to me. "You've . . . adjusted well here. We're going to . . . push you hard. But we want you to stand out. You have a . . . very interesting look. You talk lispy. Accentuate the wrist a little," he said, bending his wrist.

"You have a very . . . unique way of speaking. You need to be very over-the-top and flamboyant . . . you know what I'm saying?"

There had been rumors about me being gay in WCW. And I did have a lisp. But he was trying to make me do something that I didn't want to do. I didn't think it was a good idea. Why should I be effeminate? I wasn't. It was weird.

I went to Jericho. "Do you think this will work?"

"Hell no, man."

No one thought it was a good idea.

Everyone thought Vince was trying to humiliate me. But at the same time, you have to pay the bills.

I went to one of the writers assigned to me, Dominick.

"I don't see why they want to do this, but I guess we could try," he said.

"OK," I said, shrugging. "Let's try."

So we worked out this odd speech impediment. It seemed forced, unnatural and it really didn't work. I tried to overemphasize my own natural lisp, and it just came out wrong.

We worked on it for weeks but eventually, Dominick told Vince we couldn't do it. Later it occurred to me that maybe I couldn't do it because I didn't want to. At the same time, Vince wanted another wrestler named Bubba Ray Dudley to have a stutter. He fought that, too, and it didn't really work.

Looking back, I'm sure Vince knew I was gay. And I'm sure he tried to exploit it.

★

In August of that year, I'd reformed my tag team with Page, and together, we won the WWF Tag Team Championships over a team known as the Acolytes Protection Agency. We had the belts for exactly 10 days before we lost to the very popular tandem of Kane and the Undertaker. Shortly thereafter in San Antonio, I also lost my national title to a wrestler named Tajiri. Since we were cut loose from the WCW, Tajiri had taken on a new manager—a guy named Jim Mitchell, who kept using his sinister gimmick to manage scary characters. Tajiri was only five-nine, but he was more than 200 pounds of muscle. He was pretty good.

I knew I was going to lose, and I was disappointed. But afterward, I felt even worse when I didn't have enough time to connect with the crowd. Mitchell saw me and came over. He shook my hand.

"Hey," he said, "it's nice to have a job, isn't it?"

"Yeah, I guess," I said.

In the locker room, I couldn't hide my frustration.

"I'm losing my push within the company, aren't I?" I asked Page.

"It looks that way," he said.

I couldn't say any more. Page didn't have the authority he once had. There was no real way to affect the situation. I felt like my world was coming undone.

That was September 10, 2001.

The next day, I gained some new perspective.

✯

When terrorists hijacked four planes and sent them crashing into the World Trade Center, the Pentagon and a Pennsylvania field, we had no idea it was going on. Most of us were still asleep in our hotel rooms when it happened just after 9 a.m. EST. My phone rang.

"Kanyon!"

It was a friend from New York.

"You need to wake up!" he shouted. "Something's happening in New York."

I turned on the television. I saw flames and destruction, and I thought to myself this must have been what it looked like in Oklahoma City. I didn't know it then, but this was worse. Throughout that morning, all anyone could do was call their families, but most of the phone lines were jammed.

Like most people, I couldn't immediately get a hold of my family. My brother works blocks away from the World Trade Center so when I did reach him, it was a huge relief.

But something else happened that day, something that changed my personal life. When a disaster of that magnitude happens, you start re-evaluating your life, realizing what is important. As the towers crumpled, my desire to hide who I was from the ones I love went down with them.

I later learned that "coming out" is a long process. In fact, it can take years. My own process began September 11, when in the wake of unthinkable tragedy I felt utterly alone.

For a month I struggled whether or not to share my secret with my family. Yes, I'd told Jim and a few others I was gay, but that was out of necessity. But when I searched my soul for that month, I kept coming back to the realization I should tell someone in my family that I was gay. The more I thought about it, the more I came to the conclusion there was only one person I could talk to right now. Only one person had been there with me from the very beginning and who I could have easily lost on that horrible day in September 2001.

It was my brother, Ken.

I had to give him a call.

✱

Things went from bad to worse in the WWF. I'd been relegated to lower-card fights, and I was feeling powerless again. In a dark match — a match that is not shown on television — against Randy Orton, a six-four, 230-pound ex-Marine, I tore my left anterior cruciate ligament in my knee. The injury was so serious I was forced to travel to Birmingham, where the legendary Dr. James Andrews repaired the tear. I was officially out of the Invasion storyline.

I was facing another low. My professional career was floundering, and when I came home, I was tormented by indecision about my big revelation. I just kept thinking about how alone I felt. So I knew what I had to do. I phoned Ken.

I knew I had to get it out right away or I would explode. "I have something I need to tell you," I said.

He paused. "OK."

"Ken, I've appreciated your friendship for a long time," I began. "That's why when I needed to tell someone about this, I thought of you."

He said nothing. I went on.

"I've known this for a long time, but I always thought, for different reasons, that I needed to keep it quiet," I said. "But I think now that by keeping it a secret, I'm not being fair to anyone — not my family, my friends or myself. Plus, I think I'm going a little crazy because of it."

"Are you OK, Chris?"

"Yeah, I am," I said. "But I'm also . . . gay."

Ken didn't say a word. For a beat, then another, he stayed quiet, and I wondered if what I'd done was the right thing.

"Thanks for telling me, man," he finally said. "I know that must have been difficult. I love you, brother."

I smiled. He was cool, and he made me feel OK about it. "Yeah, it was hard," I said.

"How long have you known?" he asked.

"Since I was about six or seven."

"Wow! You kept that secret all this time?" he said. "Have you told Mom and Dad yet?"

"No."

"Oh," he said. "Wow."

"Yeah," I said. "Congratulations. You're the first."

✶

My brother took the news great. I, however, did not. Later I would learn there are resources, like books and pamphlets that could have helped me in dealing with my feelings. I didn't feel relief like I thought I would; in fact, I was more afraid than ever, and the prospect of telling my parents terrified me. I didn't want to let them down, and it felt like I was doing just that. I wouldn't be giving them any grandchildren. I wouldn't be getting married to a woman. I felt like they would be disappointed in me.

Ken assured me they wouldn't. "It won't change a thing," he told me. "But I do think they need to know."

That's when I had an idea. "Why don't you do it?" I asked Ken.

"What?"

"Why don't you tell them for me?" I begged. "It makes sense. You could prepare them and I could come in to finish the job."

"I don't know, man," he said. "I guess I could do it if you want me to."

"I do," I said. "I really do. I'll owe you big time."

"Yeah," he said. "I think you will."

✶

Ken and I decided he would tell them just before Christmas, then when I came home, we could all discuss it together. That sounded like the best plan.

In mid-December, Ken called to let me know how it went.

"They still love you," he said. "It went great."

It was a relief just to hear him say it. "Thanks, man."

"Hey, what are brothers for?" he said, laughing.

I waited a few more days to let the news sink in. I wanted to call them and make sure they were OK. Just before the weekend, I was going out of my mind, so I called them up. When they answered, we did not talk about their son being gay. We talked about everything else—weather, my travel plans, my job. Everything.

"Anything going on?" I asked.

"Same old, same old," my dad said. "When are you coming home?"

"Tomorrow," I said.

"OK," Dad said.

I had to bring it up. "Uh, Dad?"

"Yeah?"

"Didn't Ken call you up and tell you the news?"

"Yes," my dad said. "Yes, he did."

I almost couldn't believe he hadn't brought it up. "Well, what do you think?"

He paused. "I think we'll talk about it when you get home."

Hmm. I didn't know what to think about that. What did it mean? I couldn't figure out how to ask, so I left it at that.

"See you tomorrow," I said.

"Alright then," Dad said.

It couldn't have been any more awkward. It was awful. At that point I really wished we hadn't told them.

✻

Being back in New York so soon after the tragedy was reassuring. It was great seeing my old hometown again and being able to commiserate with true New Yorkers, like Danny and my other friends. There is a pride in New York that rivals that of every other place in the world, and nothing can beat that out of us.

For the entire week, my family never brought up the fact I was gay. The days crawled by, sometimes filled with awkward pauses and glances between me and my brother. Never did my parents say a word.

"What are they doing?" I whispered to Ken after dinner, when they were out of the room. "I thought you said they were OK with all of this?"

"They are!"

"Well they sure don't act like it!"

"Well, they haven't acted poorly toward you, either, Chris."

"Why don't they say *something* about it?"

"Well," Ken said, "maybe they feel as awkward as you do."

I hadn't thought of that. Maybe they did. Maybe I was the one who needed to bring it up. I decided to do it.

When the two came back into the room I stood up. "Mom, Dad—I'm gay," I said. "I want you to know that if you have any questions, just ask. I'm still the same person I've always been, but now I can be honest."

Dad and Mom looked at each other, then to me.

"Have you had sex with men?" Mom asked.

Oh boy. "Yes," I said. "A few times."

"Tell me about your first sexual experience with a man," she said.

Oh my God. I was not ready for this. Not at all.

But I told her, and when I was through, she seemed to be OK with all of it. My Dad, who had also listened, had a question too.

"You know, I've heard about how this works," Dad said. "But I was wondering—are you a pitcher or a catcher?"

Oh my God. Oh my God. Oh my God. He wanted to know if, in the course of anal sex, I gave or received. The crude baseball metaphor had been used since I was a kid.

I mustered my courage. "I'm a pitcher, Dad," I said. "I pitch. That's what I do."

I explained I had tried receiving before, but that because I was normally the bigger man, I was much more comfortable with giving the anal sex.

After that wall was broken down, we continued to talk for almost three hours, about my life and what it was like to be a gay wrestler. We talked about the pressures I faced and my constant fear of being discovered. For the first time, my family really knew me, and it felt good. But I was still afraid of the rest of the world knowing. I needed time. And maybe the world needed time too.

I didn't want to lose my job. And I was still convinced that if I did come out, my career would be over.

This is enough, I thought. *For my family to know, this is enough for me.*

I was wrong. It was not enough. My family knowing was a good thing, but it wasn't even close to being enough to help me.

✱

While I was recovering from my knee injury, I began to develop a character that was so close to home it would mean that, for me, wrestling was about to get *real*. I wanted to be an openly gay man playing a gay macho wrestler. I wanted to be me.

I had to pitch the idea to someone, so I told three wrestlers I was gay.

Two of them took it to people in Vince's office, like Michael Hayes, one of the agents and writers, without my knowledge. It was almost like Michael didn't want to be involved, I was told. He redirected it to others, because he didn't want to fool with it.

The wrestlers thought it was a good idea, but they didn't want me to do it until I was back full time. I was told Vince "didn't want me to do this on my own." I also told Jim Mitchell, who was intrigued by the idea, but he could see where Vince may not like it.

We all wondered how to go about it. But then the tone from the others changed, and people began telling me not to do it. I was sure it came from Vince, or possibly to his daughter, Stephanie. This was controversial. This was more than an angle. I was confused about asking Vince directly—I didn't know how to pitch it or how he would react. I needed people on my side, but I wasn't getting a lot of help.

Around the time I was starting to work my way back, injury struck again—I hurt my shoulder and was out for six more months. *Maybe,* I thought, *I should be more worried about getting back in the ring as any character at all.*

It seemed clear I had no support for a gay character. I'd laid aside my Mortis mask a long time go, but it looked like my Kanyon mask might be here to stay.

(38)

DID VINCE REALLY WANT TO HURT ME?

By May of 2002 I was sent down to Ohio Valley Wrestling, a developmental territory in Louisville, Kentucky, where I was supposed to continue rehabilitation and help train some of Vince's younger guys. But my career took another hit when I wrestled Lance Cade, who was another member of the Invasion and worked a cowboy gimmick.

This time I badly injured my left shoulder and neck, and a week later, I was having surgery again. I had been on a steroid cycle to speed up my recovery from my back injury, and I always used a clean needle, but I was working in a barn (literally) and I suppose that the mat was infected with staph. My left shoulder swelled up severely. At the time I thought it was a muscle pull or a tear of some kind, so I headed back to Georgia because I had a few days off. I went into the hot tub in the backyard, which I thought might help, but it didn't. I then went to a physical therapist to have it worked on, and it was way beyond painful, and worse, they broke up the staph infection and it entered my bloodstream. I ran a high fever for the next three days. By the third day I didn't know my own name.

✶

After losing two weeks and 34 pounds to my hospital stay, I realized I had to take extra time to recuperate, so I didn't push a comeback, but I was still worried. It had been more than a year since I'd been on TV, when I returned to Ohio Valley Wrestling in the fall of 2002. For four months, I wrestled my way back into shape. I wanted to go back to television and look good — and I wanted to do it all without steroids.

Those nights, alone, were the worst. I didn't know what I was feeling, but sometimes I didn't want to get out of bed for days. I know now that's called depression. It was as if I was standing on the edge of a black hole, looking down, and nothing was there. Sometimes, I wanted to jump.

I looked for companionship online, but most people wanted pictures and specifics. It was too risky. I couldn't go out to the bars because people knew who I was. I was lying to everyone (aside from family) and I felt trapped. I really didn't know if there was a way out.

I was staying with a friend of mine in Louisville. It was an old, lonely house that seemed to mirror exactly how I was feeling. Nights were spent sleeping on an uncomfortable air mattress, and that was how I felt in real life, uncomfortable in my own skin.

One morning the phone rang.

It was Pete's wife, Nellie.

"Pete had another heart attack," she said softly. "He didn't make it."

He was 54.

The rest of the conversation was lost in warped sound, like Nellie was talking underwater. I always thought Pete would be around, like Mr. Miyagi. Nellie gave me the funeral information and said she hoped to see me there.

I sleepwalked through that day. Pete was the one who got it all started for me. Emotionally, I was caught off guard, and one thought that kept coming back involved money, of all things. I never paid him the $3,000 for letting me train in his gym. And then there was the thought of attending the funeral in New York.

I wanted to — and needed to — go to the funeral. But WWE had a way of making you feel that when you're injured, these kinds of things aren't really acceptable. They even gave Kidman hell when he and Torrie wanted to go on a honeymoon.

While I was at Ohio Valley Wrestling, it seemed like I shouldn't leave.

It was a dilemma. As a pupil I knew I should be there. But I was so afraid I would be let go from the WWE if I left. After presenting my idea about a gay wrestling character, I felt like I was on everyone's bad side. I did not want to have to ask for something again.

I didn't do it.

I called up the family instead, and told Nellie I wouldn't be making it. She said she understood, and added, "He loved you like a son, Chris."

I know now I made the wrong choice.

✶

Laying in my bed was my way to avoid all of those regrets, anxieties and fears. Sometimes I would do it for six days in a row, only getting up to make an appearance in the ring — the only thing I could muster the energy to still care about.

But after four months of wrestling in Ohio Valley, my fortunes looked like they were about to change. I was back — my body felt good, and I knew I was ready to step into the ring again. That was it: I set my sights on getting back on television.

But Vince McMahon ruined everything.

✶

It was Paul Heyman, one of Vince's right-hand men, who told me they had a skit for me.

"Vince wants you to sing like a faggot," he said. He went on to tell me they wanted me to dress like Boy George and come out of a big closet.

I had been off the radar for so long, I knew that I needed to do anything they asked. But the angle was so out of the ordinary it made no sense as a storyline. Normally, when guys are out for so long, they either come back with a whimper — no storyline — or they come out with something great to get them elevated.

This angle was almost too much. This was a message: I would not be doing the gay angle I wanted to do. I would be doing the gay angle *Vince* wanted me to do. Even though it was nine months after the fact, it was another way for Vince to drive home the embarrassment.

I had to rehearse all of it, and Vince was on hand to watch, laughing his ass off. It brought me right back to the Torrie Wilson incident.

I have never felt so small. I was in a no-win situation, and I realized the gravity of it right then and there. If I said no, I could be fired, and everyone would wonder why I turned it down. If I said yes, then I would have to go through with an embarrassing act — and in my comeback to national TV, no less.

I did the only thing I could.

"I'll do it — whatever you want," I said.

✱

"I think you should do it, man." It was Jim Mitchell. I called him and told him what Vince was going to make me do. "Who gives a fuck what anyone thinks. As a wrestler, what do you always have to do? You keep the storyline going."

He was right.

"Keep it going, man," he said. "Do what you got to do."

✱

I was to wrestle The Undertaker on February 13 on McMahon's *SmackDown* show. I still wasn't quite sure how this was all going to come off. Up until that point I'd made a career of being a guy who'd do things for laughs, to make the other guy look good. But this time McMahon might be the only one laughing. The more I thought about it, the more I was certain he did this for two reasons: To see how far he could push me and to see if I would admit to being gay.

It was one of the worst beatings I ever took.

The Undertaker was a six-ten, 300-pound giant who wore a long black coat into the ring. He was known as the American Bad Ass, after the Kid Rock song.

"Do you really wanna hurt me?" I sang from the inside of the closet, which was placed in the middle of the ring. "Do you really wanna make me cry?"

When I emerged, the crowd went wild with boos and laughs. They didn't know what to make of me either. I was dressed up like Boy George, decked out in purple and pink. Makeup covered my entire face.

The Undertaker did not hold back, and it was a painful outing for me. On his chairshots, he didn't hit the flat of my back. He hit my shoulder blades, giving me yet another concussion, which kept me out of the ring again for a few weeks.

Afterward, I was convinced the whole set-up, including the beating, was deliberate. I thought it was a message from McMahon: We don't want you — or your kind — here.

✱

By that time, the rumors were all over the Internet. A Google search of "Kanyon" and "gay" brought back dozens of hits. I knew I was losing my secret. Somehow I needed to take control of it all.

I gathered my courage and went to Stephanie. I asked to do the character full time. Stephanie and the management were shocked I wanted to. The Undertaker loved the idea. But strangely, they didn't want me to — probably because I wanted to do it. I'm convinced that I turned the tables on them. When I said I was comfortable with the idea, I wasn't fun to torment anymore, so they did not allow me to do it.

After my comeback performance, I was relegated to *Velocity*, a Saturday night show for mid- and low-carders. I felt like I was finished. The show didn't lead to a storyline for me. After The Undertaker's whipping, I was a laughingstock, reduced to nothing more than an afterthought with the fans. I was out all right — out of sight, out of mind.

✶

As the days went by, I slipped further and further into myself.

I thought maybe a change of scenery would do me good, so I moved to a new beach home in Clearwater, Fla. I sleepwalked through the rest of the summer, showing up for wrestling, giving as much effort as I could muster, and coming home. But a thought always stuck with me.

I wondered if things would be better if I weren't alive. Things would be easier, wouldn't they? I got into bed and kept thinking the same thing, over and over. Could I kill myself if I wanted to? Could I do it?

It was Sept. 14, 2003. Sunday. I hadn't been out of the house — or even out of bed — since Wednesday. My bedroom was a mess, covered in newspapers and printed out e-mails from years ago, things I'd saved just because I could not throw them away. Everywhere I looked, there was another sign of my wretched life. For two straight months I had thought about ending it. My self-confidence was shaken, paranoia had set in and I had no idea how to cope with my double-life. Who was I? Was I even a person at all? I was lying to everyone because I was afraid I'd lose my job, yet I was losing my job too.

There was no escape.

I walked into the bathroom and grabbed a full bottle of sleeping pills. There were 50 pills in the bottle. *That should be enough*, I thought.

III

THE BATTLE FOR CHRIS KANYON

"Who's betta than Kanyon? Nobody!"
CHRIS KANYON

(39)

FIGHTING BACK OUTSIDE THE RING

I looked at myself in the mirror. I was covered in piss and shit and vomit.
"What the hell?" I asked. "What the hell have you done to yourself?"

✱

I tried to commit suicide. It's hard for me to admit now, but I did it. It is obvious now, even to me, that normal people don't try to kill themselves, but in my head, it seemed like the only way to have peace.

I went to a psychologist the very next day, and I told my entire life story — everything I've said here. It was in therapy that I first learned the meaning of terms like manic depression and bipolar. Suddenly my mood swings and the ways in which I dealt with problems made sense. One question remained, however: Was it something I was born with, or was this something that had sprung from hiding that I was gay for so long? From the concussions? From flirting with steroids? From my high-pressure environment? Or was it all these things together, a terrible toxic cocktail?

I didn't know. I don't think anyone could. But I know that suffering from these disorders, being gay and also being a professional wrestler didn't help. I was drowning, and finally, I was able to confide in someone who could help me understand.

My formal diagnosis was that had bipolar disorder — a condition characterized by extreme highs and lows in mood swings. The serious threat that comes along with bipolar disorder is the risk of suicide.

And the disorder is lifelong.

But I learned there is treatment. Several medications make life manageable for those with bipolar disorder, and after a while, I noticed I was feeling better, taking antidepressants and mood stabilizers. For a year I was in and out of treatment, trying to get myself better. But I still wanted to wrestle, and I may have been the best version of myself out in the ring. My only problems? I was coming off two injuries, I'd fallen out of the storylines and out of sight, and my skit only fueled rumors that I was gay.

They were big problems.

"Why don't you just come out as a gay wrestler? Who's going to care?"

Leave it to Jim Mitchell to provide another solution. Never one to care about someone's sexual preferences, Mitchell thought it may be time for an openly gay character in wrestling. After the Boy George incident, I wasn't so sure.

In 2002, two guys who called themselves Billy and Chuck had a storyline where they got married. They were called the Flamboyant Duo and when they appeared, the crowd showered them with boos. An independent wrestler, Simon Sermon, admitted he was gay, but he never wrestled as a full-time job. Another wrestler, Jordan Orlando, admitted his bisexuality on a website. He was released by WWE, and later Orlando said he was insulted at the characters he was asked to play — one character had both a girlfriend and a boyfriend.

In my therapy sessions, I would discuss the possibility of coming out as gay while in the ring. I thought maybe I could just take the mic like I used to, just grab it and shout, "I'm Chris Kanyon and I am gay!" I didn't care if the people cheered or jeered. I thought it may make an interesting storyline, and I even wondered if I could have Kanyon the character announce *he* was gay — but still keep my own sexuality secret.

Turns out I didn't have enough time.

On February 9, 2004, Vince McMahon released me from my contract.

And who's Kanyon without a contract?

Nobody.

✷

Page was kind enough to give me what I thought would be a retirement match that summer in Wayne, New Jersey. My family was there, and it was nice to have them there at the end of my career even if they hadn't been at the beginning.

But it wasn't long after I retired that I felt that familiar urge, the same one I felt when driving through Connecticut. The same one I felt after graduating college.

I called Mitchell.

"What can they take from me?" I said. "I think you're right. I think it's time the wrestling world had their first openly gay wrestler."

"Fuckin' A, man," Mitchell said.

Other athletes had come out before. It wasn't unprecedented, but it was still pretty damn rare. Billy Bean, a utility player for the Oakland Athletics baseball team in 1980s and 1990s, revealed he was gay after retiring. Glenn Burke, an outfielder for baseball's L.A. Dodgers in the 1970s came out in 1982. Former professional football players Esera Tuaolo, Roy Simmons and David Kopay — all gay. Most recently, former professional basketball player John Amaechi broke his silence in 2007 when he published a book about his gay life in the NBA.

The precedent had been set. But none of those players had actually come out while they were still participating in those activities.

And no active wrestler had ever come out — and continued to wrestle. This was something special. This was something that could get me back into wrestling. This could be the thing to end my career . . . or maybe resurrect it.

✷

In 2005 I announced the end of my retirement. I wanted to come back, wrestle on the independent circuit and — after talking to my therapist — I wanted to announce that my character, Chris Kanyon, was gay. Then, I'd also announce that I, in real life, was also gay. The feeling this time, for me, was different. I was more prepared for this, I think, than when I came out to my brother.

I began wrestling independently again, my career coming full circle. I remembered the matches Pete had set up for me, and the people my brother had gotten to come watch me in New York.

It all added up to February 4, 2006.

It was a small ring in an independent show, just like the ones I wrestled in when I was growing up. The difference this time was I was going to be honest with the crowd — mostly honest, at least.

There were only a few hundred spectators at the independent Canadian match in Greater Sudbury, Ontario, but they were in for a stunner.

In my old wrestling boots and trunks, I grabbed the mic right before the match.

"I'm tired of living in the closet," I said. "Chris Kanyon is a homosexual."

The crowd, not knowing if this was an act, responded with a mix of boos and cheers.

"I also want to say that I was not fired from the WWE due to cutbacks, as they said," I continued. "I was fired because of my sexual orientation."

More boos and cheers. I think people just had no idea how to react.

"I am the first ever active openly gay wrestler in the history of the industry," I said. "Life is about choices. I choose to be the real Chris Kanyon. You can choose to boo or cheer if you want."

I heard both that night.

✶

After coming out in Sudbury, my goal was to take that publicity and spin it into an appearance on *Oprah* or *Howard Stern* or somewhere — and then announce that I, too, was gay.

It didn't work out that way.

When I was asked after the match if I was in fact gay, or if it was just my character that was gay, I said my personal life was no one else's business. Despite my in-ring bravado, I wasn't yet ready to admit my own homosexuality. But I also wanted a bigger forum, and I wanted to use that to get back into the WWE or another market.

As it turns out, my announcement caused confusion, and a month later, I had to clarify.

On March 5, 2006, at a legends match with Page in Orlando, I came out — again — to the crowd. It wasn't any easier the second time, but with Page by my side, I knew I could do it.

"The rumors are true," I told Page and the crowd. "I'm gay. I'm the first-ever active openly gay professional athlete in this country."

As the crowd again responded with a mix of cheers and jeers, Page took the mic from me and proved, once again, why he is such a great friend.

"Give it up right now," he said, urging the crowd to cheer. "'Cause that is the baddest son of a bitch I ever knew that was gay — ever. And I don't care if you're straight, if you're gay, black, white, yellow or green — you'll always be my brother."

And he gave me a hug. It was one of the best moments of my career.

✶

A few days later, I sent out a press release, again reiterating that the real Chris Kanyon was also gay. It was awkward and I wish I could've handled it better, because I think more homosexuals could have benefited from it if I did. My "lack of clarity instantly hurt [my] cause in taking a supposed social stand," wrote James Caldwell, a columnist at Pro Wrestling Torch, which writes about wrestling and its issues.

My announcement also caused a big debate as to whether or not I was fired because I was gay and the WWE didn't want to deal with it. I can't say for sure, but I know what it looks like.

I can't see any other way to look at it.

✶

Still, I couldn't shake wanting back in the WWE. But after countless tries to contact McMahon, he would not take my calls. In September 2006 I showed up at a WWE show in Tampa with a sign that read: "Ask Vince why he fired me."

Triple H responded by saying, "Who invited Kanyon?" And after that he said, "We are better than Kanyon!"

Security then escorted me out of the arena, even though I'd paid for my ticket. I'd been thrown out of wrestling yet again.

(40)

KANYON VS. FLAIR

One of my dreams came true, though. I landed on Howard Stern's show.

I'd followed Howard's show for years, and I knew he'd always been an advocate for gay rights. When they called in 2006, I was really excited to make an appearance. I didn't know it would lead to others.

On my first appearance I told my story, explaining why I thought I was fired. But it was my second appearance a few months later that really caused people to listen. I was actually there because I bet Stern's sidekick Artie Lange that the Mets would go further in the playoffs than the Yankees. Turns out I was right, so I came on to the show to collect my bet: Artie had to make out with a 70-year-old female porn star. Howard was after more than that for the show, though: he tried to get Vince McMahon on the air so I could personally ask him why I was let go. But many of the guys were over in Japan for a special show. So instead, they sent along my boyhood hero, Ric Flair, to speak for the company via a telephone interview, which went something like this:

"The WWE is in an uproar over your allegations of why you were fired," Stern said as an introduction. "So we've got Flair on to dispute the claims."

I said I was fine with that. I said I loved Flair since I was a kid, that he was my hero, and that I respected him so much for what he'd done.

"Chris Kanyon was not fired for his sexuality," Flair stated. "I know Chris very well, but he has shortcomings in the ring, and he should not blame those shortcomings on his personal life.

"Kanyon has in-ring skills," Flair continued, "but it takes more than that."

"But your act depends on the gimmicks and storylines given to you," I said. "My act was just fine."

The topic then came up of whether anyone knew I was gay or not.

"I had no idea Kanyon was gay," Flair said. "Nor do I care."

"It wasn't a well-kept secret," I said. "Arn Anderson knew I was gay."

"Well that was your choice in life," Flair said.

"Being gay isn't a choice," I replied.

Stern intervened, redirecting the conversation. "But Chris was in wrestling for years. How could he have not been any good?"

"I lasted nine years as a national TV character," I added.

"I'm not saying he didn't make it," Flair said. "I'm just saying he wasn't fired for being gay."

"Take what they say with a grain of salt," I said. "They're just saying what they think Vince wants to hear."

Gary Dell'Abate, producer of the Stern show, then asked Flair why I was fired.

"I don't know," he answered.

"Then if you don't know, how do you know it *wasn't* because I was gay?" I asked.

"Because there are very successful people in wrestling right now who are gay," Flair said.

"Yes, but they are not openly gay," I said. "That's why I was fired."

"Look, Kanyon has all the talent in the world," Flair affirmed. "But he didn't have anything to bring to the show."

Robin Quivers, Stern's other sidekick, then asked if I could rejoin the WWE.

"No," Flair said, "his time has come and gone. You can talk all you want about who was good nine years ago, but today is different."

"Wait a minute," I said. "You just said I have all the skills in the world, but now you say I don't."

"You're not good enough right now to be on the show," he said.

"Why isn't Vince on the phone?" I asked.

Flair laughed. "I don't know."

Dell'Abate interjected, explaining he tried to get Vince McMahon on the phone, but unfortunately, everyone said he was unavailable overseas. They offered up Flair, and said he "knew enough to speak about the whole situation."

"Look, I respect you," I told Flair.

"Thank you," he said. "Look, I'm not saying you couldn't come in and get by, but it just doesn't seem you have it right now."

"But you haven't seen me wrestle in four years," I protested. "How would you know?"

"I just know that if you were good enough to be in the Show, you'd be there."

Quivers then brought up a good point. "I wonder why the WWE chose to have Flair on when he says he doesn't know why Kanyon was fired."

Stern then asked if I was attracted to Ric, and I said no. But I had one more question for Flair: If I was such a bad wrestler, why did he once ask me to train his own son?

"Asking you to 'work out' with my son and to 'train' him are two completely different things," he said.

"I respect your opinion," I told him. "And I think you're the best ever."

"Man, this was the most civilized wrestling argument of all time," Lange said.

"Kanyon is a great guy," Flair said, "but you shouldn't use Howard Stern to get publicity."

"Well, unlike you, Ric, they called me."

Then Flair hung up.

I'd always dreamed of facing off with Flair one day, and while this wasn't exactly what I had in mind, at least this was one match the WWE couldn't script for me.

✱

After dropping off the radar of the WWE, I tried further comebacks in the independent circuits, including a feud with Raven in Total Nonstop Action Wrestling and another with Joey Ryan in Pro Wrestling Guerrilla. I was prepared to participate in a *TNA iMPACT!* taping, but had to back off because my contract asked for me to sign away image and persona rights, which I would not do. I was through letting promotions determine who Chris Kanyon should be.

(41)

ENJOY THE JOURNEY, ENJOY YOUR LIFE

In the ring no one wanted to hear about my sexuality, but outside of it, people were asking me to share my experiences. I was asked to speak to about 200 college students at Northern Kentucky University for National Coming Out Day in October 2006.

I get extremely nervous speaking in front of large groups of people, and I had to plan out the entire speech, write every word and continually practice it. The day before, I was almost hyperventilating just thinking about it. I didn't want it to come out wrong.

The next day, I saw a few hundred people, some who were gay, some who were trying to convince themselves they weren't gay and some who were just wrestling fans. I told them about my career, my upbringing and how I was let go from the WWE. But what I really wanted to get across was how delicate the process is when deciding to come out. I looked out across a sea of young, eager listeners, took a deep breath, and gave it my best.

"I used to be against Gay Pride," I said.

"I wanted it to be pushed aside, so I didn't have to see it. I wanted it to go away, so I wouldn't have to deal with my own feelings and how I was hiding them. But a funny thing happened on the way to me hating Gay Pride — and hating myself.

"I realized just how dangerous all of the loathing was, and I went to therapy. Depression and being a closeted gay go hand in hand, and it is difficult to overcome. I decided I needed to come out, to make myself feel better and then I could accept what I was. But coming out isn't easy, and it doesn't always end well. You can only do it when you're ready, and when those you will tell are ready too. I actually came out in different stages, and I recommend it.

"And the beauty of it all is that when you do come out, you will continue to create a positive cycle for all gays and lesbians. The more society accepts us, the more our families will accept us, and then together we can be a strong, unified community.

"The more people come out, the stronger we can get. If you really want to affect change, come out, and we can find strength in numbers. Be comfortable and feel good about who you are — and who we all are.

"Be vocal. Show your pride. As much as I used to be against it, I now realize how wonderful it is to tell the truth — to be honest to you, and most of all, to myself.

"That's why days like today are important. It makes it easier for us to come out. Do it for gays and lesbians everywhere. Do it for me. But most of all, do it for yourself.

"Enjoy the journey and don't focus too hard on the destination. Enjoy your life."

✶

My speech went on for a lot longer than that, and when I was finished, I saw a standing ovation in front of me.

I was speechless.

It felt good to have done it, and to try to help others who were struggling. I know it helped at least one person.

Later that day, my friend walked up and said he got a phone call from a student in the crowd.

"Just tell Kanyon I said thank you," the student had said. "I came out to my parents today, after the speech. It was a shock to them, but it felt so good not to lie anymore. I couldn't have done it without hearing what Kanyon had to say."

It only took one person to make all my struggles worthwhile.

I figured if I could affect just one person's life in a positive way like that, life was worth living. Being up there in front of all those people, it was a little like performing again. The only difference? I wasn't lying to anyone.

✱

I am a person who always lived life by following my own set of rules. I'd dedicate myself to a proposition and follow through until I succeeded. I set my sights on becoming a professional wrestler who would be respected by his peers, and I gave everything I had to entertain the fans. I believe I achieved that goal. But it did take its toll on me physically, and especially mentally.

Between being bipolar, the stress and the concussions, I don't know if I am sane anymore. Knowing that I will have to deal with all this for the rest of my life, probably in a more drastic way as I get older, is too much for me to bear at times.

As I said, I am a person who lives life on his own terms, and I am prepared to meet my death following the same principles. And that leaves only one answer for me, which I do not recommend to anyone else — ending my own life.

Every couple of days I stare at the bottle of pills in my medicine cabinet, sometimes for what seems like hours. I can feel them calling me.

✱

On April 5, 2007 — 15 years to the day after I wrestled my first match in Long Island — I formally announced my retirement from wrestling.

Wrestling provided me with everything in life, and I would never trade one second of it. From meeting and training celebrities, to being featured on television, radio and in newspapers, I enjoyed everything. Through high spots and takedowns, feuds in the ring and out, it was the match of a lifetime.

I realize there is still more life to live. What lies ahead for me I don't know, but whatever it is, I'm ready. Although I won't wrestle again professionally, I'm still a fan, and I will always follow it.

All in all, I'm doing OK. I have my good days and bad days. Sometimes I still spend all day in bed. But my medication helps, and being bipolar is something I will struggle with the rest of my life. I take each day as it comes, as well as the struggles that come with it. I fight on.

So what now? I don't know. Can I hold down a nine-to-five job again? I don't really know. Part of me thinks not. But I'm willing to try.

Some ask if I'll go back to physical therapy, but the industry has grown so much now—there may be too much more for me to learn to go back. You know what everyone says about old dogs and new tricks, right?

So yes, I still have a lot to figure out. Do I have regrets? Only a few. One of my goals was to wrestle in Madison Square Garden, and I never did that. Another was to become the world heavyweight champ, and I missed the mark on that too.

I'd still like to one day be the punch line for one of Jay Leno's jokes. Then you know you're really famous. Maybe he could make fun of how I bought my parents' apartment. Or how I'm still new at the dating scene—I've got a lot of catching up to do—but I'd like to find a steady boyfriend of some kind. I'm not great with relationships, but I'm working on it.

I guess I just want to help as many people as I can, because I know that if there was an openly gay wrestler—or a gay person in any sport or job that I could look up to—it would have made it easier for me. If I can help anyone, I will feel like I've done something good.

And I hope that by telling people what I've gone through, others can find inspiration to overcome their own troubles.

Remember, whoever you are, enjoy the journey. Be you. And enjoy your life.

EPILOGUE: APRIL 2, 2010

From the *New York Daily News*:

> FORMER GAY PRO WRESTLER CHRIS KLUCSARITS A.K.A. "CHRIS KANYON" FOUND IN APPARENT SUICIDE

A popular former pro wrestler was found dead in his Queens apartment after he apparently committed suicide, officials said Saturday.

Chris Klucsarits, who wrestled as Chris Kanyon, was found dead Friday night in his Sunnyside flat, officials said.

An autopsy on Klucsarits, 40, did not immediately determine a cause of death, according to the city medical examiner. Scores of pills were found near his body and his death is being investigated as a suicide, police sources said.

The WWE responded with a statement on its website: "World Wrestling Entertainment would like to express its deepest condolences to Christopher Klucsarits' family and friends on his tragic passing."

✶

My final conversation with Chris took place three days before his death. Because I am also bipolar we used to talk on the phone every once in a while about how to deal with it on a day-to-day basis. I told him that he had to take a regular regimen of medication and see a therapist weekly. This was something that Chris was either unprepared or unable to do. I had gotten the sense that he had finally lost his grip on reality. This is very common for people who are bipolar, who (untreated) can experience lapses in reality and psychotic reactions. Add to this the approximately 10 concussions he suffered in the ring from which there had to be some kind of brain damage, and you have a recipe for danger.

I knew Chris for most of his life, and the person who I loved and treated as a member of my own family had mentally deteriorated for several years. It was hard to watch, and I always tried to help him when he asked me to.

When I was down and out, a hopeless drug-addicted mess, he took me into his home and got me sober. I owe him my life for this, and there I feel a guilt that will never go away that I wasn't there when he needed me to save his life.

Chris had become a tortured soul. He was no longer the person he used to be. He knew it, and it was apparent to all of the people that were close to him. Over the years, several times he had threatened to kill himself and I know of at least one attempt.

The weight of living with his condition became too much for him. Because you don't get better, you can only hope to contain the effects of manic-depression.

When I got the news of his passing by his own hand I was crushed, but I understood it. It wasn't until I saw him laying in the casket that I began to feel a sense of relief, because I knew deep in my heart that he was now finally at peace.

If there is a heaven then I know that Chris is there, probably working matches with the wrestling greats that have passed. "Time fears no man, except the legends of professional wrestling."

— *Mike Passariello (a.k.a. Brother P.)*

We will always love and remember you. You were always such a good person and everyone that knew you loved you.

— Mom and Dad

As with most siblings, my brother and I had a tumultuous relationship in our younger years, but became best of friends as we entered adulthood. I continually encouraged him to pursue his dream of becoming a professional wrestler and could not have been more proud when he achieved this goal. Unfortunately, when it comes to dreams, you eventually have to wake up, and this came in the form of severe bipolar disorder for my brother. It took its toll and eventually cost him his life, but instead of viewing this as a tragic and sad ending, I choose to fondly remember all he accomplished in his 40 years of life and smile when I think about him. Chris was the kindest and most giving person I ever knew and I'm sure everyone who had the pleasure of knowing him would agree.

I guess if there is one bit of advice I could give after being through this experience, it would be family and friends are the most important parts of your life. They should never be taken for granted. Let them know they are closest to your heart . . . and if they leave this earth and are no longer part of your life, cherish and hold their memories just as close.

— Ken Klucsarits

ACKNOWLEDGMENTS

The authors would like to thank, in no certain order:

Our families and friends, especially Ken and Pass, who saw us through four years and many tribulations during the completion of this project.

Robert McLearren, captain of the cause. Without you this would not have happened. Because of you we have all the interviews, and you helped in the editing process. You are wonderful.

The various and amazing wrestlers and promoters, friends all, who gave us your warm attention and helped make this possible, especially Diamond Dallas Page and Jim Mitchell. For the friends and others who knew — and were helped by — Kanyon, this book is as much yours as ours.

The representatives at our places of work who encouraged the project, including former coworkers and editors at the *Cincinnati Enquirer*, especially David Niinemets, William Croyle and Patrick Crowley.

Those officials from Northern Kentucky University who gave us so much help navigating National Coming Out Day, who put us in touch with various references, and who served as readers and editors, including: Jim Nilson and family, Chris Cole, Dr. Robert Wallace, Dr. Nancy Kersell, Dr. Jimmie Manning and Dr. Roxanne Kent-Drury, among others.

Our personal soundboard of editors and writers who offered unending support and criticism, including Jacob Bennett, Erica Walsh, Andy Miller, Megan McCarty, Tom Ramstetter, Rebecca Weatherford, Terry Boehmker, Rich Shivener, Travis Mayo and all the students, professors and staff at Northern Kentucky University, especially those in the Graduate Department of English.

Others, who without your help this book would still be an idea: Caroline Lynch Pieroni, Anthony Zelli, Sonny Brewer, Dennis Tuttle and Molly Harper White.

And to Michael Holmes and everyone at ECW Press, thank you so much for taking the chance. Because of you, Kanyon's last words can be heard.